Seeking
HIS FACE

Seeking His Face

A Daily Devotional

Charles Stanley

THOMAS NELSON PUBLISHERS®
Nashville

A Division of Thomas Nelson, Inc.
www.ThomasNelson.com

Library of Congress Cataloging-in-Publication Data

Stanley, Charles F.
   Seeking His face : a daily devotional / Charles Stanley
     p. cm.
   ISBN: 0-7852-7299-2
   1. Devotional calendars. I. Title.
   BV4811.S818 2002
   242'2—dc21   2002005957

Printed in the United States of America

03 04 05 06   BVG   12 11 10 9 8 7 6

Contents

Introduction

A Fresh Encounter with God

An encounter with God takes place when He confronts us. Through these divine encounters, the Lord comforts us, challenges us, heals and forgives us. He changes us.

We can't manipulate these encounters, but we can make ourselves attentive to His voice, listening for His instruction and direction. When we make ourselves willing and available, God will encounter us.

In our desire to grow in our relationship with the Lord, we need to set aside a time to meet Him daily, commune with Him, and seek His plan for our lives. These encounters with our holy God transform us and change the direction of our lives.

The Old Testament recounts the story of the people of Israel who were oppressed by the Midianites. They cried out to God for relief, and He demonstrated His mercy by raising up a man named Gideon to deliver them from captivity.

Gideon was hiding in the wine press when he encountered God, and he was never the same after that. "The LORD looked at [Gideon] and said, 'Go in this your strength and deliver Israel from the hand of Midian. Have I not sent you?'" (Judg. 6:14 NASB). Through this encounter with God, Gideon was transformed from a fearful man into a bold, valiant warrior for the Lord.

We, too, can experience life-changing encounters with God as we listen for His voice and follow His leading in our lives. No matter how we perceive ourselves, we sense our unworthiness whenever we encounter God. We realize He is the reason for the blessings in our lives. Nothing we have ever done has made God love us more or less. All we can do is stand in awe of His amazing love and grace for us. Realizing our unworthiness and understanding the true state of our souls open the door for God to transform us.

Mary Magdalene had a fresh encounter with God. So did David, Samuel, and even Saul. The apostle Paul had a tremendous encounter with God along the Damascus road. The apostle John's encounter is recorded in the book of Revelation, and we can draw a tremendous lesson of faith from Peter's encounter with Jesus on the Sea of Galilee.

Mary of Bethany and her sister, Martha, encountered God through the miracle of their brother's resurrection. The woman who had been plagued for years with a hemorrhage encountered Christ's healing touch along a dusty Jerusalem roadway.

We find common threads in each of these lives—a sense of desperation, a desire to know God, a sense of humility and personal unworthiness, and an awareness of personal sinfulness. Each of these people came to the Lord with a need, and in His presence they found hope and healing.

Fresh encounters with God are not limited to the people of the Bible. They are just as much ours today. John the Baptist told a crowd of listeners, "He must increase, but I must decrease" (John 3:30). Jesus entered the scene, and John instantly knew what had to be done. The same is true in our lives when we encounter God. We must recognize that no matter how far we have come in our relationship with Him, there is still room for more of Him in our lives. He must increase; we must decrease.

Our encounters with God are not designed to heap condemnation on our heads. Instead, God wants these meetings to bring about true change in our lives as we encounter His greatness. As we understand what it means to thirst and hunger for righteousness, God will teach us more about His awesome holiness. As we stand in His presence, God begins the process of washing our sins away and transforming us more and more into the people He desires us to become.

Use each day of this new year as an opportunity for a fresh encounter with God!

JANUARY

*A Divine
Encounter with God*

The Days Ahead

SCRIPTURE READING: Matthew 6:25–34
KEY VERSE: Matthew 6:25

Therefore I say to you, do not worry about your life, what you will eat or what you will drink; nor about your body, what you will put on. Is not life more than food and the body more than clothing?

Many people find themselves concentrating on the future, especially at this time of year. They wonder whether they will ever accomplish anything noteworthy in this life. Anxious thoughts quickly turn into worry and fear when they ponder whether God will answer their prayers and meet their needs in the days ahead.

Temptations also abound. We have just celebrated the birth of our Savior and Lord, but for many the most meaningful moment came when everyone gathered around the Christmas tree and opened presents. Did you get what you wanted?

Chances are that many did, or at least they thought they did. But how long did it take for the newness to wear off and discontentment to reappear? Only a divine encounter with God can satisfy the inner longing of your heart and bring a true sense of fulfillment and lasting peace.

During His earthly ministry, Jesus spoke of man's desire to gain and hold on to material things (Matt. 6:25). Somehow we have come to believe that if we are successful from a material perspective, we have achieved God's will. This is a long way from the truth.

God's will for your life is simply for you to love Him with your whole heart and seek His kingdom above the world's passions. When you do, you find a sustaining peace within your heart that nothing can remove or change.

Dear God, I love You with my whole heart. Help me to seek Your kingdom above the world's passions.

Reasons to Trust

SCRIPTURE READING: Psalm 37:1–9
KEY VERSE: John 15:9

As the Father loved Me, I also have loved you; abide in My love.

As we anticipate the coming year, let us reflect on reasons why we can trust God:

He is the one true God (2 Sam. 7:21–22). Since the beginning of time, those who seek God have found Him. No other god has revealed himself to man in this way.

He is the essence of truth (Heb. 6:17–18). God cannot lie, and He will never lead you astray. However, He has told us that there is one who deceives us, and that is Satan. Jesus called him the father of lies and rightly so (John 8:44).

He is absolutely faithful (Lam. 3:23). When was the last time God let you down? He never has, and He never will. No matter what you are facing, God knows about it, and He is near to show you how to resolve your dilemma.

He has all power (Matt. 28:18). Henry Thiessen writes, "God can do what He wills to do, but he does not necessarily will to do anything . . . To the Christian the omnipotence of God is a source of great comfort and hope."

He loves you unconditionally (John 15:9). God will never stop loving you. Even when you are unlovely, He loves you. And His love draws you away from sin and into His arms of infinite care.

He never changes (Heb. 13:8). God is immutable. Thiessen declares, "He is exalted above all causes and above even the possibility of change."

Dear heavenly Father, I thank You that You are the one true God, the essence of truth. You are absolutely faithful, have all power, love me unconditionally, and never change.

The Essence of Hope

SCRIPTURE READING: Psalm 18:1–6

KEY VERSE: Psalm 18:2

The LORD is my rock and my fortress and my deliverer;
My God, my strength, in whom I will trust;
My shield and the horn of my salvation, my stronghold.

Hope from God is an anchor to the soul. It is not something worn lightly so that it is easily brushed aside. Hope that comes from Jesus Christ resides deep within your heart. It will never abandon you, and if you look for it, you will find it there to encourage you in mighty ways. Hope is the very thing that keeps you from giving up when all the odds are stacked against you.

It also is something God begins to train you how to use and depend upon from the first day you trust Him as your Savior. We often laugh about taking baby steps as young Christians. But this is exactly what we do. We crawl, then we begin to walk. Just like any toddler, we stumble, fall, even bump our heads and cry.

God, our heavenly Father, lifts us up into His arms not because it is His duty, but because He loves us. This is the essence of hope: We have felt the brush of His love across our hearts and emotions, and we are drawn to Him again and again.

Are you hopeful today? Many are not. They worry and fret and in doing so stumble in their emotions. Oh, that you could see how the loving hands of Jesus reach out to catch you whenever you fall.

Beloved, place your hope in God for every issue, and you will find a strong and mighty refuge for your weary heart (Ps. 18:2).

Lord, help me to place my hope in You for every issue. Thank You for providing a strong and mighty refuge for my weary heart.

Trust God for Tomorrow

SCRIPTURE READING: Hebrews 6:13–20
KEY VERSE: Hebrews 11:39

All these, having obtained a good testimony through faith, did not receive the promise.

Hope miraculously comes as you let go of your anxieties and expectations and trust God for your tomorrows.

In Hebrews 11 we are given a list of people who lived their lives in the light of hope. They trusted God through valleys so dark that they could not see the path before them. Yet the darkness could not blind them to God's promises.

How did they live without the material evidence we so enjoy of God's completed work? Hope is the answer. Planted deep within them was a sense of undeniable hope that God would accomplish what He had promised.

The writer of Hebrews tells us that "all these, . . . gained approval through their faith" (Heb. 11:39 NASB). Imagine the strength that hope provided when they faced the end of their lives! Hope taught them to believe that they would soon be in the presence of God.

Today the Spirit of God, who resides within each believer, offers this same hope to each of us. His presence in our lives is the connecting point that keeps us clad in hope.

As you embrace the hope of God through faith, you are given the ability to endure the storms of life. Hope is an anchor to the soul and a gateway to peace and rest through a living God who holds your life within His loving grasp.

Thank You, Lord, for hope. I praise You that You hold my life within Your loving grasp.

Standing in Awe of God

SCRIPTURE READING: Psalm 42

KEY VERSE: Psalm 42:1

As the deer pants for the water brooks,
So pants my soul for You, O God.

God doesn't want us to fear Him in such a way that we avoid coming to Him in prayer and worship. God calls us to stand in awe of His wondrous power and ability.

In your heart, God needs to be God, the great I AM. Let a sense of worship that clings to Jesus Christ be engraved in your life. Even in small devotional times, recognize that all-powerful God is near and He is aware of your every need. Worship Him not because He commands it, but because you are driven to love and honor Him. The psalmist proclaimed, "As the deer pants for the water brooks, So my soul pants for Thee, O God" (Ps. 42:1 NASB).

God's love motivated Him to send His only Son to earth. Jesus came to teach us about His Father's intimate love for each one of us. When we ignore God or fail to honor Him with our lives, we are the ones who suffer.

Many view God as being someplace way up in the heavenlies and not present here on earth. But God is actively involved in His creation. Before His death, Jesus told His disciples, "I tell you the truth, it is to your advantage that I go away; for if I do not go away, the Helper will not come to you; but if I go, I will send Him to you" (John 16:7 NASB).

As a child of God, you're in His presence through the power of the Spirit. Therefore, fear Him for His majesty. Love Him for His eternal care over your life. And live in the truth that He will never stop loving you.

Lord, help me to live in the truth that You will never stop loving me.
Thank You for Your presence through the power of the Spirit.

Fearing God

SCRIPTURE READING: Psalm 99
KEY VERSE: Philippians 4:8

Finally, brethren, whatever things are true, whatever things are noble, whatever things are just, whatever things are pure, whatever things are lovely, whatever things are of good report, if there is any virtue and if there is anything praiseworthy—meditate on these things.

What has a hold on your thoughts? In his book, *Living Free in Christ*, Neil Anderson writes,

Suppose a secretary is intimidated by her boss. She works in fear of him all day because he is both present and potent to her. But what power does the boss have over the secretary? I suppose he could fire her. But could she overcome that power? Yes, she could quit or be willing to quit.

By not allowing her boss to hold the job over her head she would free herself from his intimidation. I am not suggesting that you rebel against your boss: I am pointing out that the New Testament teaches we can live a responsible life without fearing intimidation from others. Peter puts it this way: "Who is going to harm you if you are eager to do good? But even if you should suffer for what is right, you are blessed. 'Do not fear what they fear; do not be frightened.' But in your hearts set apart Christ as Lord" (1 Peter 3:13–15 NIV).

There is, however, a legitimate and ultimate fear in our lives, and that is God. That's because He is both omnipresent and omnipotent. When we, with reverence and awe, make God our ultimate fear object and sanctify Christ as the Lord of our lives, we will experience the freedom that Christ purchased for us on the cross.

Lord, help me to stand strong in the face of fear. I set my heart upon You!

The Presence of God

SCRIPTURE READING: Psalm 101
KEY VERSE: Proverbs 20:27

The spirit of a man is the lamp of the LORD,
Searching all the inner depths of his heart.

God never changes His mind concerning you. Through some act of sin you may grieve His Spirit, but once you are saved, God will not take His presence from you.

In his book, *The Person and Work of the Holy Spirit,* R. A. Torrey asserts,

In some, however, He dwells way back of consciousness in the hidden sanctuary of their spirit. He is not allowed to take possession as He desires of the whole man, spirit, soul, and body. Some therefore are not distinctly conscious of His indwelling, but He is there nonetheless. What a solemn, and yet what a glorious thought, that in me dwells this august person, the Holy Spirit.

If we are children of God, we are not so much to pray that the Spirit may come and dwell in us, for He does that already. We are rather to recognize His presence, His gracious and glorious indwelling, and give to Him complete control of the house He already inhabits, and strive so to live as not to grieve this holy one, this divine guest . . .

What a thought it gives of the hallowedness and sacredness of the body, to think of the Holy Spirit dwelling within us. How considerately we ought to treat these bodies and how sensitively we ought to shun every thing that will defile them. How carefully we ought to walk in all things so as not to grieve Him who dwells within us.

Father, let me be sensitive to things that would defile me. I want to be Your holy temple.

In Awe of His Grace

SCRIPTURE READING: Psalm 43:3–5
KEY VERSE: Proverbs 14:27

The fear of the LORD is a fountain of life,
To avoid the snares of death.

*E*ach time a scribe would come to a passage containing the name of God, he would lay down his stylus and go wash his hands. The scribe did not feel worthy to print God's name without cleansing and humbling himself before the Lord. There was an aspect of godly fear in this action that seems foreign to us today.

Do you fear God for who He is? Are you aware of His awesome power and presence in your life? We miss a great blessing when we fail to give Him His rightful place in our lives.

Satan eagerly entices you to become frightened of God. He lies by telling you God wants to hurt you in some way. Nothing is farther from the truth. God loves you completely.

Proverbs 14:27 (NASB) tells us: "The fear of the LORD is a fountain of life, That one may avoid the snares of death." When we fear God, we reverence Him with our lives. We are not frightened. Instead, we acknowledge His holiness and humble ourselves before Him. We also avoid anything we sense will bring sorrow or grief to His Spirit living within us.

When you yield to temptation, be quick to admit your failure, and seek His forgiveness. Because His Spirit lives within you, you can trust that He will lead you away from sin and toward righteousness when your heart is right before Him. Standing in awe of His matchless grace gives evidence that you are on the right spiritual pathway.

Lord, I am in awe of Your grace. Help me to avoid anything that will bring sorrow or grief to Your Spirit living within me.

The Divine Potter

SCRIPTURE READING: Hebrews 12:4–11
KEY VERSE: Jeremiah 18:2

Arise and go down to the potter's house, and there I will cause you to hear My words.

God is the Potter. We are the clay. He is molding us into what He wishes us to be, giving us a look that is unmistakably His.

The process is never-ending. God will add a little here, take away a little there, try you in the fire. When you feel His hand pressing into your life, there is a reason. To Him, a bit of clay is askew. He seeks to correct the flaw.

This is God's discipline in your life. It is not wrath—it is love, unconditional and immeasurable. It isn't something to fear; it is something to embrace because it is for your good.

You can be sure of God in His wisdom, His timing, His motives. God's mind and heart are perfect. Ours are far from perfect, and in discipline He is using a sure method to draw us closer to Himself. Look closely and see His fingerprint in the clay.

When we were corrected as children, sometimes it was difficult to understand exactly what Mom or Dad meant when one said, "I'm just doing this because I love you." However, when God says this to us, we know it is framed in perfect love.

His perfect blend of discipline and blessings works together for good. One does not come without the other, so when you feel His touch of discipline, don't shy away. Ask God to show you what He is trying to teach you; accept it, and grow stronger in Him.

Lord, help me to understand that Your discipline and blessings work together for my good. Show me what You are trying to teach me, and help me accept it and grow stronger in You.

The Pattern of Life

SCRIPTURE READING: Ephesians 4:1–15
KEY VERSE: Ephesians 4:14–15

That [you] . . . speaking the truth in love, may grow up in all things into Him who is the head—Christ.

The pattern Jesus gave us to live by is one of love. Paul wrote, "I . . . entreat you to walk in a manner worthy of the calling with which you have been called, with all humility and gentleness, with patience, showing Forbearance to one another in love" (Eph. 4:1–2 NASB).

As a believer, live each day in such a way that your life honors the Lord, who saved you through His mercy and grace. This means to live in a "manner worthy" of your calling. How did Jesus call you? Did He come to you with a list of demands requiring you to fulfill each one before He would consider caring for you? No. He came to you in love.

Redemptive love brought Him to earth so that you might receive eternal salvation. Love was all the motivation He needed to be crucified at Calvary.

His love watches over you, protects you, plans your future, and encourages you not to give up in times of sorrow and discouragement. You will spend eternity in the radiant goodness and greatness of His blessings, all because He chooses to love you.

Love that is from God is humble and gentle. It loves with the surety of Christ. Someone today is hurting because he thinks God could not possibly love him. You know the truth about His love; will you tell him?

Thank You, Lord, that I know the truth about Your love. Help me to share it with others.

When God Says No

SCRIPTURE READING: Matthew 7:7–11

KEY VERSE: James 1:17

Every good gift and every perfect gift is from above, and comes down from the Father of lights, with whom there is no variation or shadow of turning.

Have you ever asked God for something that He did not give you? At first, you might have felt slighted or upset, but perhaps much later you saw the reason why God said no.

God promises to give only what is good for you and no less. Why? The Lord loves you with an affection beyond imagination, and He fashioned every intricate fiber of your being (Ps. 139). It makes sense, then, that He knows exactly what you need and what blessings would benefit you.

Imagine a father taking his four-year-old son through a toy store. The little boy is overwhelmed by all the sights and sounds, and he points everywhere, shouting and dragging his dad down the aisles. In the sports section, the boy spots a sleek air gun and goes wild with delight. "Please, Dad, please!" he begs.

Of course, the wise father knows his son is far too young to handle such equipment safely and says no. After the son has finished pouting about the answer, the father takes him down another aisle and helps him select a gift that suits his age and abilities.

What would you think of a father who gave in without considering the consequences? Not much. Your heavenly Father is careful. You can relax in the assurance that God answers your requests in absolute wisdom and tenderness and always with regard to your ultimate welfare.

Dear God, teach me to relax in the assurance that You answer my requests in absolute wisdom and tenderness with regard to my ultimate welfare.

Ignoring God

SCRIPTURE READING: Psalm 40:1–8

KEY VERSE: 1 Samuel 15:22

Samuel said: "Has the LORD as great delight in burnt offerings and sacrifices, As in obeying the voice of the LORD? Behold, to obey is better than sacrifice, And to heed than the fat of rams."

What happens when you ignore God? In your mind, do you picture Him just walking away, looking forlorn and rejected? Or do you have a mental image of God getting mad at you and banishing you to forty years of wilderness wandering?

Neither is correct. God loves you perfectly, and His love for you is not based on your obedience. Though He tells us in His Word that obedience is better than sacrifice, the thing that God wants most from you is a love that comes from your heart.

He doesn't stop loving you just because you do something wrong. None of us can earn God's love by being good or trying to be perfect. We do not have the ability to be either of these on our own. We need a Savior. And that is why Jesus came to die for you and me. He does the very thing that you cannot do for yourself. He makes you acceptable in God's eyes.

When we ignore the Lord, we are the ones who suffer and miss a great opportunity for blessing. God is not a strong and mighty taskmaster who waits for us to do something wrong so He can pounce on us. He is a loving God who listens for our cry.

When He draws you to Himself, He uses love, not a rod of thunder. God knows once you drink of His love, the world's appeal will fade. Give Him your heart, and you will be blessed by what you receive from Him.

Lord, here is my heart. Let me drink of Your love. Let the appeal of this world fade.

Reverence for God

SCRIPTURE READING: Mark 9:36–37

KEY VERSE: John 17:3

This is eternal life, that they may know You, the only true God, and Jesus Christ whom You have sent.

Your reverence for God needs to be active and operational. Remarks about "the Man upstairs" and other off-the-cuff comments about God fail to communicate the attitude of a grateful heart.

When Moses approached God, he trembled at the sight of the Lord's power and strength. Yet often we easily reduce God's glory to fit within the casual context of human language. God demands our love. We are to honor Him with our lives and the gratitude of our hearts.

In the book *The Pursuit of God,* A. W. Tozer writes,

I want to deliberately encourage this mighty longing after God. The lack of it has brought us to our present low estate. The stiff and wooden quality about our religious lives is a result of our lack of holy desire. Complacency is a deadly foe of all spiritual growth. Acute desire must be present or there will be no manifestation of Christ to His people . . .

The shallowness of our inner experience, the hollowness of our worship, and the servile imitation of the world which marks our promotional methods all testify that we know God only imperfectly and the grace of God scarcely at all . . . We must put away all effort to impress, and come with the guileless candor of childhood. If we do this, without doubt God will quickly respond.

Dear heavenly Father, help me to put away all efforts to impress, and come to You with the guileless candor of childhood.

The Perils of Intervention

SCRIPTURE READING: Proverbs 3:11–13

KEY VERSE: Psalm 94:12

Blessed is the man whom You instruct, O LORD,
And teach out of Your law.

When a friend is suffering, we often seek ways to alleviate the emotional and physical pain. However, many times God wants that individual to go through the process of suffering so he will learn how to trust Him better. Does this mean He is a bad God? No. In fact, it proves the opposite.

Without the presence of difficulty, we would forget just how much we need the Lord. As long as most people have their immediate needs met, they do not think of crying out to God for His assistance. But let the winds of adversity blow across their lives, and they are quick to run to Him.

The Bible admonishes us not to despise the discipline of the Lord. God uses discipline to train us and shape our lives so that we reflect His mercy and grace to others. Therefore, stepping in and rescuing someone who is going through troubled times can actually block that person from receiving the blessings of God. Next time you are tempted to intervene, even if that person is a family member or friend, take time to pray and ask God what you should do.

He may lead you to pray for that individual, or He may show you the best way to help. Being sensitive to His Spirit puts you in a position to be used greatly by God. When you know you have given the other person to the Lord through prayer, you have given the greatest gift of all.

Dear Lord, use divine discipline to train me and shape me so that I reflect Your mercy and grace to others. Show me the best way to help others who are experiencing Your discipline.

The Goodness of God

SCRIPTURE READING: Luke 18:18–23
KEY VERSE: Psalm 86:5

You, Lord, are good, and ready to forgive,
And abundant in mercy to all those who call upon You.

Concerning the goodness of God, Henry Thiessen explains, "In the larger sense of the term, the goodness of God includes all the qualities that answer to the conception of an ideal personage; that is, it includes such qualities as God's holiness, righteousness, and truth, as well as his love, benevolence, mercy, and grace."

The rich young ruler called Jesus "Good Teacher," but the Lord was quick to reply: "Why do you call Me good? No one is good except God alone" (Mark 10:18 NASB). Faithfully, Jesus was doing exactly what the Father had sent Him to do: point men and women to their heavenly Father. He also was involved in training people to seek God not out of fear, but out of a desire to know and experience His goodness and mercy.

In *The Pursuit of God,* A. W. Tozer concludes, "Right now we are in an age of religious complexity. The simplicity which is in Christ is rarely found among us. In its stead are programs, methods, organizations and a world of nervous activities which occupy time and attention but can never satisfy the longing of the heart."

Often we seek Him because we have heard that He is "good." But we stop at this point and miss learning about the deeper goodness of God. Make sure that as you discover more about God's goodness, you also take time to grow in your devotion toward Him.

Lord, let me grow in my devotion toward You. I wait each day for a divine encounter with You.

The Revelation of God

SCRIPTURE READING: John 13:1–17
KEY VERSE: John 15:15

No longer do I call you servants, for a servant does not know what his master is doing; but I have called you friends, for all things that I heard from My Father I have made known to you.

The highest proof of true friendship," emphasizes Andrew Murray, "is the intimacy that holds nothing back and admits the friend to share our inmost secrets. It is a blessing to be Christ's servant; His redeemed ones delight to call themselves His servants. Christ had often spoken of the disciples as His servants. In His great love our Lord now says, 'No longer do I call you servants, but I call you friends, for all things I heard from my Father I have made known to you.'"

Since the beginning of time God has sought ways of revealing Himself to mankind—first in the Garden of Eden and later to the prophets. With the birth of His Son, God initiated an intimacy with man that can never be destroyed. Jesus' love for us was so great that He laid aside His royal robe in heaven and took up a towel and basin to serve those He came to save.

The next time you are tempted to think that God doesn't care if you hurt or if you are lonely, think about what it cost Him to come to earth. He did not come to judge or condemn; He came to demonstrate His personal love for you. Before He left heaven, He knew there would be a Cross, and still He was willing to come to you.

God continues to reveal Himself even when you are captivated by the things of this world. Ask Him to make you sensitive to His great love.

Lord, make me sensitive to Your great love. Thank You for Your personal love for me, for leaving heaven and coming to earth to die for my sin.

The Love of God

Come and see the works of God;
He is awesome in His doing toward the sons of men.

There are people who find it hard to believe that God is involved in the physical elements of this world. They maintain a false assumption that God is distant from His creation. But this assumption is opposite from the true nature of God. Just as God spoke life into the universe, He is actively involved in every aspect of life.

From the beginning, God's sole intent has been one of revelation, whereby He has sought to manifest Himself to mankind. And while His desire is for all men and women to love Him in return, it has never been His goal to force anyone into loving Him. To be sincere, love must come from the heart and not as a result of obligation, guilt, or other external pressure.

God draws you to Himself by loving you. However, He will never demand your love in return. He desires it, looks for it, longs for it, and welcomes it, but He will never demand it.

What an awesome God we serve! He is so sure of Himself and so confident in His power and mercy that He can trust us to make the right decision.

How do you know you can trust the love of God? One way is by taking time to study His Word. Ask Him to reveal more of Himself to you. Once you encounter God on an intimate level, the need to question His sovereignty fades, and the desire to love Him grows in a wondrous way.

Dear God, draw me to You in love and reveal Yourself to me.

The Mind of the Father

SCRIPTURE READING: John 14:16–18
KEY VERSE: John 14:26

The Helper, the Holy Spirit, whom the Father will send in My name, He will teach you all things, and bring to your remembrance all things that I said to you.

The natural or unsaved man does not have the ability to discern God's ways. Only the person who has accepted Jesus Christ as his Savior can know the mind of God, and even then there is a limitation to the knowledge given. We cannot really know all things about God. Jesus told His disciples that there are some things the Father has kept unto Himself.

Perhaps God does this because He knows that our limited, earthbound minds could not understand the vastness and power that are His. In this way, we do not need to understand all that God knows. But we do need to know Him as our personal Savior and loving Lord.

He has given us the Holy Spirit so that we might know Him better. Over the course of your lifetime, God will reveal many things about Himself. One thing you can be sure of, He will never withhold His loving care from you. He is present with you today, through the life of the Holy Spirit. You can pray to the Lord and know He hears you.

Even though those utterances may seem too difficult to speak, God is aware of each one and will minister His hope to your heart so you will not become tired or weary. God's Spirit is there, conveying His love and truth each moment. You are held safe in the arms of Christ because the Holy Spirit stands guard over your soul. Praise Him for His goodness and mercy!

Lord, I am so thankful that I am held safe in Your arms. Thank You for setting the Holy Spirit as a guard over my soul. Thank You for Your goodness and mercy!

The Life of God

SCRIPTURE READING: John 11:1–45
KEY VERSE: John 10:10

The thief does not come except to steal, and to kill, and to destroy. I have come that they may have life, and that they may have it more abundantly.

Think about your best friend for a moment. Try to remember your very first meeting. What if your best friend had handed you a long list of dos and don'ts, telling you any violation would lessen his care for you? Obviously your relationship would never have progressed. Who would want such a friend?

Yet many Christians act as if this is their view of Jesus. But He did not hand you a list of conditions when you accepted Him. What He gave you was His life.

In the New Testament, there are several Greek words for life. *Bios* (origin of *biology*), generally translated, means "lifestyle." Another Greek word for life is *zoe,* which means "life as God has it."

In John 10:10 (NASB), Jesus said, "I came that they might have life, and might have it abundantly." In John 11:25, He stated, "I am the resurrection and the life." In both cases, Jesus used the word *zoe.* How awesome to hear from our Lord Himself that the "life as God has it" is within us, a magnificent gift of His unconditional love.

Since you have this life, His life, you already have the very best. He dwells within you to encourage and empower you. As long as you are within God's will, sustaining energy will flow through you from His eternal wellspring. Within His will, you'll never tire of living for Jesus.

Father, help me walk in Your will so that sustaining energy from Your eternal wellspring will flow through me.

A Living God

SCRIPTURE READING: Psalm 36:1–9
KEY VERSE: Proverbs 22:4

By humility and the fear of the LORD
Are riches and honor and life.

He had gone to church as a young boy. However, in growing older he strayed from the things of God. After a short term in the military, he took a job with a large company and relaxed. He had job security, a lovely wife, and children. What more could he want?

That was 1950. Since then, things have changed dramatically. The security he once enjoyed waned. Economic changes forced him into an early retirement. He never prayed or asked for God's wisdom, thinking instead, *That religious stuff isn't for me.* Yet in secret, he hoped his life was "good enough" to earn him a spot in heaven.

Many things are lacking in this man's life. The most obvious is salvation. There is also a lack of understanding of who God is. The writer of Proverbs asserted, "The fear of the LORD is the beginning of wisdom, And the knowledge of the Holy One is understanding" (9:10).

People who do not fear God do not really know Him. Only when you take time to know God do you realize He is a personal, loving, living God, who is active in every area of life.

If you have never accepted Christ as your Savior, now is the right time to make that decision. Or if your fellowship has grown cold, ask Him to restore the intimacy of your personal relationship.

Father, let me come to know You in an intimate way. Renew the warmth of my fellowship with You.

God Is Good

SCRIPTURE READING: Romans 8:35–39

KEY VERSE: Psalm 33:5

He loves righteousness and justice;
The earth is full of the goodness of the LORD.

Here is the truth about God's goodness: it always seeks to encourage and lift up rather than tear down or condemn. Romans 8:1 reminds us that "there is therefore now no condemnation to those who are in Christ Jesus." God knows the times you struggle, and He longs to pour out His encouragement and hope over your life.

In the light of this goodness, nothing has the power or ability to separate you from the love of God (Rom. 8:35, 38–39). His power securely keeps you. Nothing is strong enough to deter His help when you call to Him. Does this mean that you will never face hardship? No, but it does mean that in times of difficulty, God will be near enough to hear even the whispers of your heart.

Never view Christ as a stern, unloving judge. Jesus was very quick to point out that He came to save, not to judge the world. Once you accept Him as your Savior, the only judgment you will ever attend is the one where God rewards your faithful love and devotion toward Him and His Son.

Can you step away from God's goodness? Yes. Because the Lord has given each of us a limited free will, we can choose to turn from God. However, God will never turn away from you. You may be troubled by a situation that seems uncontrollable, but God holds the solution, and He will provide the hope you need as you turn to Him.

Lord, I am so grateful that You will never turn away from me. You hold the solution to every situation. You will provide the hope I need.

Fruitless Prayer

SCRIPTURE READING: Isaiah 66:1–2
KEY VERSE: PSALM 51:17

The sacrifices of God are a broken spirit,
A broken and a contrite heart—
These, O God, You will not despise.

In Shakespeare's play *Hamlet,* King Claudius of Denmark steps into a chapel in his castle to pray, an act to which he is unaccustomed. But his nephew, Hamlet, has murder on his mind and stands outside the door, deciding whether he will rush in and kill the king. When Hamlet hears him trying to pray, he backs down from his plan for the moment and walks away.

What Hamlet misses, however, is the ending to the king's fruitless prayer: "My words fly up, my thoughts remain below: Words without thoughts never to heaven go." In other words, the king realized that he was not sincere in his prayers, and that God would not honor his unrepentant heart.

God's message to Israel through Isaiah pertains to the same issue of spiritual heart condition. God did not recognize their sacrifices because the Israelites did not offer them in true repentance, did not follow God's laws concerning sacrifices, and continued in their lifestyles of sin.

God wanted their hearts to be truly His; He desired genuine relationship with them, and He desires the same with you. Are you holding back by refusing to admit how much you need His cleansing? When you humble yourself before the Lord, you open the door for sincere and pure fellowship.

Lord, I humble myself before You today to open the door for sincere and pure fellowship with You.

Accepting God's Love

SCRIPTURE READING: Romans 5:1–15

KEY VERSE: Romans 5:15

The free gift is not like the offense. For if by the one man's offense many died, much more the grace of God and the gift by the grace of the one Man, Jesus Christ, abounded to many.

God's grace saves you. No amount of your good works can do what God does through His mercy and grace. Salvation is a free gift that He offers to all who come to Him. However, some men and women spend a lifetime trying to earn the approval of God on their own and through their own ability. They donate time, money, and energy to good causes. But at the end of their lives, if they have not accepted Jesus Christ as their Savior, they remain lost and separated from Him.

What would it be like to spend eternity apart from God? Many scholars believe once you die, you have the perfect knowledge to know either the eternal love of God or eternal separation from Him. Sin and rebellion build a deep division between God and you. Good works cannot bridge this gap, but admitting your need of the Savior who is God's Son can.

During your lifetime, God allows you to experience many opportunities—some are pleasurable, while others are painful. However, each has been chosen with the goal of bringing you into a closer relationship with Him.

He is the only One who can meet all your needs. When you refuse His love, the gulf between Him and you grows deeper. His loving grace is your only hope. Stop working to achieve a special place in God's heart. You already have it. Accept His love and you will be saved.

Lord Jesus, I accept You as my Savior. Forgive me. Cleanse me. Save me!

The Sovereignty of God

SCRIPTURE READING: 1 John 4:4–10
KEY VERSE: 1 John 4:10

In this is love, not that we loved God, but that He loved us and sent His Son to be the propitiation for our sins.

If you have felt that God has abandoned you when things go wrong, you are not the first believer to wrestle with such thoughts. Don't be afraid to ask God the hardest questions. He longs to answer you with His power and grace.

In her book, *Lord, Where Are You When Bad Things Happen?*, Kay Arthur shares her emotions as she discovered the truth of God's sovereignty:

After I came to know Jesus Christ, God sent a godly man to tutor me in the faith. I was like a dry sponge being softened by the Word, absorbing all that I could get.

One night as Dave and I sat in my living room, he took off his signet ring and put it into his hand, clinching his fingers around it until his knuckles were white. Then he said, "Kay, now that you belong to Jesus Christ, you are just like this ring, and my hand is just like the hand of God. God has you in His hand. No one can touch you, look at you, or speak to you without God's permission."

I didn't recognize it then, but Dave was teaching me the sovereignty of God. Later, as I came to understand that God is sovereign and in control of everything so that nothing can happen without his knowledge and permission, I understood more fully what Dave was saying.

I also understood that the God who held me in His sovereign hand is a God of love (1 John 4:10). Everything that came into my life would have to be filtered through His fingers of love.

God, I am thankful that everything in my life is filtered through Your fingers of love. You hold me in Your sovereign hand.

God's Waiting Room

SCRIPTURE READING: Psalm 27
KEY VERSE: Isaiah 40:31

Those who wait on the LORD
Shall renew their strength;
They shall mount up with wings like eagles,
They shall run and not be weary,
They shall walk and not faint.

Do you feel as though you're in God's "waiting room"? You've asked Him for something for years, and you just don't have a sense that He has answered you yet. Why doesn't He seem to respond?

In her book, *Adventures in Prayer,* Catherine Marshall addresses this often painful issue:

Waiting certainly plays an enormous role in the unfolding story of God's relationship to man. It is God's oft-repeated way of teaching us that His power is real and that He can answer our prayers without interference and manipulation from us.

But we have such trouble getting our will, our time schedules out of the way. Much of the time we act like a child who brings a broken toy to be mended. The father gladly takes the toy and begins work. Then after a while, childlike impatience takes over. Why is it taking so long . . . Finally in desperation, he snatches the toy from the father's hands and walks off with it, saying that he hadn't really thought his father could fix it anyway. Perhaps it wasn't even "his will" to mend toys.

On the other hand, when we are trustful enough to leave our "broken toy" with the Father, not only do we eventually get it back gloriously restored, but are also handed a surprising plus. We find for ourselves that during the dark waiting period when self-effort had ceased, a spurt of astonishing spiritual growth took place in us.

Father, here are all my broken "toys" for You to fix as You see fit.

Knowing God

SCRIPTURE READING: Ephesians 3:14–21
KEY VERSES: Ephesians 3:18–19

[That you] may be able to comprehend with all the saints what is the width and length and depth and height—to know the love of Christ which passes knowledge; that you may be filled with all the fullness of God.

It's difficult to describe things that are beyond the terms of our immediate visual experience. For example, we know that outer space is immeasurably vast, but we cannot make any concrete comparisons. When numbers get up into billions and trillions and even higher, the effect is staggering, and we lose all sense of their meaning. And there are crevices in the ocean floor that go down so far they cannot be measured.

If we cannot fully grasp the mysteries of our physical world, how much more inept are we at comprehending our all-knowing, all-powerful, eternal Lord? Yet the true wonder is that God wants you to know Him and love Him the way He loves you. He does not want to remain a distant mystery.

That was why Paul stressed the importance of understanding who He is: "[I pray that you] may be able to comprehend with all the saints what is the breadth and length and height and depth, and to know the love of Christ which surpasses knowledge, that you may be filled up to all the Fulness of God" (Eph. 3:18–19 NASB).

When you are filled with the knowledge and intimate experience of His love, the rest of life falls into perspective. His clarity and righteousness subdue the confusions and complexities of this world. God is not impenetrable or distant, and He desires your fellowship.

Dear God, I want to know You and love You the way You love me. Fill me with the knowledge and intimate experience of Your love.

God's Blessings

SCRIPTURE READING: Psalm 16
KEY VERSE: Psalm 16:6

The lines have fallen to me in pleasant places;
Yes, I have a good inheritance.

The time-worn phrase "count your blessings" is a good one to remember. It may sound trite, but it's always a good exercise to pause and consider all the wonderful things God has poured into your life.

And don't forget to include events and circumstances that did not seem positive at the moment. From the vantage point of the passing of time, you can probably see how God transformed even those negatives into blessings. Sometimes you appreciate those blessings at an even deeper level.

King David made a habit of viewing his life from a perspective of gratitude and satisfaction. In Psalm 16, he wrote, "The LORD is the portion of my inheritance and my cup; Thou dost support my lot. The [boundary] lines have fallen to me in pleasant places; Indeed, my heritage is beautiful to me . . . In Thy presence is Fulness of joy; in Thy right hand there are pleasures forever" (vv. 5–6, 11 NASB).

By nature, are you a grumbler? Do you have a habit of whining about every little thing? A spirit of complaining and dissatisfaction can pervade every facet of your being and even influence how you understand God's involvement in your life.

Instead of grumbling, you can give thanks to God as David did, and that process begins by deliberately and specifically identifying His generous blessings.

Dear Father, help me to give thanks instead of grumbling. Help me this day to specifically identify Your generous blessings.

The House That Stands

SCRIPTURE READING: Matthew 7:24–27
KEY VERSE: Galatians 6:7

Do not be deceived, God is not mocked; for whatever a man sows, that he will also reap.

Some of God's blessings are ones you receive over time as you build your life on the truth of His Word. For example, after years of obeying Him in the area of prayer, you have a richness of relationship with Him that could not be built any other way.

Many people have difficulty understanding the principle of reaping what they sow (Gal. 6:7), but it is definitely in operation, even if the consequences don't show up for a long time. That's why Jesus talked about building your life on the basis of His truth: "Every one who hears these words of Mine, and acts upon them, may be compared to a wise man, who built his house upon the rock; and the rain descended, and the floods came, and the winds blew, and burst against that house; and yet it did not fall; for it had been founded upon the rock" (Matt. 7:24–25 NASB).

From the outside, you can't necessarily determine what kind of foundation a house has. Yet as the years pass, the strength of the house reveals its true foundation. The house constructed on the sure beams of God's truth can weather any storm or trial and remain standing.

The same is true of your life. Your foundation may not be evident to all today. Yet eventually the results of trusting God will be evident to others, a powerful testimony of the blessing of believing what He says.

Lord, let the results of my trusting You be evident to others. Lord, make me a powerful testimony of the blessing of believing what You say.

The Foundation of Our Security

SCRIPTURE READING: 1 Peter 1:18–21

KEY VERSE: 1 Peter 1:18

Knowing that you were not redeemed with corruptible things, like silver or gold, from your aimless conduct received by tradition from your fathers.

A favorite hymn goes like this:

My hope is built on nothing less than Jesus' blood and righteousness;
I dare not trust the sweetest frame, but wholly lean on Jesus' name.
On Christ, the solid Rock, I stand;
All other ground is sinking sand, all other ground is sinking sand.

When darkness veils his lovely face, I rest on his unchanging grace;
In every high and stormy gale, my anchor holds within the veil.
On Christ, the solid Rock, I stand;
All other ground is sinking sand, all other ground is sinking sand.

(Edward Mote and William Bradbury, "The Solid Rock.")

What is the foundation of your security? Is it Jesus Christ or something else? If your hope, life, desires, dreams, ambitions, or affections are set on anything but God's Son, then you are not standing. Instead, you are caught—trapped— in sinking sand.

Countless Christians come to know Christ as their Savior, but they never transfer ownership rights from themselves to Him. The apostle Paul is a perfect example of a radical change (Acts 9). A short time before meeting Jesus on the Damascus road, he had been a willing and instrumental participant in Stephen's death (Acts 7). Paul never forgot what Jesus did for him, and he never returned to his old lifestyle. He found what he had been looking for. Have you?

Lord, I stand upon the solid Rock, Christ Jesus. All other ground is sinking sand. I rest on Your unchanging grace, knowing my anchor holds in every storm.

Time Out

SCRIPTURE READING Psalm 32
KEY VERSE: Psalm 32:8

I will instruct you and teach you in the way you should go;
I will guide you with My eye.

God's care for you includes His specific instructions for your life. If you think about it, we never read about Jesus hurrying here or there. He was not taken aback by the circumstances of life. Nor was He swayed by the opinions of others. That is because the focus of His life was set on His heavenly Father and not the approval of those around Him.

When you find yourself in a burdensome situation, refuse to respond to the adversity from the depths of your intellect. If you can, step away from the problem. Try to take a walk or a drive, and ask God to clear your mind of opinions and prejudices that would keep you from viewing the situation from a positive standpoint.

God always has something good in mind for the challenges we face. He is creative and in control. He wants you to learn to bring your problems to Him in prayer and not rush into a situation that produces a heated argument.

Just as we encourage our children to "have a time-out" whenever they are frustrated and overwhelmed, we should do the same.

Chances are, there is a reasonable solution for every event you will face. For the times that are too traumatic, God provides the strength and knowledge you need to get through each incident.

Lord, help me to change my focus from concern for the approval of others to concern for Your approval. I set the focus of my life on You.

Living by Faith

SCRIPTURE READING: Psalm 119:9–16
KEY VERSE: 2 Corinthians 5:7

We walk by faith, not by sight.

We think and talk about trusting and try, even though we fail many times, to walk by faith. And many times, our trying trips us up.

God wants us to learn to live by faith and not by sight (2 Cor. 5:7). This means living with the idea that God is able to do what we cannot do ourselves. What a victorious thought! It is also a marvelous invitation to experience freedom from doubt, worry, and disbelief.

Before we can trust God fully, we must come to a point of helpless dependence. It is here that we realize we simply cannot do it all, be all that is needed, and have all the answers. If we could, there would be no need for God. We would be in total control and very proud of it.

Although God gives us the ability to solve many of the problems we face, His greater desire is for us to live our lives dependent on Him. Godly dependence is not a sign of weakness but one of immeasurable strength and confidence.

There are problems that only God can solve, tasks that only He can perform, and solutions that can be discovered only through the wisdom He gives. The basic foundation to faith is this: Trust God more than you trust yourself. When you do this, you gain wisdom and hope for every area of life. You will have had a divine encounter with God.

Lord, help me to trust You to give me wisdom and hope in every area of my life.

FEBRUARY

*A Divine
Encounter with
Emotional Healing*

Your Deepest Need

SCRIPTURE READING: Luke 8:43–48

KEY VERSE: Luke 8:50

When Jesus heard it, He answered him, saying, "Do not be afraid; only believe, and she will be made well."

Jesus is very holistic in His approach to mankind. A good example of this is found in Luke 8, when He healed a woman who had hemorrhaged for twelve years.

It's hard to imagine how she maintained her hope for healing, especially with the stigma that accompanied her illness. Unclean according to Jewish law, she probably was forced to live outside the city gates, away from family and friends.

Her need for love and acceptance was overshadowed by the cruelty of Jewish tradition. Anyone who touched her was in turn considered unclean. The portrait Christ gives us is one of abundant mercy and grace. Not only did He heal her physical disease, but He healed her spiritually and emotionally as well. In no way was He repulsed by her sickness.

No matter how complex and disillusioning life may appear, Jesus refuses to turn His back on you. The woman in today's text believed if she could stretch out her hand far enough to touch the hem of His outer garment, she would be healed. What faith she had!

In His compassion, Christ turned to her and said: "Daughter, your faith has made you well; go in peace" (Luke 8:48 NASB). Jesus met her deepest need, and He will do the same for you as you have a divine encounter with Him.

I thank You, Lord, that You meet my deepest spiritual and emotional needs.

God's Promise

SCRIPTURE READING: John 17:24–26
KEY VERSE: Hebrews 13:5

*Let your conduct be without covetousness, and be content with such things
as you have. For He Himself has said, "I will never leave you nor forsake
you."*

In Hebrews 13:5, God promises to never leave you or forsake you. And
since God is truth and God is love, you can know without reservation
that He will honor His promises. There is no shadow of turning in Him; He
cannot defy His character of love.

So why are so many people devastated by loneliness?

Paul Little writes,

Isn't it ironic that in an age of the greatest population explosion the world has
ever known, more people are desperately lonely than ever before? . . . Even the
high-rise apartments in our big cities are monuments to loneliness. There is
aching loneliness behind those doors for many people. I know of those, both
in the city and in the suburb, who go to the large shopping centers simply for
the opportunity to talk to somebody in the store. At least the checker will
speak to them as they go out.

Much of the basis for loneliness stems from people's childhoods. Their parents
were too busy, were too apathetic, or for some reason were never there for them
when they were children. They have felt unloved and unneeded most of their
lives, and as they wondered about the whereabouts of their parents, they also
might have wondered about the whereabouts of God.

God has always been there, even when people failed you. He always will
be there, never leaving you, never forsaking you. It's a promise.

**Father, thank You for Your promise that You are always with me. You
will never fail me or forsake me.**

Gifts of Eternal Value

SCRIPTURE READING: Ephesians 4:29–32
KEY VERSE: Proverbs 10:20

The tongue of the righteous is choice silver;
The heart of the wicked is worth little.

One of the most important components of the Christian life is the way we communicate with one another. Paul told us: "Let no unwholesome word proceed from your mouth, but only such a word as is good for edification according to the need of the moment" (Eph. 4:29 NASB). Our words can be powerful tools of encouragement and hope or, if thoughtlessly delivered, weapons of emotional devastation.

Few people truly understand the depth of shame and guilt of the woman at the well. More than likely, she was the focus of local gossip and malicious accusations. No one took the time to look into her heart—no one, that is, until Jesus.

Instead of rejection, Christ's words brought hope and forgiveness. The result was a changed life. Many of the people we meet and pass each day need to hear of God's love and eternal forgiveness. Rather, they are often met with disapproving stares and whispers.

Those trapped in sin already know the reality of their shame. What they really need is a way out of the mess they are in. Do as Jesus did. Accept them as people dearly loved by God while refusing to justify their sin. Let your words be gifts of eternal value instead of arsenals of pain.

Lord, let my words be gifts of eternal value instead of arsenals of pain.

Shipwrecked Saints

SCRIPTURE READING: Acts 27:14–44
KEY VERSE: 1 Timothy 1:19

Having faith and a good conscience, which some having rejected, concerning the faith have suffered shipwreck.

On his way to Rome, Paul and his Roman captors were shipwrecked. God had warned the apostle that if they continued the journey, their ship would be torn apart by the pounding seas. However, the captain sailed on.

Many Christians have faced similar circumstances in their walks with God. For whatever reason, they have turned aside to temptation, complacency, or some other sin. Deep inside they know they are no longer living the life God has for them, yet they have become driven by their actions and are blind to the impending consequences.

Paul remembered what it felt like to be shipwrecked. He could recall the sensation of the ship coming apart beneath him and the screams of the frightened crew. So clear was this one event in his mind that he drew an analogy from it to warn others who were on their way to becoming spiritually shipwrecked in their faith (1 Tim. 1:19).

When you compromise God's principles, you risk running aground spiritually. If you feel as though you've already sailed onto a rocky shore, ask Him to forgive and cleanse you. Forgiveness and restoration are always God's way. Whatever your need, He is willing to meet it if you will turn to Him.

Father, strengthen my faith. I don't want to become a shipwrecked saint.

The Consequences of Compromise

SCRIPTURE READING: Judges 1

KEY VERSE: Joshua 1:7

Only be strong and very courageous, that you may observe to do according to all the law which Moses My servant commanded you; do not turn from it to the right hand or to the left, that you may prosper wherever you go.

The nation of Israel was given a command to drive out its enemies who worshiped other gods. God knew if that did not happen, then Israel would be tempted to abandon its single-minded devotion to Him.

In the book of Judges we find, however, that Israel did not obey God. While many of its enemies were defeated in battle, Israel did not drive them out of the land. Instead, the people of Israel captured many of their enemies and made them their slaves. As the years passed, they intermarried. Later, these very nations rose up against the people of Israel and took them captive.

God demands obedience. Israel's existence depended on this one thing. The Lord is not a harsh taskmaster. He knows our future, and He knows that sin, if we allow it entry, will keep us from experiencing His blessings.

Often compromise does not begin as flagrant sin. It's much more subtle but just as deadly. If you are tempted to compromise your life before God, think again of the love God has given you. Take the time to recall His commitment to you. Ask Him to show you the seriousness of the enemy's pull on your life. There is only one way to deal with thoughts of compromise: Turn and walk away. Anything else is an open invitation to sin against God.

Help me turn and walk away from the deadly sin of compromise. Lord, show me the seriousness of the enemy's pull on my life.

Fit for Battle

SCRIPTURE READING: Psalm 139
KEY VERSE: Psalm 139:23

Search me, O God, and know my heart;
Try me, and know my anxieties.

Beneath the murky waters of the port of Savannah, Georgia, lies one of the Civil War's finest relics—the wreckage of the CSS *Georgia*. In the beginning the ship was thought to be incapable of defeat. It was clad with railroad iron and contained groupings of cannons armed and posed for war.

However, history provides us with a different footnote. While the ship appeared fiercely strong and protected on the outside, there were hidden weaknesses on the inside. For one, it leaked. Pumps often were stretched to the limit just to keep standing water removed from its hull. Another flaw was its weight. It was so heavy and cumbersome that it never made it past the entrance to the port. It was doomed to be nothing more than a floating barge that might offer a degree of protection should the battle stretch up the Savannah River.

Too many Christians look and play the role of well-groomed saints on the outside while underneath there are major leaks and flaws—greed, lust, laziness, deception, and others.

Make it your goal to be fit for battle and not a shipwrecked saint. Ask God to expose any area of your life in need of repair. Accept His forgiveness and then purpose to live fully in the light of His loving grace.

Dear God, expose any area of my life in need of repair. I want to live fully in the light of Your loving grace.

Your True Identity

SCRIPTURE READING: 1 Peter 1:1–5

KEY VERSE: Luke 9:24

Whoever desires to save his life will lose it, but whoever loses his life for My sake will save it.

Researchers say that a lack of true identity is the reason for the high suicide rate among young adults. Many people spend a lifetime trying to gain recognition and a sense of belonging and accomplishment.

Because we are Christians, our identity is found only in Jesus Christ. Searching for it in another person or thing brings disappointment, insecurity, frustration, and anxiety. Far too often those who profess Jesus as Lord are entrapped by the same things enslaving our world—pride, selfishness, and materialism.

Jesus said that in order to save your life, you must be willing to lose it unto Him (Luke 9:24). You cannot experience the freedom and purity of your identity in Christ if you are still longing to be identified with the things of this world.

In reminding the early church of their identity, Peter told them, yes, it was true: They were aliens, strangers to this world. Yet they had been chosen by God to know and experience all the wonder and goodness of His glory and grace. Therefore, their identity was secure in Christ.

Have you settled the need for identity in your life? If so, rest in the power of His embrace.

Lord, my true identity is in You. I rest in the power of Your embrace.

The Father Is with You

SCRIPTURE READING: Psalm 25:16–21

KEY VERSE: John 16:32

Indeed the hour is coming, yes, has now come, that you will be scattered, each to his own, and will leave Me alone. And yet I am not alone, because the Father is with Me.

Exasperated from running and hiding among caves during his flight from Saul, David knew the grip of loneliness. He cried out to God, acknowledging that he was lonely and afflicted, and he asked God to turn to him and be gracious.

David's example is ideal for all who suffer loneliness. It is one thing to know why you're lonely, to be able to readily identify a source like divorce or death. It is quite another to question the source of your emotions and whether something is wrong with you.

But think about this: God doesn't want you to be lonely. He knew even before you were born that you would encounter this season, and He is as close as you will let Him be. Just like David, you have the privilege of calling out to the Lord, asking Him to be the friend and confidant you need.

One way to overcome loneliness is to drown out Satan's lies with the truth. Do not respond to loneliness on the basis of feelings, but go to God's Word. In John 14:16–18, Jesus promised the disciples that He would not leave them alone but would send the Holy Spirit as their Helper, a pledge He fulfilled for all believers.

In John 16:32, Jesus reminded the disciples that even in His darkest hour, even after they had deserted Him, He would not be alone "because the Father is with Me." Right now, this very moment, the Father is with you.

Heavenly Father, You are with me. Let me feel Your presence.

Super You

SCRIPTURE READING: Ephesians 2:1–10

KEY VERSE: Ephesians 2:10

We are His workmanship, created in Christ Jesus for good works, which God prepared beforehand that we should walk in them.

Sometimes feelings of low self-esteem may stem from an image of how you are supposed to be, a false and unrealistic ideal. In his book, *Healing for Damaged Emotions,* David Seamands explains:

> Super You believes the myth: "I've always got to be super-happy." But are you always happy? Never depressed? Bubbling over with "Praise the Lord"? Is there never a time of struggle . . . when you do things out of sheer duty, without happy feelings? . . .
>
> When you waste time and energy trying to be Super Self, you rob yourself of growth and the friendship of God. And you never let God accept and love the Real You for whom Christ died . . . Super You is an illusion of your imagination, a false image, an idol . . .
>
> You can be yourself in Jesus, and you need not compare yourself to anyone else. He wants to heal you and to change you in order that Real You can grow up to be the person He intended you to be . . .
>
> When you stop wasting your spiritual energies to maintain this false Super You and start using those energies in cooperating with the Holy Spirit for true growth, you will find yourself free in Jesus Christ, liberated from false oughts and shoulds, freed from the approval and disapproval of other people, freed from that awful condemnation of the performance gap between what you're trying to be and what you really are.

Dear Lord, I need to be set free from the condemnation of the gap between what I'm trying to be and what I really am. Let me be the real me.

Feeling Unworthy

SCRIPTURE READING: 2 Corinthians 3:4–6
KEY VERSE: 2 Timothy 1:7

God has not given us a spirit of fear, but of power and of love and of a sound mind.

There is an interesting aspect of inadequacy that many people face. Theirs is the reverse of having a strong sense of adequacy; they struggle with feeling unworthy. For the Christian, this is certainly counterproductive. God wants you to learn to depend on Him—not because He is forcing you to do so, but because He loves you and knows what is best for your life. He knows your potential. When you give Him all of yourself, He takes your life and makes something beautiful out of it.

Remember, when God calls you to do something, He will take care of the details. When He opens a door of opportunity, He expects you to go through it, all the while relying on Him to provide the knowledge and strength you need to do the task.

Don't be plagued by doubts and fears. These can keep you from trying something new, something that could turn out to be a wondrous gift from God. Sometimes fear may strike so that everything within you wants to pull back where it is safe. But God has not called you to be fearful or afraid (2 Tim. 1:7).

Be determined. Ask Him to encourage you and speak to your heart as you step out in faith. Keep the eyes of your heart focused on the Lord. Let Him be your Guide and Refuge. Then when doubts or fears arise, He will be your Light of protection and your King of hope.

Dear heavenly Father, please encourage me to step out in faith. Be my Guide and Refuge.

Something Worth Thinking About

SCRIPTURE READING: 2 Corinthians 5:14–17

KEY VERSE: 2 Corinthians 5:17

If anyone is in Christ, he is a new creation; old things have passed away; behold, all things have become new.

Controlling your thoughts can be difficult, especially if you open the door to thoughts that are not in keeping with the thoughts of Christ. Many people say, "Well, that's not my problem. I don't think about sinful material or things that would compromise my relationship with God."

But they overlook their negative thoughts and feelings toward themselves and others. Hidden within the vast resources of our minds is a tremendous ability to store and retrieve data. The brain is so complex that scientists still do not know all its capabilities. However, one thing is clear: we view ourselves in light of what we believe to be true. If we have a negative belief system concerning who we are, then we will act negatively.

Thus the adage "Winners never lose and losers never win" is true. Not because winners win and losers lose, but because of how each group views itself.

For the next week refuse to react to negative thoughts about yourself or others. Look in the mirror and tell yourself: "I'm a child of God, and He loves me the way I am." End of discussion! God will never belittle or embarrass you. He leads you to His altar of forgiveness so you can experience His glorious care on a personal basis. He gives you a totally new beginning. Now that's worth thinking about!

Lord, I'm Your child. You love me the way I am. I praise You.

Captive Thoughts

SCRIPTURE READING: Philippians 4:4–9
KEY VERSE: 2 Corinthians 10:5

Casting down arguments and every high thing that exalts itself against the knowledge of God, bringing every thought into captivity to the obedience of Christ.

A clear conscience brings peace to the heart and a sense of contentment to the mind. People who are continually rushing and running in and through trouble shouldn't be surprised to find it hard to relax and forsake feelings of anxiety.

One of the roles of the Holy Spirit is to lead us into all truth, an essential element in gaining a clear conscience. The apostle Paul wrote, "Whatever is true, whatever is honorable, whatever is right, whatever is pure, whatever is lovely, whatever is of good repute, if there is any excellence and if anything worthy of praise, let your mind dwell on these things. The things you have learned and received and heard and seen in me, practice these things, and the God of peace shall be with you" (Phil. 4:8–9 NASB).

The verses immediately preceding these also add insight: "Rejoice in the Lord always; again I will say, rejoice! . . . The Lord is near. Be anxious for nothing, but in everything by prayer and supplication with thanksgiving let your requests be made known to God. And the peace of God, which surpasses all comprehension, will guard your hearts and your minds in Christ Jesus" (vv. 4–7 NASB).

When your thoughts are captivated with things that are not of God, it is difficult to experience the hope of His truth. Only when you are in tune with His loving Spirit can you sense His grace and mercy at work in your life.

Lord, help me to be in tune with Your loving Spirit so I can sense Your grace and mercy at work in my life.

A Question of Motives

SCRIPTURE READING: 1 Thessalonians 5:12–24

KEY VERSES: Colossians 3:23–24

Whatever you do, do it heartily, as to the Lord and not to men, knowing that from the Lord you will receive the reward of the inheritance; for you serve the Lord Christ.

Burnout isn't a problem only in the workplace. Many times, people involved in full- or part-time Christian ministry experience the same feelings of stress and depletion of emotional and physical energy. Why? They may be the victims of a misunderstanding about the true nature of service. However, when you keep in mind a few key principles, you'll avoid some common burnout pitfalls.

The Holy Spirit empowers you to do what God has called you to do. If you fall into the personal performance trap, it won't be long until you run out of resources. Read John 14–17 for a deeper understanding of how God works through you to accomplish His purposes. The Holy Spirit gives you guidance, comfort, and confidence.

You cannot serve God and yourself at the same time. Some believers confuse selfish motivations with God's. Working for a church or ministry organization becomes an end in itself, with glory and recognition or power as the real incentives. And it's not just so-called powerful people who are guided by personal gain. It can be the person doing minor tasks too. Ask God to sift through your motives as you grow and to reveal any false ones.

The Lord—not people—is the object of service. If you're working for the good of others, you'll soon be disappointed. Your real employer is Jesus Christ (Col. 3:23–24).

Dear Lord, may You be the object of my service instead of people. You are my real employer.

Resolving Conflicts

SCRIPTURE READING: Matthew 21:12–17
KEY VERSE: Ephesians 4:32

Be kind to one another, tenderhearted, forgiving one another, just as God in Christ also forgave you.

When you are hurt, how do you defuse the emotional bomb of your anger? It may sound simplistic, but the power of Jesus Christ is the answer. He is the only One who can control your emotions and channel them in the proper directions.

It is also crucial to remember that your anger is not intrinsically wrong (Matt. 21:12–17). Anger in response to sin and its ill effects is a form of righteous anger, but when it crosses over the boundary into bitterness or a spirit of vengeance, it is not honoring to God. Much has been written on the subject of handling anger, and for good reason; it is a powerful motivator.

A key principle for keeping anger from turning into deep hurt is found in Ephesians 4:32 (NASB): "Be kind to one another, tender-hearted, forgiving each other, just as God in Christ also has forgiven you." When you let go of your desire to get revenge, you are on the road to experiencing true freedom through forgiveness.

Your health and well-being are not the only reasons for quick resolution of an angry conflict; bitterness must be avoided at all costs. When a hurt is not addressed, it works its way down into the inmost parts of your heart. Bitterness is a lack of forgiveness multiplied many times over, and it will take root and spread into every segment of your life if you are not watchful.

Lord, I don't want anger to control me. Help me to forgive as You forgave me.

Joyful in All Things

SCRIPTURE READING: Philippians 2:15–18
KEY VERSE: Philippians 4:4

Rejoice in the Lord always. Again I will say, rejoice!

Jesus often instructed those He healed to go to the temple and offer a sacrifice to God. In doing that, the people were acknowledging God's mighty work while giving praise to Him instead of just focusing on the healing itself.

There was a release of joy and praise as the people went before God, thanking Him for what He had done. Joy is foundational to the Christian life. The Bible teaches us to be joyful in all things.

Can this mean that even when we fail to see God's miraculous hand at work in our lives, there is joy? Yes. Imprisoned and away from those he loved, the apostle Paul wrote, "Even if I am being poured out as a drink offering . . . I rejoice and share my joy with you all" (Phil. 2:17 NASB). It is possible to be joyful even though your world seems to be coming apart at the seams.

Because of Christ's love and devotion to you, you can be joyful even in times of disappointment, heartache, and personal loss. Joy is not based on your circumstances; it is based on a person—the Lord Jesus Christ.

When you feel sorrowful, take your sacrifices of praise to Him. Let His arms of encouragement engulf you and hold you close. Joy is not just external; it lives deep within the heart.

Thank You, Lord, that I can be joyful even in times of disappointment, heartache, and personal loss. Your joy is not just external. It lives within my heart.

Banishing Boredom

SCRIPTURE READING: Psalm 37:1–7
KEY VERSE: Psalm 37:4

Delight yourself also in the LORD,
And He shall give you the desires of your heart.

A subtle thief of contentment is boredom. Have you ever felt that a day was so dull that you just wanted to go to bed and wait for another one? Everyone goes through emotional periods of feeling listless or lifeless. But a chronic sensation of boredom may be a sign that you are lacking much-needed spiritual freshness.

Carole Mayhall comments on boredom in *When God Whispers*:

Boredom can rob a person of joy. Apathy may not sink my boat, but it can becalm me and cause despair as the wind is taken out of the sails of my life . . .

Three things will bring rejoicing to our souls: (1) God's very presence, (2) His world around us, and (3) people! God's promise to be present with us always can bring comfort and delight. So can the complexity and variety of His creation: a flower, the misty rain, the billowing clouds. Sometimes we may have to look hard into some of the people we encounter, but as we ask, God will help us delight in them, too. These are the three pools of delight we can bathe in when we're young and strong, old and feeble, or incapacitated or ill.

Anytime. Anyplace. Any condition. I'll probably have to remind myself often when dullness of soul creeps over me, but the truth is that God provides no excuse for boredom!

If you're feeling burned out and unexcited by life, ask the Lord for His renewal today.

Lord, You have filled my life with Your exciting wonders. Renew my spirit and help me to see them.

Think Like Jesus

SCRIPTURE READING: Ephesians 6

KEY VERSE: James 4:7

Submit to God. Resist the devil and he will flee from you.

God is committed to guarding your life, especially your heart and mind. He defends you from evil, but allows you to choose what you will think and do. Some find it hard to understand why their lives fall apart. However, a quick review of their thought life reveals the real culprit. Thoughts that wander along avenues of greed, pride, and lust do more harm than we can fathom by dimming the awareness of God's love and care.

When your fellowship wavers with the Lord, it also wavers with those of the body of Christ. Ever notice how some days are filled with argument and frustration? Instead of continuing along a downward spiral, stop and ask the Lord to show you where you have gone wrong.

Sooner or later, a wrong attitude leads to wrong behavior. This is why it is extremely important to check on your thought life. As long as you refuse thoughts of evil as they pass through the resources of your mind, then you are doing what God has called you to do, and that is to walk in the light of His truth.

James declared, "Resist the devil and he will flee from you" (James 4:7 NASB). Stand firm in the armor that God has provided (Eph. 6). Rebuke the enemy's draw and temptation to pull you to a substandard lifestyle. Instead, train your mind to think like Jesus, and you will be the victor!

Lord, help me to resist the devil and stand firm in the armor You have provided.

Learning to Cry

SCRIPTURE READING: Psalm 42
KEY VERSE: Acts 20:19

Serving the Lord with all humility, with many tears and trials which happened to me by the plotting of the Jews.

King David knew how to express his grief and fear, but not all men—not even believers—understand how to feel and express tremendous sorrow, and they're secretly afraid. In his book, *Real Men Have Feelings Too,* Dr. Gary Oliver explains:

After the initial shock is over and the numbness begins to wear off, we are faced with a choice. We can either face our loss and grow through the crisis or pretend that everything is fine . . . In order to move through this acute grief phase you can't repress or suppress your memories or emotions. You need to think about your loss, talk about your loss, and weep over your loss. That's right, weep over your loss.

One of the most damaging messages to men has been "real men don't cry." However, God created us with the ability to cry. David wept, Peter wept, and Jesus wept. Max Lucado describes our tears as "miniature messengers," and he describes the pain of some of those watching the crucifixion of Christ . . .

If you want the bottom-line, here it is. Tears aren't the issue. It's what our tears represent. Our tears represent the heart and soul of the person. To stuff, repress, suppress, or ignore your emotions is to deny your humanity. Lucado does not overstate the issue when he writes, "To put a lock and key on your emotions is to bury part of your Christlikeness!"

Lord, help me to release my emotions in acceptable ways, trusting Your grace to help me through times of frustration and anger.

Bearing Emotional Burdens

SCRIPTURE READING: Galatians 6:1–5

KEY VERSE: Galatians 6:2

Bear one another's burdens, and so fulfill the law of Christ.

If you saw someone struggling with a huge box, trying to carry it to the car, you would probably offer to assist. You'd feel silly not helping, especially if you were just standing there empty-handed. It seems the natural thing to do.

In the spiritual realm, however, helping each other bear emotional burdens gets a little more complicated. How do you know someone needs help? Should you help? Are you capable? Will you only make things worse? Are you intruding on the individual's personal life? What if he doesn't ask?

There is also the possibility of feeling that you are "getting in over your head." The person's difficulties may require counseling or long-term aid that you're simply not qualified or able to give. The fear of an awkward situation keeps many from getting involved.

The Bible makes it clear that as believers, we are to help each other along, however we can, in the power of the Holy Spirit and the wisdom He provides. But there are no guidelines about what that looks like specifically in every circumstance.

What you must remember as you approach a hurting person is that God knows the real need, and He will guide you in your efforts to reach out. You will grow as you see God using you to meet a need, and the recipient will be blessed as well. And remember, someday you will be on the receiving end.

Dear Father, grant me the ability to approach hurting people and reach out to them. Use me to meet the needs of others.

Dealing with Loneliness

SCRIPTURE READING: 2 Timothy 4:9–18
KEY VERSE: Matthew 28:20

"And lo, I am with you always, even to the end of the age." Amen.

There is a critical difference between solitude and loneliness. Solitude is a time of being alone that is enjoyed for its peace and calm. Loneliness is a time of being alone, but with an aching sense of separation and being cut off from the possibility of fellowship.

At the end of his ministry, shortly before he was put to death, Paul felt a sense of loneliness in prison. He had been imprisoned before, but that time was different. Certain individuals who had labored beside him faithfully no longer supported him, and Paul felt abandoned. Still, in the midst of great emotional pain, Paul recognized that God was with him: "The Lord will deliver me from every evil deed, and will bring me safely to His heavenly kingdom; to Him be the glory forever and ever" (2 Tim. 4:18 NASB).

If you are feeling lonely, admit your emotions to the Lord. He knows what you are going through, and He wants to be the One to fill that void. At some point, God will use others to meet some of your desires for meaningful relationships. But first and foremost, He wants you to recognize Him as your ultimate Provider.

Friendships with people will come and go. People change and are sometimes selfish. Only the Lord will be there for you without fail. Jesus reassured us, "I am with you always, even to the end of the age" (Matt. 28:20).

Lord, fill the lonely void in my life, and help me realize You are always with me.

Faces of Loneliness

SCRIPTURE READING: Psalm 68

KEY VERSE: Isaiah 49:16

See, I have inscribed you on the palms of My hands;
Your walls are continually before Me.

Loneliness wears many different faces. There is the loneliness that comes from being physically isolated. There is a deep, psychological loneliness that results from emotional abandonment. We may feel spiritually alone or uneasy when we are operating outside the will of God. A spiritual sense of loneliness can be one of the ways the Holy Spirit gets our attention and motivates us to return to God.

Finding yourself in opposition to God's will can be very lonely. It also can lead to feelings of anxiety and fear. Don't let Satan and his forces confuse you. God has a way planned to lead you out of every dark situation, but it requires humility and trust in Him to be your Source of help. He will take your loneliness and use it as a tool to draw you closer to Himself.

If you have drifted in your spiritual devotion to the Lord, confess it to Him. Accept His love and forgiveness. Don't be fooled by Satan's lies. God can and will restore you fully and completely when you bring your sorrows and failures to Him. Even if you are struggling with certain feelings and have not yet given in to temptation, God can break apart the darkness that seeks to enslave you.

You have Someone who knows all about you, and He has chosen you as His beloved. Nothing comforts you more than knowing that God unconditionally loves and accepts you.

Dear Lord, be my Source of help in every dark situation. Take my loneliness, and use it as a tool to draw me closer to You.

The Pit of Self-Pity

SCRIPTURE READING: 1 Samuel 30:1–18
KEY VERSE: 1 Samuel 30:6

David was greatly distressed, for the people spoke of stoning him, because the soul of all the people was grieved, every man for his sons and his daughters. But David strengthened himself in the LORD his God.

She spent most of the day moping in her favorite chair in her room. It was a rainy day, and the dark clouds and drumming of the drops on the roof only accentuated her gloomy mood.

"Why do these things have to happen to me?" she said to herself with a sigh. She had gotten nothing but bad news the previous week. Her job was no longer secure, her car's engine needed to be replaced, and she was still bothered by a persistent and painful sinus infection.

The more she thought about her situation, the more she felt sorry for herself. She didn't want to hear the words of her best friend, who encouraged her to take her troubles to the Lord in prayer. Somehow, it seemed more comfortable to feel down and dwell on the negative.

Though she didn't know it, this woman was trapped in the pit of self-pity. This pit is especially deceptive because it often doesn't feel like a pit. It's much easier to focus on the pain than it is to examine God's solutions and seek His comfort. Sometimes it takes the tough words of a friend to pull you out of the pit onto the high ground of God's tender love.

Are you having a pity party today? Self-pity is a comfort blocker. Wallowing in depression keeps you from experiencing God's victory. Invite Him to join you, and He will turn your pity into His praise.

Turn my self-pity into praise, Lord. Thank You for Your goodness to me.

Be Like a Bird

SCRIPTURE READING: Matthew 6:25–34
KEY VERSE: Matthew 6:34

Do not worry about tomorrow, for tomorrow will worry about its own things. Sufficient for the day is its own trouble.

You're sitting by a tree in the middle of a meadow, taking in the pleasant country sights and sounds. Suddenly you see a bird rush past you, feathers all in a fluff. He has a daily schedule under one wing and a cellular phone in the other. He's looking all over the ground frantically, with his beak poking wildly at the dirt. You hear him mutter, "The bug crop better be good next February, or I'll lose my nest egg for sure!"

Can you imagine such a ridiculous scene? Of course not! Birds aren't people, and they're not capable of worry or anxiety. That's why Jesus used them as an example of how you are to trust Him for your needs: "Look at the birds of the air, that they do not sow, neither do they reap, nor gather into barns; and yet your heavenly Father feeds them. Are you not worth much more than they?" (Matt. 6:26 NASB).

God knows worry is a waste of precious time. You can't change your circumstances anyway. Worry is a useless activity that robs you of the peace of trusting in His provision. Jesus said, "Seek first His kingdom and His righteousness; and all these things shall be added to you. Therefore do not be anxious for tomorrow; for tomorrow will care for itself" (Matt. 6:33–34 NASB).

When you recognize God's control over your life, you are able to let go of the need to manage things yourself. Be like one of His little birds and place yourself entirely in His care.

Lord, help me let go of the need to manage things myself. I want to be like one of Your little birds. I am placing myself entirely in Your care.

Facing Your Fears

SCRIPTURE READING: Psalm 124
KEY VERSE: Isaiah 41:10

Fear not, for I am with you;
Be not dismayed, for I am your God.
I will strengthen you,
Yes, I will help you,
I will uphold you with My righteous right hand.

In her book, *Tame Your Fears,* Carol Kent isolates and defines five forms of fear that can paralyze an individual: (1) the fear of things that haven't happened yet, (2) the fear of being vulnerable, (3) the fear of abandonment, (4) the fear of truth, and (5) the fear of making wrong choices. She writes,

> Identifying our fears and admitting we have a problem is only the beginning . . . The first step in finding a solution is to acknowledge that there are times when we question our faith and struggle with fear . . .
>
> Fear becomes "comfortable" because it's familiar. We're used to feeling like powerless subjects in the fear monster's kingdom. Instead of taming the monster and enjoying our lives, we allow ourselves to die slowly by many of the following prescriptions: denial, addictions, withdrawal, control, shame, and self-hatred . . .
>
> Facing our fear head-on can feel intensely risky. But it can be a stepping stone to humble faith, renewed confidence, appropriate power and courage, and trusting reverence toward a sovereign, powerful, and loving God. "Perfect love casts out fear" (1 John 4:18). It's in the Bible. And it's true.

When fear attacks, claim your position as God's child and accept His victory. He has overcome the disabling power of fear, and this is your greatest asset: His power living in you.

Dear Lord, help me to face my fears head-on in Your name. Let Your power be manifested in and through me.

Running from Corduroy

SCRIPTURE READING: Psalm 27

KEY VERSE: Psalm 27:1

The LORD is my light and my salvation;
Whom shall I fear?
The LORD is the strength of my life;
Of whom shall I be afraid?

An older pastor remembers a time when, as a boy, he took a shortcut across a vacant field. His mother had warned him not to cross the field in darkness. But knowing he was late for supper, he ignored her words.

Halfway through his adventure, he noticed the wind picking up. The leaf-barren tree limbs against the night sky added a frightening setting to his journey. Before he realized it, he was walking at a very brisk pace. Then he heard footsteps coming up behind him.

He turned to look, but no one was there. The moment he resumed walking, the steps returned. He tried walking faster, but the steps kept coming, right in cadence with his own. He even tried running, but that, too, was futile.

By that point he was besieged with anxiety. There seemed to be no escape! Suddenly a thought occurred to him: *Could I be imagining an evil intruder?* When he turned and looked, no one was there. Then he heard the noise again, but it came only when he moved his legs.

Looking down, he realized he was wearing corduroy pants. It was the rubbing back and forth of the material that made the sound he thought was footsteps.

Are you running from corduroy? Put your anxieties aside. Jesus is committed to protecting you.

Dear heavenly Father, take my fears and anxieties. I thank You that
You are committed to protecting me.

Trust Your Instruments

SCRIPTURE READING: John 3:14–19

KEY VERSE: Romans 8:1

There is therefore now no condemnation to those who are in Christ Jesus, who do not walk according to the flesh, but according to the Spirit.

Fighter pilots are considered some of the world's most elite technicians. Yet the pilots repeatedly are grilled with one clear truth: Trust your instruments and gauges; ignore your feelings.

Their machines are so fast, so deft, so nimble that a human's senses and emotions cannot keep up with them. How a pilot feels can vary not only from day to day but also from moment to moment. A slight loss of equilibrium can spell disaster.

In some ways, we are like fighter pilots, and Satan knows how vulnerable we can be. He knows how easily deceived and misled our feelings can leave us. This is where the enemy attacks. He tries to get us off balance. Satan cannot claim the soul of someone saved by the grace of God through faith in Jesus Christ, so he tries to steal the believer's effectiveness.

Constantly the deceiver is attempting to get you to focus on your feelings, and then he twists them into condemnation: "You're not really saved; God isn't there for you; remember that sin?" These are lies, and he is the father of them.

Jesus' death took away your sins completely. His presence gives you hope eternally. God's Word spells it out plainly. Let yourself take flight for God. Open the Bible and trust the greatest instrument of all.

Jesus, thank You that You have taken my sins away completely. Thank You for Your presence that gives me eternal hope.

The Futility of Frustration

SCRIPTURE READING: Philippians 4:10–13
KEY VERSE: Psalm 26:1

I have also trusted in the LORD;
I shall not slip.

The philosophy of this world holds that we should strive for perfection so that even if we never reach our goal, we will at least perform well because we are reaching so far. But we should ask ourselves: *Perform well for whom? Whom are we trying to impress?*

Seeking perfectionism, longing for social or professional status, and desiring "success" as the world sees it invariably result in frustration. They often bring a gnawing feeling that you do not measure up, no matter your achievement. One accomplishment quickly fades into the demands of yet another challenge. This is not how God designed your body and spirit to function.

Frustration can be tricky. What you think is the source may be only a symptom. You may dislike yourself now because of an erroneous perception you've developed over many years. You may dislike your current circumstances because of erroneous preconceived notions. God may be allowing your frustration because you have not dealt with past sin or because you are living outside God's will.

There is no human solution for frustration. There are no adequate self-help sessions or books. Only God can reveal to you the invisible wall into which you keep colliding. Humbly kneel before Christ, and ask Him to reveal your real source of frustration and His remedy for it.

Dear heavenly Father, reveal my source of frustration and Your remedy for it. Show me the invisible walls into which I keep colliding in my Christian walk.

Get off the Treadmill

SCRIPTURE READING: Isaiah 40:27–31
KEY VERSE: Psalm 131:1

LORD, my heart is not haughty,
Nor my eyes lofty.
Neither do I concern myself with great matters,
Nor with things too profound for me.

One of the most popular and effective tools people use to burn off calories, adrenaline, and stress is a machine called a treadmill. Many people work, worry, and grope through each day seemingly in vain and then dash to the gym to hop on the treadmill. Isn't it ironic that in both pursuits they must give great effort without really going anywhere?

So it is with people who try to work their way to righteousness. One reason many Christians grow stagnant in their faith is that they expend so much energy trying to adhere to some lofty ideal they have envisioned as the "Christian experience."

Have you become a modern-day Pharisee? Do you maintain a mental or psychological checklist to ensure you do what you should do and resist what you should not do? Are you closer to living under the law than under God's grace?

Rung climbing can lead to burnout. When you act outside God's will, even performing godly tasks, you are running on finite fumes: your own strength. Exhaustion, withdrawal, and bitterness can result. The real Christian experience requires only faith in Jesus Christ and an abiding in Him, the true Vine.

In His perfect time, He will lead your steps and actions for His great glory. His flame is eternal. Even if you have burned out, it never will.

Heavenly Father, I am so thankful that in Your perfect timing You will use me for Your glory. Your flame is eternal, even when I feel burned out!

Choose Life

SCRIPTURE READING: John 3:11–21
KEY VERSE: John 3:17

God did not send His Son into the world to condemn the world, but that the world through Him might be saved.

God is able to rescue us from every sin except one—denying His Son as our Lord and Savior. God has chosen to reach out to man and provide a way for him to have eternal salvation, but it is man's responsibility to accept God's offer.

Many spend a lifetime trying to work their way to eternal life. They donate money to charities, volunteer for needy organizations, and lend support for worthwhile projects, but none of this is enough to erase the sin that comes from living a life apart from the salvation of God. There is only one way to God, and that is through faith in Christ.

Jesus came to earth as God's beloved Son, not to judge the world but to save it. He told Nicodemus: "He who believes in Him is not judged; he who does not believe has been judged already, because he has not believed in the name of the only begotten Son of God" (John 3:18 NASB).

God does not condemn us to a life apart from Him; we choose it when we refuse His gift of salvation. He could force us to obey. Instead, He has given man a free will to choose life or death. He has provided all we need to step away from sin, shame, and negative emotions, but we are the ones who must select God's way over Satan's lie.

Committing the unpardonable sin need not be a problem if you submit your life to the One who waits for you with arms open wide.

Father, I choose life! I step away from sin, shame, and negative emotions.

MARCH

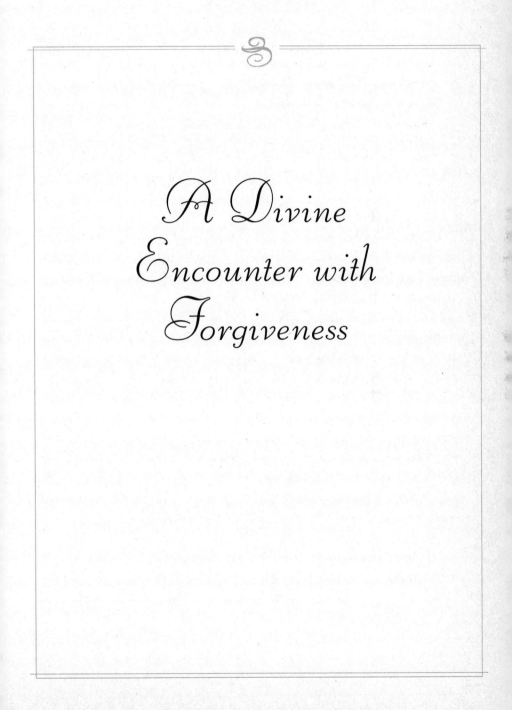

A Divine Encounter with Forgiveness

The Gift of Forgiveness

SCRIPTURE READING: 1 Corinthians 6:9–11
KEY VERSES: 1 Peter 1:18–19

Knowing that you were not redeemed with corruptible things, like silver or gold, from your aimless conduct received by tradition from your fathers, but with the precious blood of Christ, as of a lamb without blemish and without spot.

What keeps many people from rushing to embrace God's free gift of forgiveness is the pervading feeling that they have done something too awful to be forgiven.

From a human perspective, such a feeling makes sense. In legal practice, offenses against the law are categorized by their seriousness. Some crimes are just misdemeanors and carry lower monetary fines and minimal periods of imprisonment. Felonies are crimes that demand much more severe punishment, even death in some cases.

It's difficult to grasp that God does not categorize sin when it comes to His forgiveness. The tiniest, most trifling private sin is as great a transgression as the most heinous act. Jesus' blood covers them all equally, and His gift of forgiveness is absolutely free. He paid the penalty of death on the Cross so that you don't have to.

Have you ever stopped to consider that when Jesus died on that Cross, all of your sins were in the future? There's nothing that you will do tomorrow to eliminate His grace from your life. Peter told us, "You were not redeemed with perishable things like silver or gold from your futile way of life inherited from your forefathers, but with precious blood, as of a lamb unblemished and spotless, the blood of Christ" (1 Peter 1:18–19 NASB).

Father, I am so thankful that the blood of Christ covers me and that Your gift of forgiveness is free. Thank You for paying the penalty of my sins on the Cross.

Resolving Conflicts

SCRIPTURE READING: Ephesians 4:26–32
KEY VERSE: Ephesians 4:31

Let all bitterness, wrath, anger, clamor, and evil speaking be put away from you, with all malice.

Conflicts come in many packages, from children punching each other on the playground to international intrigue in times of war.

What are your "hot spots" of conflict? You might have difficulty getting along with others at home or on the job, with someone whose personality just doesn't fit with yours.

Whatever the case, conflict is a part of your life. Some Christians mistakenly believe that since Jesus lives in and through them, they'll be able to end all disagreement and trouble with others.

But that's not what Christ promised. He never intended for you to spend your energy trying to avoid tension. He wants you to let Him help you work through your anger with His grace.

When you are angry with someone, the Lord wants you to resolve the conflict as soon as you can: "Be angry, and yet do not sin; do not let the sun go down on your anger, and do not give the devil an opportunity" (Eph. 4:26–27 NASB).

Have you ever gone to bed at night with an argument unsettled? How did you feel the next morning?

Your own health and well-being are not the only reasons for quick resolution. The deeper principle at work is one of avoiding bitterness. When you don't address a hurt, bitterness takes over and spreads its poison into your innermost parts.

Dear Lord, give me grace to work through my anger. Help me to resolve the conflicts of my life.

Taking Responsibility

SCRIPTURE READING: Genesis 3

KEY VERSE: Psalm 32:5

I acknowledged my sin to You,
And my iniquity I have not hidden.
I said, "I will confess my transgressions to the LORD,"
And You forgave the iniquity of my sin. Selah.

When you are hurt by someone, you probably tend to focus more on the hurt done to your heart. What is more difficult to do is to examine the offense you may have caused him. It's all too easy to overlook your own responsibility in a conflict.

Blaming others encourages further sin. If you don't admit your responsibility, you may develop a "victim" mentality. You come to believe that you had no choice in your situation, and you may rationalize with statements such as, "Anyone in my position would have done the same thing."

Instead of concentrating on the other person's wrongdoing, be honest about your sin. If you sense the Holy Spirit telling you that you also are in the wrong, He wants you to confess that sin to Him.

When the urge to blame comes to mind, refuse it. Pray a prayer something like this one: "Lord, it doesn't matter how much (*name*) hurt me, I am the one who responded the way I did. Please forgive me, and through the power of Your blood, I forgive him."

This statement may be the hardest one you've said before the Lord, but it will free you from being bound up with inner hostilities and enable you to restore relationships. Only when you humble yourself before Him are you ready for the healing to begin.

Lord, it doesn't matter how much (name) hurt me, I am the one who responded the way I did. Please forgive me, and through the power of Your blood, help me to forgive him.

The Blame Game

SCRIPTURE READING: Genesis 3:8–13

KEY VERSE: Psalm 32:10-11

Many sorrows shall be to the wicked: but he that trusteth in the LORD, mercy shall compass him about. Be glad in the LORD, and rejoice, ye righteous: and shout for joy, all ye that are upright in heart. (KJV)

The mother came into the living room carrying a broken bud vase. Her daughter continued playing as though she did not see her. Finally her mother asked, "Catherine, do you know how this got broken?" The little girl thought for a moment and then replied, "Yes, Mickey did it." The mother knew that her daughter was speaking of an imaginary friend.

Obviously the woman's daughter had devised a scheme to avoid punishment. And while we think such stories are cute, they are not far from the actions of adults who try to cover up their sin by blaming others. In the Garden, Adam blamed Eve. Eve blamed the serpent.

How many of us have played the blame game by saying, "If only he had not made me do this or feel this way"? No one can force you to do anything. You can say no to anger, resentment, jealousy, divisiveness, fear, and much more. Blaming others for your actions leads only to heartache and feelings of anxiety. Take responsibility for what you have done. Learn to be honest with yourself and others, and you will discover a marvelous freedom.

After all, Eve chose to disobey God, and Adam made the same decision. Let obedience rule your heart. When this is your principal goal, you will be blessed.

Let obedience rule my heart, Lord. Help me seek Your forgiveness instead of blaming others for my faults.

Whom Are You Blaming?

SCRIPTURE READING: Genesis 3:14–24

KEY VERSES: Matthew 5:23–24

If you bring your gift to the altar, and there remember that your brother has something against you, leave your gift there before the altar, and go your way. First be reconciled to your brother, and then come and offer your gift.

Even when you are certain you have been wronged, even when you are certain you are right about a subject, do you realize God turns a deaf ear when you play the blame game?

This deadly game began after the very first sin in the history of mankind. Eve stumbled when tempted; Adam did likewise. But when an all-knowing God began seeking their explanations, Adam blamed Eve, and Eve blamed the serpent. Somehow, nobody was guilty!

God would hear none of it. They were cast out of the Garden of Eden, with man left to endure the toil of subsistence and woman left to endure the intense pain of childbirth. Sin ruined man's unspoiled fellowship with God. And making excuses had not one iota of effect upon God's swift judgment.

The same holds true today. Our society decays, yet no one will take responsibility. All too many marriages in the United States end in divorce, and courtrooms are filled with people seeking damages in the most trivial cases. The blame game is at the height of popularity.

God doesn't listen to our accusations of others, nor does He RSVP to our pity parties. All He wants is our proper fellowship with Him. In Matthew 5:23–24, Jesus outlined this commandment. The best way to point fingers is skyward in worship of our loving, forgiving Father.

Father, teach me to accept responsibility for my own sins.

Forgiving Yourself

SCRIPTURE READING: Psalm 51:1–7

KEY VERSE: 1 John 1:9

If we confess our sins, He is faithful and just to forgive us our sins and to cleanse us from all unrighteousness.

Did you know that learning to forgive yourself is just as important as forgiving others? It's true, although it is an aspect of forgiveness that is overlooked frequently. When you forgive yourself—that is, you stop allowing guilt to tear you apart—you are letting God heal the brokenness hidden deep within.

Refusing to "let yourself off the hook" nurtures guilt. Along with guilt come shame, feelings of worthlessness, and a desire to hide from God. You may even harbor the subconscious idea that being free from guilt would foster a carefree attitude, which might steer you back into the same sin.

There is hope for you today. God desires for you to live in the freedom, security, and holiness that are yours in Christ. Through the Savior who paid for your sin, you are truly righteous and blameless. Romans 8:1 gives you this promise: "There is therefore now no condemnation to those who are in Christ Jesus."

If your self-image is blurred because you don't feel forgiven, embrace this promise as well: "If we confess our sins, He is faithful and righteous to forgive us our sins and to cleanse us from all unrighteousness" (1 John 1:9 NASB).

As you learn to forgive yourself as Christ forgives you, you may need to reaffirm these truths periodically. Remember, Christ came to set the captives free (Isa. 61:1).

Lord, help me to forgive myself. Take my guilt and shame.

A Shining Light

SCRIPTURE READING: Genesis 6:1–13

KEY VERSE: Matthew 5:14

You are the light of the world. A city that is set on a hill cannot be hidden.

Contrasting colors are more noticeable than colors that are similar. For example, a white dot really shows up on a black background; it almost pops off the page.

That's the way Noah was, compared to the society around him. The first few verses of the sixth chapter of Genesis paint a bleak picture of the world, with great evil and sin abounding: "Then the LORD saw that the wickedness of man was great on the earth, and that every intent of the thoughts of his heart was only evil continually" (Gen. 6:5 NASB).

Yet in the midst of this great darkness, Noah was the bright spot: "But Noah found favor in the eyes of the LORD . . . Noah was a righteous man, blameless in his time; Noah walked with God" (vv. 8–9 NASB). Noah desired to please God in all his ways, and his continual desire was to walk in complete fellowship with Him.

Is that your desire as you live in a world that operates on an entirely different basis? When you focus on abiding in Christ and seeking His purposes every day, your life becomes a shining light in a society of sometimes overwhelming darkness (Matt. 5:14). Of course, you may not be consciously aware that you are being a light, but you can be sure that others are watching what you say and do. That is why you must learn to forgive.

Lord, others are watching what I say and do. Teach me to forgive so I can demonstrate Your forgiveness to them. Let me be a shining light in this dark world.

Renewing Your Mind

SCRIPTURE READING: Ephesians 4:17–24

KEY VERSE: Romans 12:2

Do not be conformed to this world, but be transformed by the renewing of your mind, that you may prove what is that good and acceptable and perfect will of God.

Wouldn't it be wonderful if the moment Jesus became your Savior, He lifted out your old mind and gave you a brand-new one, a kind of heavenly transplant?

You wouldn't struggle with thinking old thoughts. No more sinful images would crowd in on your prayers. You wouldn't even be able to come up with negative words to say, and you would be able to forgive others easily. But God did not choose to do this. Instead, He wants you involved in the process of transformation, step-by-step.

Paul urged us: "Do not be conformed to this world, but be transformed by the renewing of your mind, that you may prove what the will of God is, that which is good and acceptable and perfect" (Rom. 12:2 NASB).

The gradual change involved in renewal is not the same for everyone, so there is not a set formula for replacing the old with the new. The Lord knows exactly what your trouble spots are, however, and He will make you sensitive to areas of your thought life that need His attention.

What you must do continually is to choose truth over error and deliberately set your mind to the task of meditating on His Word. That way, when old falsehoods try to ruin your thinking, you will be alert to the patterns and ready to replace them with God's unchanging truth.

Father, help me to choose truth over error and set my mind to meditate on Your Word. Make me alert to replace false patterns with Your wisdom.

Refusing to Forgive

SCRIPTURE READING: Isaiah 43:1–21

KEY VERSE: Isaiah 43:18

Do not remember the former things,
Nor consider the things of old.

What happens when you can't seem to let go of pain and hurt from past years? Bitterness is a common symptom, the refusal to forgive. Far more often, however, the refusal to move forward results in depression and even despair. When you dwell on pain, it's not long before your entire experience of life is defined by that pain, and that clearly is not what God has intended for you as His child.

There is another way, and it's not any quick remedy or simple formula from a self-help book. The key is looking to God for encouragement and the gift of His renewal: "Do not call to mind the former things, Or ponder things of the past. Behold, I will do something new, Now it will spring forth; Will you not be aware of it? I will even make a roadway in the wilderness, Rivers in the desert. The beasts of the field will glorify Me . . . because I have given waters in the wilderness And rivers in the desert, To give drink to My chosen people. The people whom I formed for Myself, Will declare My praise" (Isa. 43:18–21 NASB).

God is ready to do a work of renewal in your heart and life, and He asks you, "Will you not be aware of it?" You may be in the desert, and you may have been scorched too long by its hot, blowing sands. But God has prepared a river of relief for you if you will only ask Him to open your eyes to His refreshment.

Thank You, Lord, for Your river of relief. Open my eyes to Your refreshment.

The World Is Not Winning

SCRIPTURE READING: Romans 8

KEY VERSE: Romans 8:37

In all these things we are more than conquerors through Him who loved us.

As you go about your daily routine, do you sometimes feel as though the world is winning? From the irritations and conflicts of your personal circumstances to bad news in the marketplace and the media, it's easy to become discouraged and focused on the negative.

The victory over sin and death that Christ won on the Cross can seem remote from daily application. But the truth remains: "Whatever is born of God overcomes the world; and this is the victory that has overcome the world—our faith. And who is the one who overcomes the world, but he who believes that Jesus is the Son of God?" (1 John 5:4–5 NASB).

You are more than a conqueror through Jesus Christ (Rom. 8:37). Does this mean that you will feel successful in every encounter and conflict? No. God may allow you to go through times when His truth working within you is obscured to another's eyes. He may need to do more work in the other person's heart before he is ready to listen. God is taking care of the consequences; your job is to trust Him for the outcome.

Ultimately the victory is yours in the Lord. In the meantime, you can cling to this promise: "Commit your way to the LORD; trust in him and he will do this: He will make your righteousness shine like the dawn, the justice of your cause like the noonday sun" (Ps. 37:5–6 NIV).

Thank You, Lord, that I can trust the outcome to You. Victory is mine through You.

The Steps of Forgiveness

SCRIPTURE READING: Hebrews 12:12–15
KEY VERSE: Hebrews 12:14

Pursue peace with all men, and holiness, without which no one will see the Lord.

You've heard of the stages of grief that a person experiences when someone close to him dies. Death brings out a host of emotions that must be dealt with honestly as they arise.

The same is true for dealing with an offense when someone hurts you. The pain is very real, and even if you know the incident was unintentional, the ache is still there. See if you can recognize these common stages in the process of coming to forgiveness:

Confusion. At first, you may be bewildered by the offense. You may try to find an explanation and relive the scenario in your mind to try to find answers. When the offender is someone close to you, the assault may be all the more troubling.

Denial. Another term for this is *detouring,* and it involves telling yourself that the offense did not even occur. You explain it away and try to convince yourself that you should not have felt hurt.

Discovery. Through the truth of God's Word, you come to realize what you're doing. Jesus urges you to forgive immediately and put the past behind you.

Forgiveness. You come before the Lord, confessing your sin of resentment and at the same time releasing the other person from all obligation to you. You are now free to love as Christ intends.

Lord, help me to identify where I am and move me through the steps of forgiveness.

Spiritual Security

SCRIPTURE READING: John 3:1–19
KEY VERSE: 1 John 5:13

These things I have written to you who believe in the name of the Son of God, in order that you may know that you have eternal life (NASB).

There is a familiar sound in this passage. It is the combination of words and the way they are stated that bring thoughts of our Lord to mind: "These things I have written to you who believe in the name of the Son of God, in order that you may know that you have eternal life" (1 John 5:13 NASB).

Jesus often used the phrase "These things I have spoken to you . . ." Christ's words always reflected the truth of God, and the Lord's messenger, John the Beloved, continued the work of putting forth the truth.

Keep in mind, the apostle John was an eyewitness to the miracles and teaching of Christ. We could say that He literally sat in God's classroom. It is from this point of view and the fact that God's personal anointing was on John's life that he wrote to the early church and to all who place their faith in the Lord Jesus Christ.

Certain things in God's Word cannot be overlooked or denied. The truth John gave us is not truth expounded by man but truth taught and illuminated by the Holy Spirit. God has made the way of salvation clear. Faith in Jesus Christ saves us (John 3:16).

Truth has been given "so that you may know that you have eternal life." There is no hesitation here. God forgives and saves all who call upon the name of the Lord Jesus Christ. This is a point of spiritual security that no one can remove.

Father, thank You for the truth that forgiveness guarantees my spiritual security.

The Love of God

SCRIPTURE READING: Jeremiah 31:1–8
KEY VERSE: Jeremiah 31:3

The LORD has appeared of old to me, saying:
"Yes, I have loved you with an everlasting love;
Therefore with lovingkindness I have drawn you."

God told the Israelites that He loved them with an "everlasting love." And God has the same type of love for *you*. No matter what you have done in the past or where you stand in your walk with Him, God loves you. This is His eternal message that reaches across all emotional, physical, and spiritual boundaries.

God loves each one of us, and you cannot change the nature of His love. Doubt, fear, regret, feelings of hopelessness, or sin will not alter His feelings toward you. Love is one of His attributes, which means love is a core aspect of His nature.

You may not always act lovingly toward Him, but He will always care about you. This does not mean He is unmindful of your sin. Instead, it is a testimony of how God honors who He is. He looks at your life and unashamedly declares His love for you. The kind of love God extends to you is the same love He has for His Son.

In the Greek, this love is called *agape*. Bible expositor W. E. Vines writes, "*Agape* expresses the deep and constant love and interest of a perfect Being towards entirely unworthy objects." God loved you even when you were lost in sin. True freedom and peace come when you accept the eternal love and forgiveness of God. The good news is that it is available to you right now and forever.

Dear Lord, I thank You that You loved me even when I was lost in sin.
I accept Your eternal love and forgiveness.

The Name of Jesus

SCRIPTURE READING: Luke 10:1–17
KEY VERSE: Philippians 4:13

I can do all things through Christ who strengthens me.

There is power in the name of Jesus. We can see it in the lives of the seventy disciples mentioned in Luke 10:1–17. The evidence of their ministry was dramatic, but they did not have success because of their own abilities. "Even the demons are subject to us in Your name" was their testimony to Jesus.

It is keenly important for you to understand the significance of Christ's name. Just saying the name of Jesus does not make a significant difference in and of itself. A powerful change takes place when you acknowledge His lordship and sovereignty.

The seventy disciples were sold out for Christ. And because of their dedication, they experienced something that was miraculous in nature. This moving of God's Spirit is available to you as well.

The apostle Paul proclaimed, "I can do all things through Him who strengthens me" (Phil. 4:13 NASB). Paul made a conscious decision to lay aside his personal desires and rights in order to follow Jesus Christ. The life of Christ within him gave him the ability to meet all demands, reach all goals, and accomplish all things.

Are you aware of who is in control of your life? Or are you still clinging to the reins and hoping that somehow your human ability will make a difference? Nothing but Jesus will ever satisfy your longing, and only the name of Jesus will bring true peace and forgiveness.

Take control of my life, Lord. I want to experience true peace and forgiveness.

God's Discipline

SCRIPTURE READING: 2 Samuel 24
KEY VERSE: Psalm 119:67

Before I was afflicted I went astray,
But now I keep Your word.

*E*ach of us will face times of discipline. Usually we can trace the origin back to some area of sin. God had to discipline even His greatest servants. David was not an exception. When he decided to count his fighting men, God became angry. David's faith was supposed to be in God's ability and not in his own power or military strength.

As a result of David's sin, the nation of Israel faced the disciplining hand of God. Pressure always builds within when we become involved in things that God has warned us to steer clear of. Many times you can avoid His discipline by asking Him to make you sensitive to the leading of His Spirit.

When discipline does come, realize that it is not His arbitrary punishment against you. God loves you and has a purpose in mind for any instruction He sends your way. He is your loving heavenly Father, who uses discipline only as a tool to bring you closer to Himself.

Your attitude toward His discipline is crucial to future spiritual growth. Take it seriously. Endure it until God releases you because it's an expression of His perfect love toward you. Submit to it and accept it as something He will use greatly in your life.

Blessing is the reward that comes as a result of your obedience. God's great and wondrous grace and forgiveness are yours today.

Father, I want to be blessed. Extend Your grace and forgiveness to me today.

The Tool of Discipline

SCRIPTURE READING: 2 Chronicles 7:12–14

KEY VERSE: 1 Peter 5:6

Humble yourselves under the mighty hand of God, that He may exalt you in due time.

When God sends His discipline, you can be assured that He has something wonderful in mind for your life. And while this may be hard to envision, especially when you are enduring the trial, it is true. God is on your side. He never works against you. Even in times of discipline, God is directing your life.

Discipline is the tool He uses to bring focus to your life when you have drifted from His chosen path or when you are refusing to follow His instruction in a particular situation. Through discipline, you learn how to live a godly life.

Peter admonished us to humble ourselves "under the mighty hand of God." Why? So that once we have learned the lesson God wants us to learn, we will experience the overflow of His blessings throughout our lives.

This does not mean that the goal of discipline should be only to receive a blessing and nothing else. The greatest benefit of discipline is the potential for intimacy it brings between you and the Lord.

If you do what Peter advised by humbling yourself before the Lord, then you will experience a deeper level of fellowship with God. Your heart and mind will be opened, and you will hear His voice leading you.

Are you facing a difficult time? Greet your adversity with humility. Submit yourself to God, and He will exalt you at the proper time.

Dear Lord, I submit myself to You. Use the tool of discipline in my life.

Keep Out of Satan's Territory

SCRIPTURE READING: Luke 22:31–32

KEY VERSE: Ephesians 6:12

For we do not wrestle against flesh and blood, but against principalities, against powers, against the rulers of the darkness of this age, against spiritual hosts of wickedness in the heavenly places.

She had spent a long, hard day at the office. After-hours work caused her to get caught in heavy traffic, the aftermath of an earlier accident. Plans for an early dinner date with her husband were running afoul. Through it all, she tried to remain at peace, knowing circumstances were beyond her control.

However, by the time she arrived home, her husband's concern for her tardiness had turned to irritation. As the conversation degenerated, both took a defensive posture.

After tempers had cooled, they called to mind Ephesians 6:12. Satan took subtle advantage of the circumstances, turning concern and weariness into personal conflict.

When such conflicts arise between two people, it is hard to keep in mind that the devil is slyly working behind the scenes. We seek to solve problems in our own abilities, ignorant of the reality of the spiritual realm. When we begin to understand the spiritual forces that are at work, we can then be more tolerant and forgiving of others, thwarting Satan's plan of strife.

Allow Christ to fight your battles in the heavenlies, keeping you out of Satan's territory.

Lord, fight my battles in the heavenlies. Keep me out of Satan's territory!

Meeting Your Needs

SCRIPTURE READING: Genesis 16

KEY VERSES: Psalm 130:3–4

If You, LORD, should mark iniquities,
O Lord, who could stand?
But there is forgiveness with You,
That You may be feared.

Abram and Sarai thought they were doing a good thing. After all, God promised them a son to be the heir of the promise and God's special covenant. He didn't specify exactly how this birth would come about, they must have reasoned.

Maybe Sarai was impatient. Maybe she struggled with waiting for such a long time. She could have simply felt inadequate for the task. So she proposed to Abram that he try to have a child with her maidservant Hagar, and he readily agreed.

What was the result? Hagar bore a son named Ishmael, who grew up to be a rival of Abram's covenant family through Isaac. There has been no end of trouble and fighting through the outworking of their sin in not trusting the Lord to fulfill His promise in His timing. God did bless them fully, but they always had the heartache and reminder of their attempt to go around God's ways.

Have you ever tried to meet your needs outside God's legitimate plan? You probably know the pain of that mistake, and you quickly learned why it is so important to trust the Lord fully. What is more important now is that you grasp His forgiveness through Christ. There is no such thing as a misstep so big you can never go back.

Don't waste time living in guilt. Let God's forgiveness free you to enjoy His good for you today.

Lord, I don't want to waste time living in guilt. Forgive me so I can
be free to enjoy the good things You have planned for me today.

Obedience Is Better

SCRIPTURE READING: 1 Samuel 15
KEY VERSE: Romans 6:16

Know ye not, that to whom ye yield yourselves servants to obey, his servants ye are to whom ye obey; whether of sin unto death, or of obedience unto righteousness? (KJV)

Obedience can be a tough command. Saul discovered this, and in 1 Samuel we learn that he failed the test of obedience miserably. As a result of his disobedience, God took steps to remove him from Israel's throne. The Lord commanded sacrifices to be done a certain way. Yet Saul disobeyed God's instruction, citing the fact that he was afraid of the people.

Peer pressure is deadly and tempts us to turn from what is right. In addressing Saul's error, the prophet Samuel told him: "To obey is better than sacrifice."

Oswald Chambers affirmed, "It is a great deal better to fulfill the purpose of God in your life by discerning His will than to perform great acts of sacrifice."

It was extremely important for Saul to remain true to the Lord's commands and not compromise his life before God. Each of us will be tested just as Saul was. You may not be a king or a ruler, but you are a child of God. And He demands obedience. To settle for anything less is to miss His will.

Many think they can compromise their lives with sin, and nothing will happen. But sin carries with it horrendous consequences.

God knows the temptation you are facing has the power to destroy your life. But He has provided a greater way of escape through His Word and the power of His Holy Spirit. Cry out to Him. He is your Defender.

Forgive me, Lord, for disobeying You. I cry out to You. You are my Defender.

The Words of Your Mouth

SCRIPTURE READING: Psalm 19

KEY VERSE: Proverbs 4:23

Keep your heart with all diligence,
For out of it spring the issues of life.

The words of your mouth often reveal the contents of your heart. Some people work hard at being in control of what they say. They are careful not to allow any distasteful or deceitful word to be used. However, at some point emotions rise, and the quickness of speech uncovers what is hidden inside.

The psalmist wrote, "Let the words of my mouth and the meditation of my heart Be acceptable in Thy sight, O LORD, my rock and my redeemer" (Ps. 19:14 NASB). All of us have experienced a time when we have said something that hurt another and we felt badly for doing it. But when your life is fully submitted to Jesus Christ, God will protect your words and teach you how to walk in purity of thought and deed.

In Romans 12:2, the apostle Paul addressed the need to renew our minds in Christ. What does this have to do with the words we say? Everything! When our minds are set on Jesus, all that proceeds from us will be laced with love, patience, joy, hope, and kindness. Then even in difficult times, the words we say will reflect an inner peace that comes from the Savior.

Proverbs 4:23 (NASB) is a good reminder: "Watch over your heart with all diligence, For from it flow the springs of life." Ask the Lord to forgive anything you have said in thoughtless haste to another. And pray that He will bring you close to Himself.

Lord, forgive me of anything I have said to others in thoughtless haste.
Draw me close to You.

God Will Make a Way

SCRIPTURE READING: James 1:5–12

KEY VERSE: Psalm 18:30

As for God, His way is perfect;
The word of the LORD is proven;
He is a shield to all who trust in Him.

When life takes a sudden shift, don't become discouraged. God has a way marked out that you have not thought of taking. This holds true when relationships end without warning, finances hit an all-time low, and job offers do not materialize. He knows your needs, and He has promised to make a way for you through whatever wilderness you are traveling.

F. B. Meyer pointed out: "Dare to trust Him; dare to follow Him! And discover that the very forces which barred your progress and threatened your life, at His bidding become the materials of which an avenue is made to liberty."

Often we look for quick solutions. A problem or discomfort occurs, and we draw back from the emotional pain. No one likes to suffer, but God's greatest lessons can be learned in times of adversity and strife.

Are you willing to learn how to love the person who has hurt you? Can you say to her, "I forgive you"? Or if that is not a possibility, can you tell God you are ready to learn how to forgive so you can continue without bitterness of heart?

Trials prick you. Disappointment stuns you. And adversity can leave you feeling broken with pain. When life goes wrong, the greater test is how you will deal with its coming. God uses every piercing difficulty to teach you one thing: "Surely I will be with you always" (Matt. 28:20 NIV).

Lord, teach me to forgive so I will not be bitter. I want to be able to love others with a sincere heart.

No Fishing Allowed

SCRIPTURE READING: Hebrews 10:16–18
KEY VERSE: Mark 11:25

Whenever you stand praying, if you have anything against anyone, forgive him, that your Father in heaven may also forgive you your trespasses.

In the book, *Tramp for the Lord,* Corrie Ten Boom addresses the subject of forgiveness: "Forgiveness is the key which unlocks the door of resentment and the handcuffs of hatred. It breaks the chains of bitterness and the shackles of selfishness. The forgiveness of Jesus not only takes away our sins, it makes them as if they had never been." This is the same principle mentioned in Hebrews 10:17 (NASB): "THEIR SINS AND THEIR LAWLESS DEEDS I WILL REMEMBER NO MORE."

Hanging on to past failures and sins distorts God's view of who we are in Christ. He tells us that we are new creatures, saved and redeemed, but guilt and shame keep us from looking up into His wondrous face of love and acceptance. By focusing on the past, we block God's future intent for our lives.

Buying into false guilt leads to feelings of defeat that may end in hopelessness and fear. People who struggle with lingering guilt often have a hard time accepting God's love. They cannot imagine how the Lord could possibly use them for His glory, especially when they think about their past sins.

But think for a moment. If this were true, God would have never chosen Moses, David, and Paul as vessels for His work. Corrie had a saying that many people have come to love: "When God forgives your sin, He buries it in the deepest sea and puts up a 'no fishing' sign." When Christ forgives, He also forgets!

Dear Lord, please break the shackles of selfishness from my life. Take my sins and cast them into Your sea of forgetfulness.

Confronting Your Sin

SCRIPTURE READING: Romans 7:4–25

KEY VERSE: Romans 7:24

O wretched man that I am! Who will deliver me from this body of death?

*M*an's natural state is one of sinfulness. It is a direct result of the fall of mankind and the rebellion Adam and Eve demonstrated in the Garden of Eden. Our fallen nature is evident in feelings and emotions such as jealousy, anger, fear, resentment, unforgiveness, and more.

When the apostle Paul became aware of the depth of his sin, he cried out: "Wretched man that I am! Who will set me free from the body of this [spiritual] death?" (Rom. 7:24 NASB).

Confronting your sinfulness should bring the same response from you. Left on our own with no thought of God, we would be controlled by sin. It is only by the grace of God and the mercy of Jesus Christ that we can say with the apostle Paul, "Thanks be to God through Jesus Christ our Lord!" Only Jesus Christ saves us from the clutches of sin. And only He can change hearts and provide an opportunity for new life.

We can choose to live for Him and turn from evil, but first we must come to a point where we see our sin as He sees it. There's nothing glamorous about sin. It separates us from God and keeps us from experiencing His marvelous blessings.

Ask the Lord to surface anything in your life that reflects the old nature. Pray for Him to give you the strength to walk in the light of His grace.

Lord, only You can set me free. Save me from the clutches of sin. Change my heart and give me a new life.

A Second Chance

SCRIPTURE READING: John 8:1–11

KEY VERSE: John 8:11

She said, "No one, Lord." And Jesus said to her, "Neither do I condemn you; go and sin no more."

Although scholars argue whether or not the woman caught in adultery was a setup by the Pharisees in order to trap Jesus going against the Law of Moses, the overarching theme is forgiveness. God's love, mercy, and grace were all present and active. He did not condemn the woman but instead challenged her accusers to throw the first stone if one among them could be found without sin.

After the Pharisees departed, Jesus looked at the woman lying at His feet. It was not the first time she had committed such an act, but it was the first time she had appeared before Jesus. There was no doubt in her mind that He was a man of God. How exposed and embarrassed she must have felt, that is, until the Savior revealed His word of forgiveness and hope to her heart.

Perhaps there is something in your life you wish you could erase. Just the thought of it brings feelings of condemnation and sorrow. Adultery was an act that was punishable by stoning, according to the law, yet Jesus set the woman free.

He gave her a second chance, and this is what He gives each of us. If there is something you have done, know that when you bring it to God in prayer seeking His forgiveness, it is forgiven. God will never bring up the matter again. His Son's death at Calvary was sufficient payment for all your sins. Only almighty God can love us this much.

O Lord, I thank You that Calvary paid for all my sins. Only You could love me this much.

Extend Your Arms

SCRIPTURE READING: Matthew 6:12–14
KEY VERSE: Luke 6:37

Judge not, and you shall not be judged. Condemn not, and you shall not be condemned. Forgive, and you will be forgiven.

Corrie Ten Boom tells of a time she learned an important aspect of spiritual growth. It was 1947, and she had just finished speaking of God's forgiveness to a group in a small German church.

The audience was still haunted by memories of war. Yet the message they heard that day brought a sense of hope. They could forgive those who treated them so cruelly and go on with life.

As the service concluded, Corrie noticed a heavyset man coming toward her. Instantly she remembered him. He had been a guard at the concentration camp where she had been imprisoned.

"I know God has forgiven me for the things I did," he said. "But I would like to hear it from your lips. Will you forgive me?"

"It was the most difficult thing I had ever had to do," she writes. "I thrust my hand into the one stretched out to me. And as I did, an incredible thing took place. A healing warmth seemed to flood my whole being, bringing tears to my eyes. 'I forgive you, brother!'"

One of the ways we measure spiritual growth is by the way we extend our arms of forgiveness to others. In doing so, remember that Jesus extended His arms completely for you at Calvary.

Dear Lord, thank You for extending Your arms of forgiveness to me at Calvary. Help me to extend that same forgiveness to others.

Confessing Your Sin

SCRIPTURE READING: 1 John 1:8–10

KEY VERSE: 1 John 2:12

I write to you, little children,
Because your sins are forgiven you for His name's sake.

Confessing sin isn't something you do in order to be forgiven. In Christ, you are already forgiven of all sin—past, present, and future. Confession means that as you sin, you agree with God that it was wrong. You experience humble gratitude for Christ's gift, a fresh feeling of forgiveness, and renewed fellowship with God. Do you know how to confess your sins in this way?

Assume full responsibility for your actions. Only when you realize that you are guilty can you feel His forgiveness. Self-justification and blame of others become stumbling blocks to spiritual freedom.

Don't generalize the sin. Instead of saying, "Forgive me for what I did wrong," be open and honest. Take time to think through your actions and isolate the real sins involved. Say, for example, "Forgive me, Lord, for lying to my friend." Of course, God doesn't want you to dwell on your sin, but identifying it clearly will help you be more wary in the future.

Don't wait until a better time. Confession before the Lord is an activity for right now, the moment the Holy Spirit convicts you of a sin. Why? The longer you carry the guilt, the farther away from God you feel. Go to Him for restoration immediately. Keeping the lines of communication open between you and your Savior is a vital part of your spiritual health.

Lord, never let me carry around needless guilt. Help me to be honest.

Healing Memories

SCRIPTURE READING: Matthew 18:21–35
KEY VERSE: Matthew 18:35

So My heavenly Father also will do to you if each of you, from his heart, does not forgive his brother his trespasses.

Forgiving others is not something we do automatically. It takes a conscious effort on our parts. Yet Jesus was very clear on this subject: We are to forgive those who hurt us. Peter thought he could limit the amount of forgiveness he extended in going beyond what was expected by Jewish custom. However, Jesus quickly put a stop to this line of thinking.

For a moment, think about God's forgiveness toward you. You make mistakes. Yet Romans 8:1 tells us God's goal is not to condemn. First John 1:9 tells of His willingness to restore you each time you come to Him and confess your sinfulness. Christ's death was sufficient payment for every wrong you will ever commit. So what keeps you from forgiving those who hurt you? Seeking personal revenge or maintaining a "get-even" mentality only brings more heartache.

David Seamands writes,

Memory healing means being delivered from the prison of past hurts . . . We cannot change the facts we remember, but we can change their meanings and the power they have over our present way of living . . . A major part of the healing process is the discovery that God can take even the most painful of our experiences and work them out for our good and His glory . . . This does not mean God is the Author of everything that has happened to us. But it does mean that He is the Master of it all.

Help me, Lord, to forgive those who have wronged me. Heal my memories.

$\mathcal{L}$earning to $\mathcal{F}$orgive

SCRIPTURE READING: Genesis 50:14–20

KEY VERSE: Genesis 39:2

The LORD was with Joseph, and he was a successful man; and he was in the house of his master the Egyptian.

$\mathcal{I}$f you have been deeply hurt, you know healing takes time. But did you know that you cannot completely heal until you are willing to forgive the individual who hurt you? By forgiving, you are not saying that what he did was acceptable or even right.

Those who have suffered abuse know it is not easy to get past painful memories. However, if you want to experience true freedom, there must come a point at which you decide to let go of the bitterness and anger.

Joseph suffered during his imprisonment. He had been betrayed by his brothers and left in a pit. Rather than leave him there to die, they sold him to a group of traders, who took him to Egypt. For the first time in his life, Joseph was alone. The thought of his brothers' rejection must have seemed incomprehensible.

However, "the LORD was with Joseph, so he became a successful man" (Gen. 39:2 NASB). Joseph did not spend his time thinking about what he could do to get even. He made the most of his situation without self-pity. By the end of the story, we learn that he not only forgave those who sought to harm him but also was used by God to save them.

God may not require this same type of action from you. Yet He does want you to learn to forgive. Until you do, you will remain captive. Forgiveness sets the heart and spirit free.

Father, place in my heart the ability to forgive as You forgive me. Help me let go of bitterness and anger.

Your Dearest Friend

SCRIPTURE READING: John 15:12–17

KEY VERSE: John 15:9

As the Father loved Me, I also have loved you; abide in My love.

True friendship includes many things: love, a sense of closeness, forgiveness, openness, and availability. A true friend knows how to listen and, if necessary, be silent about his own needs at times. Only God can use a friend to help heal a hurting heart. Friendship also includes acceptance, flexibility, commitment, and a sense of unselfishness,

George Matheson said of a friend: "If I would know the love of my friend I must see what it can do in the winter." Loving someone else can be difficult. We are not easy to love at times. We have flaws in our lives that need God's attention, forgiveness, and care. But we also contain something worth sharing with another.

Because of the love of Christ that has been given to us, we are worthy to be loved and to love. It is God's love that motivates you to care for someone else. It is His example of pure love that spurs you to forgive when you have been unjustly hurt or accused. God loves you even when you act totally unlovely. He forgives and offers you another chance. In the purest sense, God winters with you.

He wants you to have this type of love for others. Next time you are tempted to stay angry at a friend, ask the Lord to help you understand the way He loves you. Jesus came because of His forgiveness and willingness to restore even the most hardened sinners. He is our dearest Friend.

Lord, teach me to see others through Your eyes of love and to forgive when I have been unjustly hurt or accused.

Responding to Failure

I pray for them. I do not pray for the world but for those whom You have given Me, for they are Yours.

Did you ever realize that the Lord knows about your failures before they even happen? When you really blow it, whether your failure is internal and spiritual or external and observable by everyone, you often feel an immediate sense of worthlessness or stupidity. Even worse, you feel as though you have disappointed God, and He expected better from you.

God knows your weaknesses and fallibilities. Even when your fellowship with Him is rich and full and you feel His direction in a powerful way, you are still prone to making silly blunders along the way. God is interested in your heart attitude after you make a mistake. Are you angry, sullen, or irritable, or do you pause to think things through and thank Him for another learning opportunity?

Yes, it can be painful to mess up, and you do feel silly sometimes. But your response to failure is the key to your future success. Look at the life of Peter, who denied that he ever knew Jesus. He committed a deliberate act of rejection, and Jesus welcomed him back with tenderness and open arms.

God allows you to mess up for many reasons, one of which is to encourage you to turn to Him for wisdom. Mistakes and goof-ups are continual reminders of your dependence on Him and of your need to accept yourself and others on the basis of His love and forgiveness.

Lord, use my mistakes as continual reminders of my dependence upon You and my need to accept myself and others on the basis of Your love and forgiveness.

Accepting God's Forgiveness

SCRIPTURE READING: John 21:15–17

KEY VERSE: Psalm 103:12

As far as the east is from the west,
So far has He removed our transgressions from us.

*P*eter had to make a difficult decision. The risen Lord was with him, and he found himself having to come to terms with his earlier denial. The Lord directed three questions toward Peter with the desire of revealing the disciple's heart devotion.

"Simon, son of John, do you love Me more than these?"

"Yes, Lord; You know that I love You," was the reply (adapted from John 21:15 NASB). Then there were a second and finally a third question. After each affirming response, Jesus gave Peter a course of direction to follow.

"Tend My lambs."

"Shepherd My sheep."

"Tend My sheep."

Jesus was restoring the fellowship between Peter and Himself. It was clear He had not given up on His disciple. He was still a part of the team. However, it was up to Peter to accept the Lord's forgiveness and act of restoration. If he had stalled, citing his unworthiness or past sinful behavior, the entire process would have been for nothing.

Is there something in your life that has bound you in fear and condemnation? Jesus forgives you when you express your sorrow and sadness over your sin. God forgives on the basis of what Jesus did for you at Calvary.

Forgive yourself and be restored. The freedom you long for is waiting. Will you take the hand of Christ and allow Him to bring you into the light of His love?

Lord, I confess my need of Your cleansing. Restore my fellowship with You.

APRIL

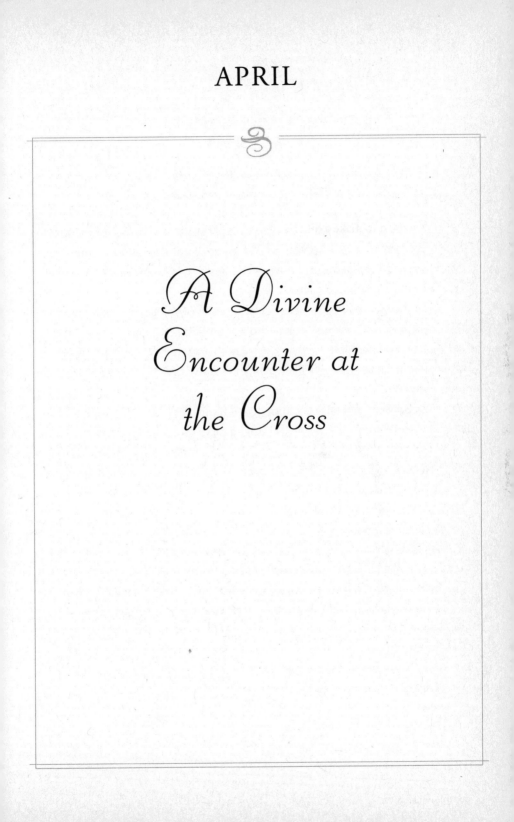

A Divine Encounter at the Cross

April Showers

SCRIPTURE READING: 1 Corinthians 13

KEY VERSE: Romans 8:35

Who shall separate us from the love of Christ? Shall tribulation, or distress, or persecution, or famine, or nakedness, or peril, or sword?

It has been said that April showers bring May flowers. If you've had April showers, don't be surprised if God awaits with a gorgeous bouquet of May flowers. It could come tomorrow. Perhaps it won't come until sometime later. But don't be discouraged.

Jesus Christ will bring His elegant bouquet, everything perfectly arranged. He may resolve your turmoil just as you prayed. He may resolve it in a different, much better way. Or He may choose not to resolve it at all. Still, you can be assured His thoughts are higher than your thoughts and His plan is perfection. He knows what is best for you.

Someday He will knock, holding your bouquet of May flowers. They will be your favorite color, beautiful and bright and wonderfully scented, a sweet savor unto the Lord.

Your April showers could be anything: trouble, sickness, sin. Perhaps they have left you feeling unworthy of God's attention and love. Understand that His is an unconditional love, and you have done nothing for which He won't forgive or restore you.

God's May flowers are a symbol of His eternal love that was demonstrated at the cross. He is able to cultivate them in season and out of season. They will have been planted, fertilized, and grown with the greatest of care by the ultimate Gardener. Jesus will bring the flowers after using your April showers to water them perfectly.

Lord, I thank You for the April showers that bring May flowers in my life.

Jesus Is Alive!

SCRIPTURE READING: 1 Corinthians 15:12–19
KEY VERSE: John 20:25

The other disciples therefore said to him, "We have seen the Lord." But he said to them, "Unless I see in His hands the print of the nails, and put my finger into the print of the nails, and put my hand into His side, I will not believe."

After the Resurrection, the disciples were overcome with joy that sprang from the realization that God had not forgotten them. Jesus was alive! However, not everyone shared the same enthusiasm. Thomas, one of their own, proclaimed, "Unless I shall see in His hands the imprint of the nails, and put my finger into the place of the nails, and put my hand into His side, I will not believe" (John 20:25 NASB).

Eight days later, Jesus came once again to them. That time Thomas was among those present. Turning to him, Jesus said, "Reach here with your finger, and see My hands; and reach here your hand, and put it into My side; and do not be unbelieving, but believing" (John 20:27 NASB).

In *Lectures in Systematic Theology*, Henry Thiessen writes, "The Resurrection is the fundamental doctrine of Christianity . . . In 1 Corinthians 15:12–19 Paul shows that everything stands or falls with Christ's bodily resurrection. If Christ has not risen, preaching is vain (v. 14), the Corinthians' faith was vain (v. 14), the apostles were false witnesses (v. 15), the Corinthians were yet in their sins (v. 17), those fallen asleep in Jesus have perished (v. 18), and Christians are of all men most to be pitied (v. 19)."

We are made fully alive because Jesus Christ lives within us. Death had no authority over Him. As Thomas learned, He truly is our risen Lord and Savior!

Jesus, I praise You that I am fully alive because You live within me. You are my risen Lord and Savior.

A New Level of Love

SCRIPTURE READING: Matthew 16:21–26

KEY VERSE: Romans 5:8

God demonstrates His own love toward us, in that while we were still sinners, Christ died for us.

Peter was privy to the greatest spiritual teaching. He also was the first disciple to proclaim Jesus as Messiah. The spiritual insight he gained helped to build his faith and self-esteem. Therefore, when Jesus began to talk of His death, Peter did not hesitate to say, "God forbid it, Lord! This shall never happen to You" (Matt. 16:22 NASB).

However, Peter miscalculated his spiritual maturity. He thought he understood the ways of God, but in actuality he understood only what made him feel good on the inside. He liked being close to Jesus.

There is something very rewarding in finding our self-worth in Christ. Yet we must be sensitive to the complete will of God. The life of Christ was given as a gift to demonstrate God's great love. It is only through Jesus that we have eternal salvation. He paid the price for our sins. Peter missed the bigger picture that Christ had to die so that we could live for eternity with the Father. Often God takes a different route from the one we think is necessary. Acceptance of His will positions us for spiritual maturity and blessing.

Are you trusting your feelings and wishing that God would work a certain way? Let Him have the entirety of your life and the lives of your loved ones. When you do this, you will find that you have grown to a new level of loving a holy, infinite God.

Lord, I give You the entirety of my life and the lives of my loved ones. Move me to a new level of loving You.

God's Guarantee

SCRIPTURE READING: John 14:1–4

KEY VERSE: Hebrews 11:13

These all died in faith, not having received the promises, but having seen them afar off were assured of them, embraced them, and confessed that they were strangers and pilgrims on the earth.

Have you ever known the frustration of canceled hotel reservations? Sometimes even the "guaranteed late arrival" system isn't foolproof. You hustle through two airports, fumble with bags all the way, grab a rental car, drive through unfamiliar territory, and finally make it to the hotel, only to hear the clerk say, "I'm sorry, but no rooms are available."

When Jesus told His disciples about His impending death, He gave them special assurance for the future: "In My Father's house are many dwelling places; if it were not so, I would have told you; for I go to prepare a place for you" (John 14:2 NASB). This promise was not for the disciples only; it is for everyone who accepts Christ as Savior and trusts Him for salvation.

Once you do this, your name is written in the Lamb's Book of Life, and it cannot be erased (Rev. 21:27). Your reservation is secure. And you can rest in the fact that the place Jesus is preparing for you is custom-made! Consider heaven as your real home and earth as a mere way station.

Hebrews 11:13 (NASB) tells us that the heroes of faith regarded themselves as "strangers and exiles on the earth." They had great comfort in knowing that there was an eternal destination waiting for them.

You have God's guarantee: no mansion on earth will ever compare to the one He has waiting for you.

Lord, I thank You that the Cross guarantees my destination. Heaven is my eternal home.

The Object of Your Faith

SCRIPTURE READING: Psalm 23
KEY VERSE: Psalm 23:4

Yea, though I walk through the valley of the shadow of death,
I will fear no evil;
For You are with me;
Your rod and Your staff, they comfort me.

There is always a time limit to the darkness we face. When God's purpose is accomplished, He brings fresh light. The psalmist asserted, "Even though I walk through the valley of the shadow of death, I fear no evil; for Thou art with me" (Ps. 23:4 NASB). For faith to be real, it must have an object. It also must be tested.

Who or what is the object of your faith? If your faith rests in anything other than Jesus Christ, it will crumble when it is tested. David's faith was rock solid because God and the accomplished work of the Cross was the focus of his life. He did not spend hours worrying about enemy forces and the winner of the battle. He knew God was with him. Therefore, he would not go down in defeat. This strong, tenacious belief was David's greatest strength in perilous times.

He also realized that though the darkness surrounded him, it was not his destiny to remain there. His faith told him that he was walking through darkness to reach the light. A. W. Tozer writes, "The true friend of God may sit in His presence for long periods in silence. Complete trust needs no words of assurance."

There will be times of darkness in your life. However, realize that God is with you (Ps. 139:11–12; Heb. 13:5). He never leaves you alone to fight any battle. His design for your life will often include darkness training sessions where you learn to trust Him even when you don't feel that He is near. The truth is, when you feel Him the least, He is just as close as ever.

Dear Father, I am so glad that You are with me, even in times of darkness.

Our Eternal Gift

SCRIPTURE READING: John 10:7–14

KEY VERSE: John 10:11

I am the good shepherd. The good shepherd gives His life for the sheep.

Scripture tells us that Jesus felt compassion for the multitude before Him because they were distressed and downcast like sheep without a shepherd. At that point, Jesus was well into His earthly ministry. Hundreds followed Him, countless individuals sought healing from Him, and thousands heard Him speak. For John to record words that tell of obvious distress among so many, there had to be evidence that this was true.

Jesus did not simply come in contact with people. He had the divine ability given to Him by His heavenly Father to touch the heart and soul of every individual whose path crossed His. He never looked at a crowd of people without seeing individual hearts and lives. Had He wanted to, and the time of eternity allowed Him, Christ could have immediately ministered emotional and spiritual healing to all.

But God's plan involved a greater possibility. Through Christ's life and death, we are given an eternal gift, the opportunity to live and know Jesus as our personal Shepherd and loving Lord through the presence of the Holy Spirit. We have His undivided attention every minute of every day. Take time to praise Him for His patience and love toward you.

Father, I praise You for Your patience and love toward me. Thank You for the eternal gift of knowing You.

What Is Your Choice?

SCRIPTURE READING: Luke 23:39–44

KEY VERSE: Luke 23:43

Jesus said to him, "Assuredly, I say to you, today you will be with Me in Paradise."

People often say, "If I only had one day to live, this is what I would do." They go on to list various activities and desires. The truth is, none of us knows when we will draw our last breath. Only God knows this.

The two thieves sentenced to die at the same time as Jesus were totally unprepared for what they were about to face. At the end of their earthly lives, one continued to resist God's saving love while the other humbled himself and asked Jesus to save him. What a difference that request made in his spiritual life.

One of the men died without God; the other died with the peace of knowing that that very day he would walk with the Lord Jesus Christ in paradise.

Some scholars believe that hell is a place where some will live for eternity with the realization of what they have done by denying God's love. A destiny like this is more horrendous than the mind can imagine—eternal separation from everything that resembles hope, light, and love. Jesus Himself called hell a fiery place.

Life does not have to end with this type of destiny in mind. Just as Jesus was willing to save both men, He will save you. There are two choices, but only one leads to eternal life and the wonder of experiencing God's glory and love for eternity. Which one will you choose?

Lord, I choose the path that leads to eternal life and the wonder of experiencing Your glory and love for eternity. Thank You for showing me the way.

Your Sentinel of Victory

SCRIPTURE READING: John 16:29–33

KEY VERSE: John 16:33

These things I have spoken to you, that in Me you may have peace. In the world you will have tribulation; but be of good cheer, I have overcome the world.

Oswald Chambers writes of adversity: "The typical view of the Christian life is that it means being delivered from all adversity. But it actually means being delivered in adversity, which is something very different . . . If you are a child of God, you will certainly meet with adversities, but Jesus says you should not be surprised when they come."

It's not a question of *if* tough times will come; it's a question of *when*. At some point, you will face a severe heartbreak, a problem you can't solve, a broken relationship that won't heal, the death of a loved one, a serious illness, or some other difficulty beyond your control.

Jesus wanted to be sure His disciples understood that they would face many trials. That was why He told them, "Take courage; I have overcome the world" (John 16:33 NASB). Jesus has overcome the sorrows of this world. He has put an end to the power of sin, banished the sting of death, and exposed the empty threats of fear.

In His hands are the keys to eternal life, victory over every illness, and eternal hope for every problem you face. After His crucifixion, the disciples found this hard to imagine—that is, until they saw the risen Lord. Today, you serve a mighty God, One who loves you completely and fully. If there is a need for peace or wisdom, Jesus will provide it for you. He is your Sentinel of eternal victory!

You are my Sentinel of eternal victory, Jesus. Thank You for this assurance.

The Message of the Cross

SCRIPTURE READING: Philippians 4:8–13
KEY VERSE: Philippians 2:5

Let this mind be in you which was also in Christ Jesus.

As Christians, we need never suffer with thoughts of low self-esteem or defeat. There may be times when we feel down or battle worn, but never defeated. Jesus Christ has conquered the power of sin and death. He is our sufficiency for every need we face. No matter what the circumstance, He is with us and for us.

The most powerful message we can feed our minds is the message of the Cross. God loves us eternally and unconditionally. Paul learned to be content in every situation of life because he knew the Son of God was watching over him. How could he possibly fail?

Whether in need or in abundance, Paul's sufficiency was rooted in Jesus Christ. His mind was tuned in to the powerful possibilities of God, not the doubt and discouragement of the world. Through times of suffering, even to the point of death, Paul remained firm in his faith.

Ask God to help you exchange any negative thoughts you may have for God's perspective. You will find that God never uses words of confusion, doubt, fear, or hopelessness. Instead, He always gives us words of hope, victory, peace, blessing, triumph, and love. Cultivate God's blessing by learning to walk in light of His victory.

Lord, let me tune out confusion, doubt, fear, and hopelessness. Help me receive Your words of hope, victory, peace, blessing, triumph, and love.

A Divine Bridge

SCRIPTURE READING: Ephesians 2:1–9

KEY VERSE: Romans 5:2

Through whom also we have access by faith into this grace in which we stand, and rejoice in hope of the glory of God.

The American mind-set is predominantly bootstrap oriented. When placed into difficult straits financially, emotionally, or otherwise, we seek yet a higher level of grit and determination to see us through the calamity.

However, the Christian faith offers no boot or strap for the sternest of problems—sin and death. It declares the chasm between unsaved man and God uncrossable. No human resolve, labor, innovation, or initiative can span its immeasurable darkness.

The sole bridge over such estrangement was built by God Himself with two pieces of timber at the Cross. The only hands that can rescue man were nailed to that Cross.

You cannot be saved apart from grace. It is a gift given by the holy love of God through the death of His Son. Only when you realize your utter helplessness can you receive the free gift of eternal life.

It is also the grace "in which we stand" today. When you sin, grace forgives. When you are weak, grace makes you strong. When you are confused, grace points the way. When you are depressed, grace lights your heart. Everything you are and will be is the work of God's grace.

Dear Lord, give me grace to stand today. When I am weak, let Your grace empower me and make me strong.

Filling the Empty Life

SCRIPTURE READING: John 4:3–18
KEY VERSES: John 4:13–14

Jesus answered and said to her, "Whoever drinks of this water will thirst again, but whoever drinks of the water that I shall give him will never thirst. But the water that I shall give him will become in him a fountain of water springing up into everlasting life."

Jesus motioned in the direction of the well by which He was standing and said to the woman: "Everyone who drinks of this water shall thirst again; but whoever drinks of the water that I shall give him shall never thirst" (John 4:13–14 NASB). The water Jesus offers is continuous. It wells up inside a person, satisfying the deepest needs of the heart.

The woman to whom Jesus was speaking was very needy. Her life was emotionally frayed and spiritually and morally bankrupted. Instead of feeling free to join the other women as they drew water from the well, she chose to come at a time when no one else was there. Sin always separates us from others.

Yet she was the very type of person who drew the love of God in a very compassionate way. Instead of bypassing Samaria, Jesus directed His band of disciples right into the heart of the region. There He waited for this woman to make her appearance.

She had been married five times, and the man she was living with was not her husband. It was obvious that she had tried in vain to fill the emptiness within her heart; still it remained. Instead of condemning her, Jesus offered her a way out of the bondage that had held her life captive.

Is there an emptiness in your life that needs the Savior's touch? Depression, anxiety, frustration, disappointment—even these are points of healing when we turn to Him. Jesus' death on the Cross assured that your empty life can be filled!

Fill the empty places in my life, dear Lord. Take away my depression, anxiety, frustration, and disappointment.

The Provision of the Cross

SCRIPTURE READING: Lamentations 3:22–26
KEY VERSE: Psalm 106:1

PRAISE the LORD!
Oh, give thanks to the LORD, for He is good!
For His mercy endures forever.

A scene from a children's musical depicts a group of angels discussing the believers on earth. One angel turns and asks the others, "Do they know how much the Father loves them? Do they realize how much He cares?"

God promises to eternally provide for you, yet there is one condition He places before you: obedience. Every need of Adam was attended to, yet he disobeyed God. All that Israel could ever dream of obtaining was theirs, yet they abandoned the ways of God, and disobedience ruled their hearts.

Throughout history, a discomforting glitch has remained in the heart of mankind. We have continued to seek the pleasures of other gods while pushing away what God offers so freely: His love and devotion. We have ignored the reality that we are His redeemed, purchased at Calvary's Cross.

The guarantee He offers us is the same one He gave to Abraham, Isaac, David, Mary, and the disciples: "Come unto Me. Drink My living water and find refreshment for your souls."

Trace His provision through the Bible. Start with Genesis and follow it through to Revelation. He will provide all that you need if you will place your trust in Him.

Father, thank You for the living water that brings refreshment for my soul. You will provide all I need. I place my trust in You.

The Finality of the Cross

SCRIPTURE READING: Romans 8:31–39

KEY VERSE: Romans 8:31

What then shall we say to these things? If God is for us, who can be against us?

It may seem to be an obvious statement, but Satan does not want you to experience the strong faith that comes when you realize the finality of Christ's work at the Cross. Kay Arthur writes in her book *Lord, Is It Warfare?*:

When you were nothing but a sinner—helpless, ungodly, and without hope—God justified you. Even though you were His enemy, when you repented and believed that Jesus Christ was God and that He died for your sin, God immediately transferred you from Satan's domain of darkness into His glorious kingdom . . . Sin and death are not like oil and water—they mix. Death follows sin . . . Therefore, if your sins had not been paid for in full, if you had not been made righteous, you would die and be eternally separated from God.

One of Satan's most effective strategies is to keep our sin before us. He'll remind us of sins we've already confessed or convince us that because of them God doesn't want or cannot use us. Sometimes he tries to convince us that God will never forgive us, our sin is too terrible. To believe any of this is to go into battle without your breastplate.

So, when condemnation or difficulties come and you think it's because God doesn't love you or is punishing you, you must recognize who's the instigator of those accusations. Romans 8:31–39 is always a comfort and help to me. Read it carefully.

Dear heavenly Father, I am so thankful that You love me. Thank You for sending Your Son to die for me.

Communion with the Father

SCRIPTURE READING: 1 Corinthians 11:23–28
KEY VERSE: 1 Corinthians 11:26

For as often as you eat this bread and drink this cup, you proclaim the Lord's death till He comes.

Whenever we celebrate the Lord's Supper, we must remember its sacred significance. It is a holy remembrance of Christ's shed blood and its inauguration of a new covenant based on the forgiveness of sin through Christ's death.

When you drink of the cup, realize that your fellowship with the Father is grounded on the blood of Christ. You may talk with Him and receive His friendly guidance and eternal embrace all because God chose to crucify His Son on your behalf.

The barrier of sin could not be removed except by the death, burial, and resurrection of Jesus. The stain of sin could not be taken away apart from His blood. The red blood of Christ on your black sin clothes you in white robes of God's righteousness.

As you eat of the bread, think upon the fathomless love of God that divinely initiated the blood-soaked beams of Calvary. God's love sent Jesus to the Cross for you, and God's love forgives and restores you to communion with the Father.

Because Jesus was broken and bloodied for you, you can enjoy the wholeness, joy, and peace of a personal, living relationship with Christ. Christ's blood is God's love demonstrated.

Father, Your love was demonstrated through Christ's blood. Thank You for the provision of peace that Your gift brought to me.

Freedom to Love

SCRIPTURE READING: 1 John 2:4–10
KEY VERSE: 1 Thessalonians 3:12

May the Lord make you increase and abound in love to one another and to all, just as we do to you.

How free are you in your love? Do you give love without needing or expecting love in return? While each of us desires love, it is far better to love unconditionally than always to expect a return on our love.

Amy Carmichael writes about love toward others:

A few minutes ago I read words that sum up my desires for you: 1 Thessalonians 3:12, "The Lord make you to increase and abound in love one toward another." This poor world is a cold place to many. I pray that no one who comes to us may ever feel chilled here, but rather that all chilliness may melt, melted by the blessed glow of heavenly love. Don't let us ever be afraid of being too loving. We can never love enough.

So I pray, "Lord, keep us free to love. Never let the slightest shade of suspicion shadow any heart. Help each to think the best of every other. Through all the chances and changes of life, hold all together in tender love. Let nothing quench love. Let nothing cool it. Keep every thread of the gold cord unbroken, unweakened, even unto the end, Oh my Lord, Thou Loving One, keep my beloveds close together in Thy love forever."

How you love others reflects your love for Christ. Be patient in love, willing to receive little to no thanks for something you have done in love for another. Remember, no act of love is ever wasted.

Lord, set me free to love. Don't let suspicion shadow my heart. Help me to think the best of others.

The Garden near the Cross

SCRIPTURE READING: John 19:38–42
KEY VERSE: Song of Solomon 8:5

Who is this coming up from the wilderness,
Leaning upon her beloved?
I awakened you under the apple tree.
There your mother brought you forth;
There she who bore you brought you forth.

In the book, *Candles in the Dark,* a collection of letters to friends, other missionaries, and family, Amy Carmichael writes,

How tangled life can be, and nobody can disentangle such tangles. Sometimes I wonder how I can spend one single moment on trifles; I should be all the time praying for those who are in tangles. But I do believe it is true that whatever I am doing, awake or asleep, the underlying thought is always there for those who are going through hard ways.

"Now in the place where He was crucified there was a garden." It comforts me to know that you have found the garden, the garden that forever lies so near the cross. And you will find it a place where the south wind blows as well as the north. It isn't all north wind.

But my chief word for you these days is the Song of Songs 8:5, "Who is this that cometh up from the wilderness, leaning upon her Beloved?" I have just noticed afresh that He on whom we lean did Himself "come out of the wilderness." He doesn't ask us to walk in any path where He has not walked before.

When Peter saw Jesus walking on the water during the zenith of the storm, he wanted to walk out to Him. Halfway there, however, Peter became frightened and began to sink; then he cried out to Jesus. Never be ashamed to call to the One who loves you. As He was with Peter, He is with you.

Lord, help me to lean on You today, knowing You have already been where I am going.

Love Demands Our All

SCRIPTURE READING: Ephesians 2:8–10

KEY VERSE: 1 John 4:16

We have known and believed the love that God has for us. God is love, and he who abides in love abides in God, and God in him.

You are God's workmanship. He did not create you or allow you to be born as the result of a whim. Just as He planned heaven's creation, He planned you. Some who read these words may feel as though their lives do not count for much. But from God's perspective there is no greater potential than what is contained in your life.

Each one of us has an opportunity to experience the love of God, not just in an ecclesiastical sense but in an intimate, personal way that goes beyond the hallowed halls of a church or a worship service. We can know God, talk with Him, and tell Him all our concerns. We can worship Him and pray to Him without getting all dressed up.

Jesus comes to you right at the point of your greatest need. His ideas are fresh and victorious. You may struggle for years, searching for an answer to a particular problem. When you think you have reached your limit, God will surprise you with His solution and blessing.

How do you experience such goodness? It begins with love. Jesus loved you so much that He was willing to submit to the Father's will. He came to earth with a principal goal in mind—to die so that you might know the love of His Father. His love and death take away the punishment of your sin. Love like this demands our all. He gave us nothing less. Now will you give Him all of yourself?

Dear Lord, I give You my all. I submit to Your will.

The Life of Faith

SCRIPTURE READING: Hebrews 11:1–8
KEY VERSE: Hebrews 11:8

By faith Abraham obeyed when he was called to go out to the place which he would afterward receive as an inheritance. And he went out, not knowing where he was going.

When the foundation of all that you believe is firmly grounded in Christ, your faith will hold no matter what the trial. Oswald Chambers writes about faith:

In the Old Testament, personal relationship with God showed itself in separation, and this is symbolized in the life of Abraham by his separation from his country and from his kith and kin. Today the separation is more of a mental and moral separation . . .

Faith never knows where it is being led, but it loves and knows the One who is doing the leading. It is a life of faith, not of intellect and reason, but a life of knowing who makes us go. The root of faith is the knowledge of a Person, and one of the biggest snares is the idea that God is sure to lead us to success.

The final stage in the life of faith is attainment of character. There are many passing transfigurations of character; when we pray we feel the blessing of God enwrapping us and for the time being we are changed, then we go back to the ordinary days and ways and the glory vanishes.

The life of faith is not a life of mounting up with wings, but a life of walking and not fainting. It is not a question of sanctification; but of something infinitely further on than sanctification, of faith that has been tried and proved and has stood the test.

Abraham believed God. Can you say the same about yourself?

Lord, let me stand the test. I want a faith that will enable me to walk and not faint in the midst of adversities.

A Crucified Life

SCRIPTURE READING: Philippians 1:15–18

KEY VERSE: Psalm 98:1

Oh, sing to the LORD a new song!
For He has done marvelous things;
His right hand and His holy arm have gained Him the victory.

What do you do when you find you are misunderstood? Do you look for a way to escape or retaliate? Or do you feel hurt and secretly hold the pain inside?

For a great deal of His life on earth Jesus was misunderstood. The emotional persecution He faced ended in His death. But God won the victory. The focus of Christ's life and work was not on His circumstances. Instead, He was totally committed to the Father's will. That was the heartbeat of His ministry, regardless of whether someone agreed with Him. His desire was for all men and women to know the forgiveness and love of God.

Paul was persecuted. In the end, his faith in Christ cost him his life. Stephen died believing and proclaiming the truth he had learned through the power of the Holy Spirit. What set men like Paul and Stephen apart from the others was their determination to do God's will over the will of the world. Jesus set a pattern for each of us to follow.

In the book, *Gold by Moonlight,* Amy Carmichael writes, "A crucified life cannot be self-assertive. It cannot protect itself. It cannot be startled into resentful words. The cup that is full of sweet water cannot spill bitter-tasting drops, however sharply it is knocked."

Father, I have so much to learn. Teach me the lessons of a crucified life.

The Importance of Relationship

SCRIPTURE READING: Luke 19:1–10

KEY VERSE: Luke 19:8

"Behold, Lord, half of my possessions I will give to the poor, and if I have defrauded anyone of anything, I will give back four times as much" (NASB).

The story of Zacchaeus is usually taught with an emphasis on his complete enthusiasm to see Jesus. The picture of this short man climbing a tree just to get a glimpse of the Messiah is an example of how eager we should be to meet with the Savior.

It can be easy to overlook the life change that Zacchaeus experienced after Jesus called him down from the tree and asked if He could come to his house. Zacchaeus's heart flooded with joy when Jesus loved and accepted him.

As they were on their way to his house, Zacchaeus said, "Behold, Lord, half of my possessions I will give to the poor, and if I have defrauded anyone of anything, I will give back four times as much" (Luke 19:8 NASB). Zacchaeus knew in his heart that his account of sin had been wiped clean because he placed his faith in Jesus. In that first moment of exultant freedom, he wanted to set accounts right with his fellowmen.

Notice that Zacchaeus changed his viewpoint only after he experienced the unconditional love of Christ. Before that day, Zacchaeus could not possibly have understood God's priorities. Even if someone had explained the truth to him logically and carefully, he could not comprehend it until he had a one-on-one heart encounter with Jesus.

Only on the foundation of a relationship with the Lord can you grasp the application of His truth and the power of the Cross in your life.

Father, deepen my relationship with You. Let me grasp the application of Your truth in my life.

How Good Is Good Enough?

SCRIPTURE READING: Romans 3:10, 20, 23

KEY VERSE: Matthew 5:17

Do not think that I came to destroy the Law or the Prophets. I did not come to destroy but to fulfill.

How many times have you heard someone say, "When I die, I'm going to heaven because I have lived a good life"? Well, many good people do go to heaven, but so do a lot of other folks who lived a "so-so" life.

That is because the key to salvation is not how good you are, but in whom you place your trust. When Paul first preached this message, the Jewish leaders called him a heretic and wanted him stoned to death. Their lives had been molded according to the Law of Moses and Jewish tradition. They could not conceive tossing it away for the sake of salvation by grace.

The problem we run into when we try to live good lives is, how good is good enough? There is no way to measure it. What may be regarded as good to you is deficient to someone else.

Christ did not come to destroy the law but to fulfill it, living the only life good enough to satisfy God's demand for perfection (Matt. 5:17). His death on Calvary was the beginning of the new age of grace (Luke 22:20). Christ is the only way to heaven. Don't spend a lifetime hoping that somehow you will end up in heaven through good deeds. Believe in Christ and know that you are saved!

Father, I can never be "good enough." Thank You for the righteousness You secured for me at the Cross.

Don't Stop with the Rubbish

SCRIPTURE READING: John 15:1–8

KEY VERSE: John 15:5

I am the vine, you are the branches. He who abides in Me, and I in him, bears much fruit; for without Me you can do nothing.

In her book, *Gold Cord,* Amy Carmichael wrote of the time she stayed at the China Inland Mission (C.I.M.) compound:

One morning after breakfast, the veteran missionary, Mr. J. W. Stevenson, Deputy Director of the C.I.M., rose from his seat . . . He stood for a moment silent, then said, "And there was much rubbish."

Everyone understood. Part of the C.I.M. compound was not quite finished, and where there is building there is rubbish. However, Stevenson continued, "People will try to discourage you. They will say, 'Oh, your converts are all nice or soft Christians.' Don't be discouraged. Of course there is rubbish—there always is where anything is being done. Don't stop because of the rubbish; get on with the building."

Carmichael added, "God holds us to that which drew us first, when the Cross was the attraction, and we wanted nothing else." There will always be rubbish in the world, but the call of Christ is not to let rubbish deter you from being all He has called you to be.

One of the reasons God prunes His saints is to prepare us for ministry. He trains us by allowing us to be battered by rain and wind and rubbish. Have you decided to abide in Christ regardless of the rubbish surrounding you?

Dear Lord, don't let me be affected by the rubbish of this world. Help me continue to build Your kingdom.

The Anchor of Hope

SCRIPTURE READING: Hebrews 6:17–19
KEY VERSE: Hebrews 6:19

This hope we have as an anchor of the soul, both sure and steadfast, and which enters the Presence behind the veil.

The writer of Hebrews drew a clear, concise point in encouraging us in "laying hold of the hope set before us" (Heb. 6:18 NASB). He used an anchor as a word picture to emphasize his point: "This hope we have as an anchor of the soul, a hope both sure and steadfast and one which enters within the veil" (Heb. 6:19 NASB).

Most members of the early church understood how anchors were used to hold a ship firmly, not allowing it to drift far. However, even this analogy, when placed alongside the surety of God's love, is limited and flawed.

Material anchors cannot hold us securely the way Jesus is committed to doing. When the storms arise, earthly anchors slip and drag along the bottom of the sea. But God is your eternal Anchor. He is your strong, immovable hope when the storms of life hit. You don't have to worry about drifting off course as long as you are firmly anchored in Christ.

Will He ever let you go? No. Jesus loves you with an eternal love that is not bound by human desire, expectations, or possibilities. He is the true Anchor to your soul, One who is not earthbound, but One who extends to the very heart of God.

You don't have to run for cover when the winds of doubt, low self-esteem, or discouragement blow. Nothing that touches your life is stronger than the power of the Cross.

Thank You, Father, for Your eternal love, which is not bound by human desires, expectations, or possibilities.

Take a Closer Look

SCRIPTURE READING: John 3:1–19

KEY VERSE: John 3:5

Jesus answered, "Most assuredly, I say to you, unless one is born of water and the Spirit, he cannot enter the kingdom of God."

Many scholars believe Nicodemus eventually became a secret follower of Jesus, while a few cite a lack of evidence concerning his conversion. Considering the consequences, Nicodemus took a huge risk in coming to Jesus that evening. Had his peers found out, he could have faced banishment from the Sanhedrin.

Each time Nicodemus heard Jesus speak, the message pointed in one direction: The kingdom of God was now among them. But how could that be? And if it was, how did one gain access?

Jesus' answer was baffling: "Truly, truly, I say to you, unless one is born of water and the Spirit, he cannot enter into the kingdom of God" (John 3:5 NASB). Christ was speaking of a spiritual rebirth, something Nicodemus had never heard before.

There is only one way to enter the kingdom of God, and that is through faith in His Son and the finished work of the Cross. We know Nicodemus took a critical look at his faith because the next time he is mentioned, he was preparing the Lord's body for burial.

Only one thing could move a man to join in such an effort, and that is the love of God. Have you taken a critical look at your faith? Is Jesus the central focus of your life? Anything less demands a closer look.

Jesus, You are the central focus of my life. Thank You for the finished work of the Cross.

The Risen Christ

SCRIPTURE READING: Acts 2:23–24, 32–36

KEY VERSE: 2 Timothy 2:9

The word of God is not chained.

In her book, *Shadow of the Almighty*, Elisabeth Elliot offers penetrating insights into the life of her husband and missionary martyr, Jim Elliot. Ever the seeker, Elliot disliked any attempt to contain or confine the fires of God in the human life. He wrote this while a student at Wheaton College:

> 2 Timothy 2:9 says, "The word of God is not bound." Systematic theology— be careful how you tie down the Word to fit your set and final creeds, systems, dogmas, and organized theistic philosophies!
>
> The Word of God is not bound! It's free to say what it will to the individual and no one can outline it into dispensations which cannot be broken. Don't get it down "cold," but let it live—fresh, warm, and vibrant—so that the world is not binding ponderous books about it, but rather the world is shackling you for having allowed it to have free course in your life.

Although Jesus was not a revolutionary, what He began on Resurrection Sunday has transformed millions of men and women through the centuries.

When you are regenerated by the Holy Spirit, you are filled with the power of the risen Christ. You are joined with a Savior with whom nothing is impossible. Never be surprised at what He will do next.

Father, I claim the power of the risen Christ in my life. Renew my strength by Your Spirit.

Transforming Thoughts

SCRIPTURE READING: Ephesians 4:17–24
KEY VERSE: Ephesians 4:23–24

. . . and be renewed in the spirit of your mind, and that you put on the new man which was created according to God, in righteousness and true holiness.

In 1758, when Robert Robinson was a vibrant and energetic twenty-three-year-old pastor, he penned the words to the beloved hymn "Come, Thou Fount of Every Blessing."

Many years later on a stagecoach trip, he sat next to a woman singing his hymn. When she asked him if he was familiar with the song, he began to cry and replied, "Madam, I am the poor unhappy man who wrote that hymn many years ago, and I would give a thousand worlds to enjoy the feelings I had then."

The man who wrote the words "Prone to wander, Lord, I feel it" experienced the same discouragement in his walk with the Lord that we often feel. But God does not want us to ride an emotional roller coaster; He wants us to abide in the security of His truth.

God's desire is "that you be renewed in the spirit of your mind, and put on the new self, which in the likeness of God has been created in righteousness and holiness of the truth" (Eph. 4:23–24 NASB).

The Lord renews your mind when you acknowledge your position in Christ that was secured at the cross and choose to set your mind on this truth. Read and study God's Word each day, and let Him transform your thoughts with His perspective.

Father, please renew my mind. I want to put on the new me that is in Your likeness, created in righteousness and holiness of the truth.

Giving In

SCRIPTURE READING: 1 Kings 11:1–8
KEY VERSE: James 1:15

When desire has conceived, it gives birth to sin; and sin, when it is full-grown, brings forth death.

When faced with temptation, we often rationalize or justify what we want to do, thinking that giving in on small things is not harmful. But disobedience of any kind is a compromise, a partial surrender to sin that hinders our relationship with the Lord and can grow into bigger sin.

King Solomon, the son of David, was the wisest man who ever lived. But God specifically commanded Solomon not to take foreign wives because He knew the end result: "For it came about when Solomon was old, his wives turned his heart away after other gods; and his heart was not wholly devoted to the LORD his God, as the heart of David his father had been" (1 Kings 11:4 NASB).

What started out as admiration from afar led to association, which soon led to close relationships. Eventually Solomon built altars for false gods; he was totally possessed by his sin. And he paid a price. To punish Solomon's disobedience, God took the kingdom away from his children.

The good news is that wherever you may be on the road of compromise, the Lord will restore you to right fellowship with Him if you ask Him. No sin is too big and no failure too large for the power of the Cross. Recognize your sin, repent, and let the Holy Spirit rebuild your life and ground your heart in His truth.

Lord, there is no sin too great for the power of the Cross. I repent.

Satan's Final Defeat

SCRIPTURE READING: Luke 22:31–34

KEY VERSE: 1 John 5:19

We know that we are of God, and the whole world lies under the sway of the wicked one.

Since his fall, Satan's corrupt activities against man have been intended for one purpose: to prevent the salvation of mankind through the life, death, and resurrection of Jesus Christ. However, it was during Jesus' ministry that Satan's attacks against the Messiah were most intense. Once Jesus went to the Cross, Satan's defeat would be ensured.

The devil attacked overtly in the wilderness, trying to get Christ to yield to his temptations. But each time Satan attacked, Christ used the Holy Scriptures to ward off Satan's attacks.

He dealt covertly against Jesus through those closest to Him. Peter's seemingly strong defensive stand for Christ (Matt. 16:22–23) was nothing more than a last-ditch effort on Satan's part to stop Jesus' divine destiny. However, with one straightforward statement—"Get behind Me, Satan!"—Christ exposed the deception of His adversary.

But Satan could not thwart God's plan. Satan already has been judged and condemned; the sentence of eternal death has been pronounced. All that remains is the execution of the sentence. Satan has been conquered by the Conqueror. Christ's victory is yours today.

Father, when Satan attacks, help me use the power of Your Word. Your victory is mine today!

The Way of the Cross

SCRIPTURE READING: 2 Corinthians 6:17–18
KEY VERSE: 2 Corinthians 5:17

If anyone is in Christ, he is a new creation; old things have passed away; behold, all things have become new.

C oncerning the message of the church, A. W. Tozer writes in *The Divine Conquest:*

The gospel is too often preached and accepted without power, and the radical shift which the truth demands is never made. There may be . . . a change of some kind . . . but whatever happens is not enough, not deep enough, not radical enough.

The "creature" is changed, but he is not "new." And right there is the tragedy of it. The gospel is concerned with a new life, with a birth upward onto a new level of being, and until it has effected such a re-birth it has not done a saving work within the soul . . . For there is in divine truth an imperious note, there is about the gospel an urgency, a finality which will not be heard or felt except by the enabling of the Spirit.

We must constantly keep in mind that the gospel is not good news only, but a judgment as well upon everyone that hears it. The message of the Cross is good news indeed for the penitent, but to those who "obey not the gospel" it carries an overtone of warning . . . For sinners who want to cease being willful sinners and become obedient children of God the gospel message is one of unqualified peace.

Salvation comes only one way, through faith in Jesus Christ and His atonement on the Cross of Calvary. If He is your Savior, allow Him also to be your Lord and intimate Friend.

I am coming the way of the Cross. I declare my faith in You, Jesus. Come and be my Savior and intimate Friend.

Come on Back

SCRIPTURE READING: Revelation 2:1–7

KEY VERSE: Revelation 2:4

Nevertheless I have this against you, that you have left your first love.

The church at Ephesus was commended for many things. It was a wonderful body of believers, known for their service, sacrifice, perseverance, and suffering. Yet the Lord had a key criticism of them: "I have this against you, that you have left your first love" (Rev. 2:4).

Their "first love" was Jesus Christ. Their activities and demonstrations of grace to others were admirable, but outside of a growing, intimate relationship with Jesus, those things were of no real value.

That is how important Jesus considers your relationship with Him. Whether you slowly drift away from closeness with Him or make the conscious choice to be consumed with other things, the result is the same—a feeling of distance from the Lord and a hollowness to your days.

Rest assured, however, that God has not pulled away from you. He longs for fellowship with you; He sent His Son to die for that purpose. If you feel you have lost your first love, or are somewhere in that process, do not be discouraged. Satan would love nothing more than for depression and thoughts of defeat to drive you away from the Lord.

Don't believe statements such as, "I've wandered too far to come back," or "It will take a while before God wants to hear my prayers." He wants to talk to you right now. Come on back to the Cross!

I'm coming back to the Cross, Lord. Renew my first love as I have a divine encounter with the power of the Cross.

A Divine Encounter with Christian Devotion: Prayer, Worship, and the Word

A Divine Encounter in Prayer

SCRIPTURE READING: Matthew 6:9–15
KEY VERSE: Matthew 6:6

When you pray, go into your room, and when you have shut your door, pray to your Father who is in the secret place; and your Father who sees in secret will reward you openly.

Prayer's greatest reward is the chance it gives us to experience the heart of God.

The most important activity we can engage in as Christians is prayer. Everything connected with God evolves out of time spent alone with Him in praise, worship, devotion, and petition.

We cannot truly experience the wonder of praise or the peace that comes from meditating on His Word unless we have first spent time with Him in prayer. Without prayer, there is no depth in our relationship with God, and our knowledge of Him becomes empty and stale within our hearts.

Only prayer can revive a weary soul. When David was on the run from Saul, the first place he went was to God in prayer. When Jesus became physically tired, He sought the Father through prayer. Nothing has the potential to change the face of your environment like prayer.

Arrested, thrown into prison, and waiting for execution, Peter prayed, as did those who knew him, and God sent an angel to help him escape. Prayer is not merely coming to God with a wish list. It is, instead, a time when you make yourself available to be used of Him in whatever way He chooses.

Dear heavenly Father, thank You for the privilege of being used by You. I am making myself available.

Learning to Wait

SCRIPTURE READING: Psalm 103
KEY VERSE: Psalm 103:1

Bless the LORD, O my soul;
And all that is within me, bless His holy name!

Have you ever wondered whether God hears you when you pray? He does, even if you feel as though your prayers are simply bouncing off the ceiling and back down to you. God loves you with an unconditional love, and He hears your every word whispered, cried, or simply spoken to Him in prayer.

God uses our prayers to teach us more about Himself. One of the most difficult lessons to learn is to wait for His answer to our prayers. Waiting is something few enjoy, but there are seasons when God wants us to do just that—wait.

The temptation is to jump ahead and try to meet our needs our way. Of course, we rarely view it from this perspective. We say things like, "I prayed about it, and if God did not want me to do it, He would stop me."

As we grow in our faith, God is persistent in His desire to teach us to listen for His still, quiet voice, no matter how long we must wait. Moving ahead without His surety ends in disaster.

When you seek God's wisdom, be sure to ask Him to affirm His will or plan for your life through Scripture. He uses the circumstances of His Word to guide and direct you safely along the pathway of life. Always praise Him for His answers to your prayers. He finds glory and honor in the praises of His people.

Lord, affirm Your will for my life through Your Word. Guide and direct me along the pathway of life.

Waiting on God

SCRIPTURE READING: Psalm 27:1–4
KEY VERSE: Psalm 62:1

TRULY my soul silently waits for God;
From Him comes my salvation.

When you think about the principles of God, there is one you don't want to overlook. It is the principle of waiting. Many times it is something we fail to understand and enjoy. Impatience can come from the feverish pace set by our society. Cell phones, E-mail, and the World Wide Web have changed the way we live and communicate. No longer do we take time to be still and listen to the dreams and hopes of a friend. Instead, we hurry away and shout over our shoulders, "E-mail me and I'll get back with you!"

This attitude can have disastrous results. God created us for fellowship with Him and with others. Certain principles hold eternally true, and learning how to wait before the Lord is one of the wisest and healthiest things you can do.

A. B. Simpson once confided to a friend, "I am nothing without time alone with God." No one is at his best when he lays aside time alone with God in order to meet a deadline or pursue another activity.

Learning to be still before God is not just a devotional dream. Those who do it discover the deep richness that is theirs at the feet of Jesus. If you are having difficulty finding time to be alone with the Lord, ask Him to open up your heart and mind to His plan. He is very creative, and you will be surprised at the opportunity He provides.

Run your race with endurance. Never give up. God has a plan for your life. If you will maintain your course of faith, He will reward your obedience. The only way you can continue to go forward is to maintain a spiritual gaze that is set on Jesus, the Lover of your soul.

Teach me how to wait, Lord. I set my spiritual gaze on Jesus, the Lover of my soul.

A Heart of True Praise

SCRIPTURE READING: John 12:1–8
KEY VERSE: Psalm 68:4

Sing to God, sing praises to His name;
Extol Him who rides on the clouds,
By His name YAH,
And rejoice before Him.

Pouring perfume on Jesus' feet may seem an awkward or overly emotional act to some of us today, but it was a pure expression of the love and worship in Mary's heart. Cultures and traditions may change through the years, but God always wants you to pour out your heart to Him in praise and adoration.

True praise longs to give something of value. Have you ever had a close and intimate relationship with another person? It was the natural inclination of your emotions to want to give something of great personal worth to that individual. It didn't have to be something that cost a lot, either. In the same way, God wants you to give yourself to Him.

True praise is not inhibited by the attitudes of others. Mary wasn't concerned about how many people were watching or what they thought. And some around her certainly had strongly negative opinions. Jesus recognized the purity of her gesture. If you're concerned about possible condemnation from others, ask God to help you focus on Him alone.

True praise moves you to love God for who He is. The book of Psalms is filled with descriptions of God's eternal character and unchanging righteousness as the basis for praise. When you praise Him for His attributes, you put your attention on His worthiness, and that's the very purpose of your worship.

God, I worship You for who You are. You are worthy of my praise.

The Purpose of Fasting

SCRIPTURE READING: Matthew 6:16–18
KEY VERSE: Isaiah 58:6

Is this not the fast that I have chosen:
To loose the bonds of wickedness,
To undo the heavy burdens,
To let the oppressed go free,
And that you break every yoke?

The point of fasting is to submit ourselves to God in such a way that we personally sacrifice something to Him. It is not a matter of working to gain His attention. It is, instead, a proclamation of love and dedication to Him, our Savior and Lord. Done with the proper attitude, fasting is a sure means of drawing closer to the Lord.

There are different ways to fast. Those who struggle with certain physical problems may not be able to give up food intake. Therefore, traditional fasting could prove difficult. However, there are other ways a person can fast: giving of time, money, or some other personal item could be considered a type of fast.

The benefits of fasting include a purified mind, heart, and body. Jesus fasted and prayed, but away from the eyes of His followers. God wants fasting to remain a personal commitment between you and the Lord.

Not every time you fast will there be a need for self-examination. Yet God often uses fasting to teach you how to submit the entirety of your life to Him. Through fasting, He may direct you to ask for His wisdom concerning a certain situation.

How serious are you in your spiritual walk? Times of fasting reveal this and lead you to pray, "Try me . . . and see if there be any hurtful way in me" (Ps. 139:23–24 NASB).

Lord, try me and see if there is any hurtful way in me.

Prayer and Anxiety

SCRIPTURE READING: Psalm 69:1–3
KEY VERSE: 1 Peter 5: 7

Casting all your care upon Him, for He cares for you.

Prayer plays an important role in handling anxiety. Prayer is an out-cropping of faith. When you pray in faith, you declare your need to God. Anxiety, however, represents the absence of faith.

Peter instructed us, "[Cast] all your anxiety on Him, because He cares for you" (1 Peter 5:7 NASB). Older saints such as Charles Spurgeon, Amy Carmichael, and Hudson Taylor would use the term "to roll" all your cares on Him. This act of rolling gives us a mental picture of what it means to give our troubles to the Lord. We actually release them into His care and walk away from the situation in such a way that we are no longer anxious over the matter. We say, "Lord, I want to roll this problem onto You." What a great sense of encouragement awaits you when you give Jesus the problems and trials of your heart!

He is your Burden Bearer, and He will accept every care perfectly onto Himself. He is sovereign. All-powerful. Holy. Righteous. Infinite in wisdom. His mercies never cease, and He has an eternal love for you that will never end. Sounds like someone you can trust? Try Him and you will see!

Lord, You are holy, righteous, and infinite in wisdom. Thank You that Your mercies never cease.

Nehemiah's Pattern

SCRIPTURE READING: Nehemiah 1:1–11

KEY VERSE: Nehemiah 1:11

"O Lord, I pray, please let Your ear be attentive to the prayer of Your servant, and to the prayer of Your servants who desire to fear Your name; and let Your servant prosper this day, I pray, and grant him mercy in the sight of this man." For I was the king's cupbearer.

Nehemiah received word about the city of Jerusalem and how it had been ravaged by war. Jerusalem's walls lay in ruins. In Old Testament times, the walls surrounding a city were extremely important. They were a formidable means of protection from enemy attack. Any hope Jerusalem had for future survival depended on getting its walls put back in place. The thought of Jerusalem being open with no way of defense caused Nehemiah to cry out to God.

From the moment Nehemiah heard of Jerusalem's fate, he set his heart on seeking God for a solution. He was ready, if necessary, to return to the city and work on the walls.

Most of us know Nehemiah's story. God granted him favor in the king's presence. He returned to Jerusalem to lead in the rebuilding of the city's walls. The crucial point in this story is found in the prayers of Nehemiah. He held nothing back before God. He was honest about his love and desire for the city. There was a brokenness within his heart that God could not resist.

Do you want God to use you? Follow the pattern of Nehemiah. Humble yourself and confess your need to Him. Then be willing to go when He opens the door. God blesses those who are willing to be used by Him.

Lord, I love You. I am willing to go where You open the door as long as You go with me.

A Love for the Word

SCRIPTURE READING: Nehemiah 8:1–9
KEY VERSE: Psalm 119:105

Your word is a lamp to my feet
And a light to my path (NASB).

One of the most beneficial prayers you can pray is to ask God to give you a love for His Word. Many try to read and study the Word of God through human effort. They struggle through Genesis, fight their way through Exodus, but lose momentum in Leviticus.

However, when there is a deep, abiding love for God's Word, even the genealogies take on a life of their own. God's principles lift off the pages and fill your heart with insight and hope. After all, God inspired His Word to be written so you would have proof of His loving desire toward you.

The psalmist exclaimed, "How I long for your precepts!" (Ps. 119:40 NIV), and "Your word is a lamp to my feet and a light for my path" (Ps. 119:105 NIV).

Something about the Word of God changes lives. According to the book of Nehemiah, after the walls of Jerusalem had been rebuilt, the book containing the Law of Moses was brought out and read to the people.

For years, they had thirsted to hear God's Word read aloud. Memories of their exile in a foreign land made that moment in time like none other. The nation of Israel—what was left of it—stood together "as one man" (Neh. 8:1 NASB), and as Ezra read God's words, the people began to weep.

Have you uncovered the sweetness of God's presence through His Word? It's there, and it awaits your discovery.

Thank You for Your Word, Lord. It is a lamp unto my feet and a light to my path.

The Joy of the Lord

SCRIPTURE READING: Nehemiah 8:9–17
KEY VERSE: Psalm 71:5

You are my hope, O Lord GOD;
You are my trust from my youth.

In these verses, we read how a sincere sorrow swept through the people of Israel as they heard God's law being read. That was when Nehemiah stepped forward and spoke words of encouragement.

God had witnessed Israel's humility and how their desires had changed. Their longing to return to the ways of the Lord was a sweet fragrance to God's ears and heart.

Nehemiah and Ezra began to speak to the people: "This day is holy to the LORD your God; do not mourn or weep . . . Go, eat of the fat, drink of the sweet, and send portions to him who has nothing prepared; for this day is holy to our Lord. Do not be grieved, for the joy of the LORD is your strength" (Neh. 8:9–10 NASB).

Our devotional time is very serious. We sense an urgency to tell God our feelings, to study His Word, and then to listen for His guidance. But there are other aspects of worship we need to practice. Joy and thanksgiving are key elements of loving God.

The Lord hears your prayers. He understands your burdens. If you have drifted, as Israel did, in your devotion to God, He wants you to return to the joy of His love with celebration. God is not a hard-to-get-to-know Savior. He is your loving heavenly Father who wants nothing more than to hold you in His arms. Bless Him today with praise and adoration!

I praise You, Lord. I adore You. I worship You and bless Your name!

Passing Along the Praise

SCRIPTURE READING: Psalm 92:1–5

KEY VERSE: Proverbs 27:2

Let another man praise you, and not your own mouth;
A stranger, and not your own lips.

Praise sometimes can seem intoxicating. Although we all want to feel accepted and loved, our focus occasionally can be misdirected.

It is wise to worry less about what men think and to keep our hearts set on Jesus. The best praise we could ever hear is, "Well done, good and faithful servant," and there is nothing wrong with making that a motivating goal.

God loves you so much, so unconditionally, that no praise on earth can compare to the approval and acceptance His love brings. His Holy Spirit will warm you when you have done well and will convict you when you need improvement. Waiting for man's nod is waiting for second best.

The proper response to earthly praise is to take it for what it is: a momentary acknowledgment from someone to whom you ultimately do not have to answer. Say something like, "Thank you very much. You're very kind," or "Thank you. That is an encouragement to me." That is all you need to say. Meanwhile, inside your heart make it a practice to funnel the praise directly to God.

Even as the person is complimenting you, simply think, *Thank You, Father. You are so good to me.* You will pass along the praise to whom it really belongs instead of letting it settle in and ferment.

Thank You, Father. You are so good to me. I am passing along the praise.

Trusting for the Impossible

SCRIPTURE READING: Colossians 4:2–4
KEY VERSE: Psalm 67:6

The earth shall yield her increase;
God, our own God, shall bless us.

In 1911, when Evelyn Forrest, along with her husband, Richard, established Toccoa Falls College, she never dreamed there would be such heartache and disappointment in her life. Training young people for Christian service was her one desire. Soon she realized that those whom God uses, He tests with difficulty to see if their devotion will remain firm.

In March 1913, a horrendous fire swept through the three-story hotel that housed Evelyn's school. The building and all of its contents were destroyed. Later, in looking back on that moment, Evelyn wrote,

With men this is impossible; but with God all things are possible (Matt. 19:26). God loves to have His children pray for the impossible. That is God's invitation to ask Him to do that which no man can do . . .

We have lost the eternal youthfulness of Christianity and have aged into calculating manhood. We seldom pray in earnest for the extraordinary, the limitless, the glorious. We seldom pray with real confidence for any good to the realization of which we cannot imagine a way. And yet we suppose ourselves to believe in an infinite Father.

When confronted with a closed door, do you trust God for the impossible? Evelyn did, and her school remains today as a testimony to what God can do if only we will trust Him.

Lord, let me trust You even in the face of a closed door. I am believing for the impossible.

Patience That Won't Let Go

SCRIPTURE READING: Luke 22:31–34

KEY VERSE: Luke 22:32

I have prayed for you, that your faith should not fail; and when you have returned to Me, strengthen your brethren.

Amy Carmichael addressed the events related in these verses:

Our Lord Jesus prayed for Peter that his faith might not fail, and within a few hours his faith did fail. The more we think of those last hours of our Lord just before Calvary, the more we see every kind of trial compressed into them. It was not only that His cup was filled to overflowing with suffering, but that every variety of suffering was there.

It is easy to escape from the intolerable sense of such suffering by saying, "He was God." And where Peter was concerned, we may say that Jesus saw across to the victory that would be given. But we know, though we cannot understand it, that Christ was man, too, and the word in Hebrews says that He suffered being tempted. To suffer means to endure or experience pain, so there is no escape by that door.

Is there one for whom we are praying who seems to be unhelped by that prayer? Are we suffering, enduring, experiencing the bitterness of disappointment? Our dear Lord has been this way before. We shall find Him there. He who "turned, and looked upon Peter" will give to us . . . His own eternal tenderness of spirit, the love that cannot be fired out of loving, the patience that will not let go.

Peter did not fully understand God's plan. Only later did he learn that God's greatest source of strength was found in looking beyond himself and into the eyes of Jesus.

Dear Lord, help me to be faithful in prayer. Give me patience that won't let go!

Fervent Intercession

SCRIPTURE READING: Colossians 1:7–13
KEY VERSE: Colossians 4:12

Epaphras, who is one of you, a servant of Christ, greets you, always labor-ing fervently for you in prayers, that you may stand perfect and complete in all the will of God.

*E*paphras, an associate of Paul, was instrumental in founding the church at Colosse. His report to Paul on the condition of the Colossian church prompted Paul's letter to the fledgling believers. At the conclusion of his epistle, Paul used Epaphras's example to give us a grip on a few of the basics of intercessory prayer.

Epaphras was "one of [their] number" (Col. 4:12 NASB). When we are involved in the lives of others through friendship, service, or other means of contact, intercession is much more natural. We can pray for others because we are aware of their concerns.

Epaphras was a "bondslave of Jesus Christ" (Col. 4:12 NASB). God's agenda needs to be ours. When we seek His will first, intercession for the needs of others will be woven into our lives. When our focus drifts from Christ, it is hard to pray for ourselves, much less another.

Epaphras was "always laboring earnestly for [the Colossians] in his prayers" (Col. 4:12 NASB). Intercession is hard work. Intercession is spiritual warfare. It doesn't come easily because Satan does not want you to pray for others.

The end result of fervent intercession is that others may be "fully assured in all the will of God" (Col. 4:12 NASB). That goal fits every need.

Teach me to pray, Lord; to intercede with fervency for the needs of others.

Confidence in Prayer

SCRIPTURE READING: Psalm 40:1–8
KEY VERSE: Psalm 40:8

I delight to do Your will, O my God,
And Your law is within my heart.

"I know God hears my prayers," you may say, "but how do I know my requests are according to His will?"

That sentiment can do more to undermine our confidence in prayer than any other thought. If we knew God's will to begin with, we reason, we would have no problem trusting God for the answer. Actually we know more about God's will than we think.

It is God's will to give thanks in all things (1 Thess. 5:18). Do you have a grateful heart no matter your circumstance? Giving thanks acknowledges His sovereignty and expresses a steadfast faith in Christ.

It is God's will to walk in purity and holiness (1 Thess. 4:3). Do you walk on a thin edge of immorality, giving place to illegitimate thoughts? Don't.

It is God's will to be filled with the Spirit (Eph. 5:18). The verb tense emphasizes such filling as a continuous action, stressing our complete dependence on the Spirit and our unceasing need for His help and guidance.

Prayer is precisely the place where we discover the will of God. We seek His mind, sift through His Word, and thank Him that God is faithfully at work in our lives.

Lord, give me renewed confidence in prayer through increased knowledge of Your will.

The Dynamics of Prayer

SCRIPTURE READING: Psalm 62:1–8

KEY VERSE: Psalm 62:8

Trust in Him at all times, you people;
Pour out your heart before Him;
God is a refuge for us. Selah.

*D*o you remember when you were asked to outline books or reports in school? The outline did not exhaust the topic or theme but merely thumbnailed the essential aspects. We should view in the same light Jesus' teaching on prayer before those gathered for His Sermon on the Mount (Matt. 5–7).

He could not, of course, plumb the depths of prayer in a few verses. He provided the audience with an outline of the basic components of prayer: worship, petition, confession, and obedience.

How you apply these to your life are the real dynamics of prayer. God wants you to pray because He wants to do something special in your life—to meet your needs, to teach you His ways, to correct your shortcomings, to reveal His character, to transform your thinking.

God launched you on a fantastic adventure when you were saved. Prayer is the frontier of personal experience where you continue that adventure.

Prayerlessness is the seed whose fruit is barrenness, drudgery, and mediocrity. Your prayers regarding the specific circumstances of your life fill in the outline of the Lord's Prayer.

Forgive me for my prayerlessness, Lord. Teach me the dynamics of effective prayer.

Our Father in Heaven

SCRIPTURE READING: Matthew 7:7–11
KEY VERSE: Matthew 7:11

If you then, being evil, know how to give good gifts to your children, how much more will your Father who is in heaven give good things to those who ask Him!

A teenager does not ask his neighbor for money. He goes to his mom or dad hoping for an extended hand, and on most occasions finds at least a portion of his request granted.

Uppermost in our thinking regarding prayer is the encouraging truth that our supplications and needs are received by our heavenly Father, not a distant deity.

The fatherhood of God forms the foundation for biblical prayer. That is why Jesus taught us to say, "Our Father who art in heaven," and explained that our requests are heard and answered by our "Father who is in heaven" (Matt. 7:11).

You do not have to wrench a response from a reluctant God; you can come to Him as your kind, loving, generous, and understanding Father. Such is the intimacy that God desires with you.

If His response is not what you expected, don't pout. If He withholds your request, stay thankful. God knows what is best for you, even when you don't.

Prayer is talk between Father and son, Father and daughter. God is never cold or distant, but always accessible, available, and ready to give His best.

Lord, You are a kind, loving, generous, and understanding Father. Thank You for being accessible, available, and ready to give Your best.

Divine Authority

SCRIPTURE READING: John 14:12–18

KEY VERSE: John 14:13

Whatever you ask in My name, that I will do, that the Father may be glorified in the Son.

A passport is an official document that allows you to move freely from one country to another. It is the means of access without which international travel is virtually impossible.

When Jesus instructed us to pray "in My name," He implied that His full work on the cross was the sole means by which the forgiven and justified believer can legitimately come to the Father and expect an answer.

E. M. Bounds, a noted writer on prayer, described Jesus' comment in such a fashion in his book *Purpose in Prayer:*

> Christ taught us also to approach the Father in His name. That is our passport. It is in His name that we are to make our petitions known.
>
> . . . How wide and comprehensive is that "whatsoever"? There is no limit to the power of that name. "Whatsoever ye shall ask." That is the Divine declaration, and it opens up to every praying child a vista of infinite resource and possibility . . . And that is our heritage. All that Christ has may become ours if we obey the conditions.

Asking in Jesus' name means we come on the merit and mediation of the Cross and in the divine authority of His name. We ask, wanting the Father's will to be done above our own.

Lord, I come to You on the merit and mediation of the Cross in the divine authority of Your name. I ask, wanting Your will to be done above my own.

In Times of Need

SCRIPTURE READING: James 1:2–8
KEY VERSE: James 1:6

Let him ask in faith, with no doubting, for he who doubts is like a wave of the sea driven and tossed by the wind.

Fall semester had come and gone without a hitch. However, spring semester was beginning on a different note. A federal grant would pay his college tuition, but he had no idea where he would get the money needed for books and other expenses.

He recalled how God had made it clear that he was to return to school and complete his degree. He prayed, "Lord, I know You have led me here. So I'm trusting You to meet this need in my life."

He had two choices: give up or go forward by faith. When God leads us along a certain path, our only responsibility is obedience. His responsibility is to work out all the details.

F. B. Meyer wrote, "Believe that God is there between you and your difficulty, and what baffles you will flee before Him, as clouds before the gate."

Later, at registration, the student was asked to sign a form for funds he was about to receive. He had been awarded a small scholarship, one that would pay for his books with extra to spare.

No matter how great or small the request may seem, God is always accessible to those who call out to Him in times of need.

Lord, I am so thankful that no matter how small my request, You are always accessible to me in times of need.

God's Viewpoint

SCRIPTURE READING: 2 Corinthians 4:15–18

KEY VERSE: 2 Corinthians 4:18

We do not look at the things which are seen, but at the things which are not seen. For the things which are seen are temporary, but the things which are not seen are eternal.

While God is infinite and sees your life from beginning to end, you are definitely finite. While He certainly has the answers, you sometimes have to pray for months or years before you can comprehend your situation from God's viewpoint.

A respected theologian once remarked: "We understand life backward, but we must live it forward." In other words, getting God's viewpoint for our specific situation is not always easy or simplistic. As a result, we must persevere and remain steadfast in God's unfailing love for us and trust resolutely in Him, even when we don't have a hint of His perspective.

Realize that God's Word consists of eternal principles that give realistic guidelines. You may want to know whether or not to buy a certain home. God can arrange circumstances and counsel to make such a choice clear, but more often He will use scriptural principles of finance and contentment to steer you in His direction.

Understand that God's work is done in your spirit. Circumstances will fluctuate, but God is unceasingly at work in your heart to bring about the likeness of Christ. That is His ultimate purpose.

Focus on principles and focus within. God's viewpoint will become far more evident when you do.

Dear heavenly Father, I want Your viewpoint. Clear my spiritual vision and help me to focus on the principles of Your Word.

A Tool of Defense

SCRIPTURE READING: Colossians 2:1–7

KEY VERSE: Colossians 2:7

Rooted and built up in Him and established in the faith, as you have been taught, abounding in it with thanksgiving.

A major portion of Paul's writings was a tool of defense against the growing infiltration of apostasy in the early church. Christianity was not the only religion of the day, but it was the only faith that offered evidence of eternal, infallible truth.

Early Christians were so eager to grow in the knowledge of Christ that they often unknowingly accepted false doctrine as truth. Acutely aware of the problem, Paul sent men like Timothy, Titus, Silas, and others to exhort and encourage struggling believers.

The cruelty of false teaching knows no limits. In Thessalonica, believers had received word from false prophets that the Rapture had already occurred. This ploy of Satan set off such a wave of disillusionment that only a letter from Paul dissipated its erroneous influence (1 Thess. 4:13–18).

Apostasy is as alive today as it was in the New Testament era. In fact, as we approach the return of Jesus Christ, it will only grow and become more shrewd in its deception. The one sure way to equip yourself against the enemy's deception is to saturate your mind with the Word of God. No other source is the origin of eternal, unchangeable truth. Don't be deceived! Ask God to give you His discernment for every situation you face.

Saturate my mind with Your Word, Lord. Give me discernment for every situation I face today.

The Fear of the Lord

SCRIPTURE READING: Psalm 113
KEY VERSE: Psalm 112:1

PRAISE the LORD!
Blessed is the man who fears the LORD,
Who delights greatly in His commandments.

The word *fear* in the Bible has a double meaning. The fear of the Lord mentioned in the Old Testament leads to reverence and is the evidence of our worship and reliance on God. The second type of fear is emotional and can come as a result of real or imagined danger.

The fear that God wants us to experience as believers leads to worship and admiration of Him. It is a fear based on love, not terror. When Moses approached God, he did so in humility, honor, and worship. The sacred awe he felt was powerful and very real because he stood in the presence of the Lord God almighty.

The fear of the Lord that resided in the heart of Moses was a sign of the bonding that had taken place between him and God. However, this kind of fear did not render him useless before God; it motivated him to step out in faith and put his entire trust in the unseen and unshakable things of the Lord.

Until we fear God with a holy reverence, we will never experience the fullness of His glory and grace in our lives. When you learn to trust Jesus with your entire life, you will find, as Moses did, you have learned to fear Him with a holy reverence that obeys His simplest command.

Teach me to fear You, Lord. Motivate me to step out in faith and put my entire trust in You.

It Begins with Access

SCRIPTURE READING: Ephesians 3:11–12
KEY VERSE: Psalm 34:15

The eyes of the LORD are on the righteous,
And His ears are open to their cry.

How confident are you in your prayer life? Is it a vague spiritual realm where you are unsure? Is it merely a rote spiritual exercise you perform because the Bible teaches its importance?

This is certainly not the mind-set or spiritual atmosphere that God intended for prayer. He designed prayer so we might experience His reality, power, and care for our lives.

We often lack confidence because we do not understand some of God's basic principles of prayer. It all begins with access (Eph. 3:11–12). Through faith in Christ, you are in His presence and can boldly bring Him your petitions. Through this access to God's very throne, you can be confident He hears your prayers, every one of them. Not one falls on deaf ears.

If you have habitually sinned, God's kindness can bring you to repentance. God's forgiveness cleanses you from sin's guilt. You are holy and righteous in His eyes, even when your behavior is unholy and unrighteous.

Your conduct does not alter your access, though it may hinder your communion. Since you have such fearless access through Christ, you can confidently pray with the assurance that God has heard your plea.

Heavenly Father, I praise You that through Christ I can confidently pray with the assurance that You have heard my plea.

The Power of the Word

SCRIPTURE READING: Romans 3:23–25
KEY VERSE: Hebrews 4:12

The word of God is living and powerful, and sharper than any two-edged sword, piercing even to the division of soul and spirit, and of joints and marrow, and is a discerner of the thoughts and intents of the heart.

Though the book of Romans was written around A.D. 57, it is just as relevant today. So powerful is its message that many have come to a deeper understanding of God's personal love through reading this book.

Warren Wiersbe writes,

On May 24, 1738, a discouraged missionary went, very unwillingly, to a religious meeting in London. There a miracle took place. "About a quarter before nine," he wrote in his journal, "I felt my heart strangely warmed. I felt I did trust in Christ, Christ alone, for salvation; and an assurance was given me that He had taken away my sins, even mine, and saved me from the law of sin and death."

That missionary was John Wesley. The message he heard that evening was the preface to Martin Luther's commentary on Romans. Just a few months before, John Wesley had written in his journal: "I went to America to convert the Indians; but who shall convert me?"

That evening his question was answered. And the result was the great Wesleyan revival that swept England and transformed the nation.

Paul's epistle to the Romans is still transforming people's lives. You and I can read and study the same inspired letter that brought life and power to Luther and Wesley! You and I can experience revival if the message of this letter grips us as it has gripped men of faith in centuries past.

Lord, thank You for the power of Your Word. Let it grip me as it has gripped men of faith in centuries past.

Cherish the Word

SCRIPTURE READING: Deuteronomy 6:1–9

KEY VERSE: Deuteronomy 6:6

These words which I command you today shall be in your heart.

Are you a list maker? Most people at least jot down their grocery items on a piece of paper before heading to the store. It's so easy to forget the little details that we need to keep checklists to help us remember.

We're just as "forgetful" concerning God's Word many times too. The Lord understands our natural weaknesses and our tendency to mentally push aside thoughts we don't deem urgent at the moment. That is why He commanded His people to keep His words ever before them: "These words, which I am commanding you today, shall be on your heart; and you shall teach them diligently to your sons and shall talk of them when you sit in your house and when you walk by the way and when you lie down and when you rise up. And you shall bind them as a sign on your hand and they shall be as frontals on your forehead. And you shall write them on the doorposts of your house and on your gates" (Deut. 6:6–9 NASB).

In other words, they were to put God's Word in the paths of their daily lives, everywhere they went, and as a part of all they did. How can you do the same today? Find some verses that pertain to your personal circumstances, and write them out on cards. Keep the cards with you or in a prominent place in your home. You'll be surprised how quickly they become a part of your everyday thinking.

Write Your Word on my heart, O Lord, and teach me to cherish it.

Learning God's Truth

SCRIPTURE READING: 1 John 4:1–6

KEY VERSE: 1 John 5:1

Whoever believes that Jesus is the Christ is born of God, and everyone who loves Him who begot also loves him who is begotten of Him.

Since you were small, you've probably been told not to believe everything you read or hear. And for the most part in the world around you, that is true. From newspapers to the evening news to what you hear at work or next door, you must be discriminating in what you choose to believe.

The same applies to the teaching of God's Word. When you hear a sermon or a lesson in Sunday school, do you ever think to question what you learn? Questioning does not necessarily mean doubting; you may have wonderful, godly teachers. Questioning in this sense means subjecting the material to your own inquiry into Scripture to see if the teaching lines up. If you are not sure how to proceed, the following are some helpful guidelines:

Check Scripture references. If your teacher gives you a list of related Bible passages, look them up when you get home. Remember, however, that your objective is not to find innocent, human errors; you are making sure that you understand how the verses relate to the topic at hand.

For deeper questions, consult a Bible dictionary or concordance or supplementary teaching material. If in your study a "caution flag" is raised about something you've been told, consider asking another credible source.

God always wants you to be informed and discerning as you learn His truth.

Dear heavenly Father, teach me to rightly divide Your Word of truth and apply it to my life.

In His Timing

SCRIPTURE READING: 1 John 5:14–16
KEY VERSE: 1 John 4:16

And we have known and believed the love that God has for us. God is love, and he who abides in love abides in God, and God in him.

The mother knew her son was not doing well at college. His grades were fine, and he had even made the football team. But between studying and practicing he had not made time for church or personal Bible study as he had in high school. How could she help him get back on track spiritually?

The apostle Paul faced the same challenge. In a Roman prison cell, Paul heard discouraging news from Epaphras, the pastor of the new and growing church in Colosse. The Colossian believers were falling into the trap of false teaching and losing their focus on Jesus Christ. Yet Paul knew that even from prison he could directly minister God's truth to the struggling Christians, through continuous and specific prayer.

The greatest privilege and blessing you have as God's child is to talk with Him in prayer. You can praise Him and bring Him your needs, your hurts, your desires. He promises to hear you in whatever you ask (1 John 5:15–16).

When you ask Him to work His truth into the lives of those you love, you will see the results. And be prepared! God may call you to long-term intercession. The Lord will give you His patience and strength as He answers in His good timing.

Dear Father, thank You for Your promise that You will hear me in whatever I ask. Give me patience and strength to wait for the timing of Your answers.

Prayer Power

SCRIPTURE READING: James 4:3–7

KEY VERSE: James 4:7

Submit to God. Resist the devil and he will flee from you.

 atan's strategy includes the destruction of the church body, society, and nations, not just the torment of the individual believer. That was why Paul implored the Ephesians to be in constant prayer for all saints.

By craftily waging war on an individual basis, he can turn our focus of prayer away from the body of Christ to the problems of self. This breakdown of prayer focus can be the beginning of a snowball effect of carnal selfishness.

Society shows proof of this tearing down in many areas. Anthony Evans explains in *America's Only Hope:*

> The loss of mankind's fellowship with God and participation in His will has staggering repercussions for individuals, families, and nations. Fellowship with God alone produces purpose in life. A lack of purpose in life eventually leads to despair that we try to alleviate with drugs, sex, and materialism. Purposelessness in families is evidenced by no-fault divorces, abuse of wives and children, incest, and a desire for perpetual entertainment.

Pray daily for your brothers and sisters in Christ. Ask God to keep you sensitive to the spiritual needs of others.

Dear God, keep me sensitive to the spiritual needs of others. Remind me to pray daily for my brothers and sisters in Christ.

Time Alone with God

SCRIPTURE READING: Luke 12:16–21
KEY VERSE: Luke 12:31

Seek the kingdom of God, and all these things shall be added to you.

As a young man, he set a goal to retire before age thirty-five. He worked seven days a week in an effort to build up his business. After several years, he found himself alone. Fed up with his workaholic attitude, friends and family members had moved on and left him wondering how he had become so out of step with God's will. From the world's perspective, he was a success, but from God's viewpoint he was a spiritual and emotional pauper.

A wondrous mystery is hidden within the cliché that beckons us to "stop and smell the roses." The memory of a sunset spent with a loved one lasts longer when we take the time to enjoy it. The sweetness that comes from sharing our lives with those around us is a part of the good things in life.

However, even this can become blurred and out of focus if we are out of fellowship with Christ. Taking time to worship God and listen for His voice through the indwelling of the Holy Spirit is not something we can switch on or off.

Ask yourself how long it has been since you have spent quality time alone with the Lord. If your schedule has you tied up and out of reach of the good things in life, then maybe it's time to take a serious look at where you are going. Will you like yourself once you get there? Love and friendship are two of the most priceless treasures we will ever know.

Thank You for the privilege of having fellowship with You, Lord. I value the time I spend alone in Your presence.

Pray Without Ceasing

SCRIPTURE READING: Psalm 30
KEY VERSE: 1 Thessalonians 5:17

Pray without ceasing.

Once Paul entered Macedonia, he immediately established a church in Philippi and then turned his attention to the port city of Thessalonica. More than 200,000 people lived and worked there. The city was a melting pot of cultural differences. It was also an area where immorality and crime thrived. Therefore, most believers saved under Paul's ministry came from pagan backgrounds.

The apostle worked quickly to help new believers understand their spiritual foundation. One of the ways he accomplished that was through prayer. Paul admonished the church to "pray without ceasing," which means to maintain an attitude of constant prayer. Much more than constant mumbling, unceasing prayer means living in conscious awareness of God's personal love and availability.

Paul's strategy was simple: When temptation comes—pray. When fear approaches—pray. When someone falsely accuses you—pray. When you are happy or sad—pray. No matter what you're facing, pray because God answers prayer!

You get to know your heavenly Father through prayer. You can come to Him with anything, at any time of the day or night.

Dear Lord, teach me to pray when temptation comes, fear approaches, and someone falsely accuses me. Teach me to pray no matter what I am facing.

What Does It Cost?

SCRIPTURE READING: 2 Samuel 24
KEY VERSE: 2 Samuel 24:10

David's heart condemned him after he had numbered the people. So David said to the LORD, "I have sinned greatly in what I have done; but now, I pray, O LORD, take away the iniquity of Your servant, for I have done very foolishly."

In numbering the people of Israel, David shifted his trust from faith in God's ability to human resources. And in His anger, God sent a pestilence that killed 70,000 men: "When the angel stretched out his hand toward Jerusalem to destroy it, the LORD relented . . . And the angel of the LORD was by the threshing floor of Araunah the Jebusite. Then David spoke to the LORD when he saw the angel who was striking down the people, and said, 'Behold, it is I who have sinned, and it is I who have done wrong; but these sheep, what have they done? Please let Thy hand be against me'" (2 Sam. 24:16–17 NASB).

When David realized his sin, he went to God in prayer. When God withdrew His anger, David prayed once again.

He purchased the threshing floor of Araunah the Jebusite so he could offer sacrifices, and he said, "I will surely buy it [the threshing floor] from you for a price, for I will not offer burnt offerings to the LORD my God which cost me nothing" (2 Sam. 24:24 NASB).

When your back is against the wall and every avenue closed up before you, do you say a quick prayer to gain relief, or do you offer prayer that costs you something? David humbled his heart before God, and the Lord heard his cry.

I'm not after instant relief, Lord. I want Your will and purposes worked out in my life.

Having Your Needs Met

SCRIPTURE READING: Psalm 34:1–7

KEY VERSE: Psalm 34:1

I will bless the LORD at all times;
His praise shall continually be in my mouth.

There is a method to having your needs met, but it doesn't begin by drawing money out of the bank. It begins with worship and prayer. A heart that is truly focused on Christ will be quick to turn to Him in prayer. The very act of praying is a signal to God that there is a willingness to trust Him.

David began Psalm 34 with adoration to God: "I will bless the LORD at all times; His praise shall continually be in my mouth." This also is where we should begin—adoring God and worshiping Him. When we acknowledge the Lord for who He is, we establish a tone of faith for our lives.

When a material need arises, we are not so quick to rush to the nearest store and wave a credit card. Ask God to teach you how to be dependent on Him and not on your resources or ability to provide for yourself.

God loves for us to need Him. His greatest desire is to build a one-on-one relationship with us. Coming to Him for even trivial needs is a blessing to Him. And often this type of action is a marvelous source of encouragement.

You may not want to pray about everything you do. However, if you will commit your day to the Lord and pray your way through the moments, you will be surprised at the closeness of His presence and at the surety that is yours because you are walking in faith in Him.

Lord, I adore You. I worship You. I wait in Your presence for a divine encounter.

JUNE

*A Divine
Encounter in
Intimacy*

The True Light

SCRIPTURE READING: John 14:21–23

KEY VERSE: John 1:9

That was the true Light which gives light to every man who comes into the world.

Too many people go to church and come home without discovering the personal love of Jesus Christ. Some may even be baptized and still not know the intimate love of the Savior. They never develop a one-on-one relationship with the Lover of their souls. God has called us to worship Him, but even before this He calls us to intimate fellowship with Him. In the Garden of Eden He walked in the cool of the day with Adam and Eve. Throughout history, He has continued to reach out to mankind.

His greatest display of love and devotion comes to us through the life of Jesus Christ. However, as A. W. Tozer writes in *The Pursuit of God,* "To most . . . God is an inference, not a reality. He is a deduction from evidence which they consider adequate, but He remains personally unknown to the individual."

The responsibility of relationship is not all God's. We must have a desire to know Him, walk with Him, and enjoy His company. He habitually reveals Himself to us, but are we seeking His presence?

"As we . . . focus upon God, the things of the spirit will take shape before our inner eyes," continues Tozer. "Obedience to the word of Christ will bring an inward revelation of the Godhead (John 14:21–23) . . . There will be seen the constant shining of the 'true Light, which lighteth every man that cometh into the world' (John 1:9)."

Lord, give me the desire to know You better, walk with You, and enjoy Your company. Reveal Yourself to me as I wait in Your presence.

ℋe Comes to Us

SCRIPTURE READING: John 4:7–26

KEY VERSE: John 3:3

Jesus answered and said to him, "Most assuredly, I say to you, unless one is born again, he cannot see the kingdom of God."

One of the first people to whom Jesus revealed Himself as the Messiah was the Samaritan woman. Typically Jews looked down on the Samaritans because they were a mixed race, part Jew and part Greek. Samaritans also refused to worship in the Jerusalem temple.

However, this woman was of special interest to Jesus. She had been married several times, and the man she was living with at that point was not her husband. Warren Wiersbe sets the scene:

> Because He was on a divinely appointed schedule, it was necessary that Jesus go through Samaria . . . He would meet a woman there and lead her into saving faith, the kind of true faith that would affect an entire village.
>
> Our Lord was no respecter of persons. Earlier, He counseled a moral Jewish man (John 3), and now He would witness to an immoral Samaritan woman! . . . In that day, it was not considered proper for any man, especially a rabbi, to speak in public to a strange woman (John 4:27). But our Lord set social customs aside because a soul's eternal salvation was at stake.

Jesus had only one purpose in mind when He came to earth, and that was to rescue us from sin. Through the life of this woman, we are given a picture of ourselves. Each of us deserves death, but because of God's mercy and grace, He has granted us eternal life. Just as Jesus came to the woman at the well, He comes to us.

Thank You, Lord, for coming to me to reveal Yourself and Your plan for my life.

Abiding in Christ

SCRIPTURE READING: John 15:7–11
KEY VERSE: John 15:7

If you abide in Me, and My words abide in you, you will ask what you desire, and it shall be done for you.

Jesus encouraged His followers with these words: "If you abide in Me, and My words abide in you, ask whatever you wish, and it shall be done for you" (John 15:7 NASB). What does it mean to abide in Christ? In the Greek, the word *abide* means "to continue, to stay, or to remain."

Christ's words imply a decision on the part of the hearer. You must decide whether to abide in God's love or be drawn away by the tinkering sounds of the world. Every day there is opportunity to draw close to God or to distance your heart from His.

You can be sure of one thing: God will never withdraw His love from you. This alone is enough to fill you with unspeakable joy. The God of the universe personally and intimately loves you. Oswald Chambers noted, "Be rightly related to God, find your joy there, and out of you will flow rivers of living water."

Many Christians believe that living up to all the rules and regulations will somehow bring a lasting sense of joy. But Jesus tells us it is enough to simply live and love God.

Lasting joy is never a result of human achievements but a result of a life devoted to the Savior. Are you tired and weary from traveling the road of discouragement? Look to Jesus, abide in Him, rest in His care, and you will experience His tremendous joy.

Father, I am tired and weary from traveling the road of discouragement. Help me to look to You, abide in You, and rest in Your care.

Your Perfect Friend

SCRIPTURE READING: John 15:12–15
KEY VERSE: John 15:3

You are already clean because of the word which I have spoken to you.

Where did you meet your best friend? Often you make friends in your own neighborhood. Sometimes you find them at school, in college, or at work. The friendship isn't perfect, yet it is an integral part of your life.

But if you could find the perfect friend, what would be your blueprint? You would probably choose someone who loves you just as you are, someone who overlooks every negative act and still loves you without condition. You'd pick someone who accepts you without regarding qualifications or stature.

No doubt, your friend would understand you fully and know why you're hurt, discouraged, or tempted, and he would understand even when you err. He doesn't agree with it, but he understands because he's been there.

Your ideal friend would be someone to whom you could tell your innermost desires and secrets without fear of rejection or criticism. The person would be committed to you, no matter the circumstance, and would be completely open with you.

Your new friend would be selfless, showing you love every day and encouraging you to love others. He would offer inspiration and comfort simply by listening before answering. If you haven't met such a friend, it's time for an introduction.

This is Jesus Christ. He is your perfect Friend!

You are the perfect Friend, Jesus. You offer inspiration and comfort. Thank You for being my Friend.

Quality Time

SCRIPTURE READING: Romans 12:1–2
KEY VERSE: 1 Thessalonians 5:24

He who calls you is faithful, who also will do it.

Ours is a world of satellites, lasers, cell phones, and ATMs. Faxes zoom across telephone lines, and computers arrange daily schedules with supreme accuracy. Because of all these things, we have learned to demand instant results.

The tendency to try to become super Christians within a very short time is grave. It is almost as if we believe that to please God, we must become "better" quickly. However, God does not work this way.

He wants love and devotion to overflow from our hearts naturally, not forcibly, turned toward Him. We cannot hurry or fax our way into spiritual growth. It takes time, quality time, spent with God.

This is how God weeds out old, sinful habits and replants His renewing truths within our hearts and minds. He knows that to produce maximum growth there must be maximum care and nurturing. God slowly reshapes our lives until they are molded into the image of His Son.

Never become discouraged by what seems to be a long time during your spiritual growth. God's timetable is not ours. And if you will seek Him above everything else, you will receive all He has for you within His timing.

Lord, I want a relationship with You above all else. I want to receive all that You have for me.

Sharing Life's Loads

SCRIPTURE READING: 2 Corinthians 12:1–10
KEY VERSES: Ecclesiastes 4:9–10

Two are better than one,
Because they have a good reward for their labor.
For if they fall, one will lift up his companion.
But woe to him who is alone when he falls,
For he has no one to help him up.

If you've ever had the experience of moving furniture around a room, you know how tedious it can be to try lifting it by yourself. Most pieces you can push around the carpet with a lot of shoving, but it's time-consuming (and not very good for the carpet). Some pieces require another set of muscles. When two or more people are lifting, the job can be done without too much strain on any one person.

The same is true with spiritual and emotional load bearing. You were not designed to hold up under such stress; that is why you need a Savior who loves you and wants to carry you along in His strength. Many times, the Lord supports you through friends and family (Eccl. 4:9–10).

Maybe it was sharing a meal or just sitting there listening to you talk and share your feelings. Comfort comes in many forms, but all displays of true, godly comfort have in mind the goal of pointing the sufferer to the One who is able to bear every burden.

Paul declared, "He has said to me, 'My grace is sufficient for you, for power is perfected in weakness.' Most gladly, therefore, I will rather boast about my weaknesses, so that the power of Christ may dwell in me" (2 Cor. 12:9 NASB).

Spiritual loads are opportunities for Jesus to demonstrate His all-sufficient love and power and to reassure you that you are never alone.

Lord, help me to realize that spiritual loads are opportunities for You to demonstrate Your all-sufficient love and power. I thank You that I am never alone.

You're on the Team

SCRIPTURE READING: Romans 5

KEY VERSE: Romans 5:1

Having been justified by faith, we have peace with God through our Lord Jesus Christ.

Though the events of baseball in the U.S. in the spring of 1995 were hardly of earth-shattering importance, the players' strike did provide unexpected lessons. The major-league baseball owners wanted to begin the season on schedule, with or without their star players. When the strike did not end, the managers made the key decision to replace them with some average guys who wanted to play.

Who were they? In *The Grip of Grace,* Max Lucado tells how these men were an example of God's major-league grace:

These weren't minor-leaguers. The minor leagues were also on strike. These were fellows who went from coaching Little League one week to wearing a Red Sox uniform the next . . .

These guys didn't make it to the big leagues on skill; they made it on luck. They weren't picked because they were good; they were picked because they were willing . . . They were just happy to be on the team . . .

Shouldn't we be, as well? Aren't we a lot like these players? If the first four chapters of Romans tell us anything, they tell us we are living a life we don't deserve . . . We aren't skillful enough to make the community softball league, but our names are on the greatest roster of history! Do we deserve to be here? No. But would we trade the privilege? Not for the world.

Father, thank You for putting my name on the greatest roster of history. I'm so glad I'm on the winning team!

Ability and Capability

SCRIPTURE READING: 2 Corinthians 12:7–10

KEY VERSE: 2 Corinthians 12:10

I take pleasure in infirmities, in reproaches, in needs, in persecutions, in distresses, for Christ's sake. For when I am weak, then I am strong.

You don't notice God's ability as much in your areas of capability. For example, let's say you are gifted with your speech and are able to strike up a conversation with anyone and set him at ease. It's not a challenge for you to enter a social setting in which you do not know many people. You have several new friends before you leave the room.

As a result, you often do not think of asking God to give you His strength and wisdom when you interact with people. He is the One who gifted you in that way, of course, but you are not as conscious of His involvement. But let's also imagine that you are not a good cook. No matter how closely you follow a recipe, something always goes wrong. People politely don't say much when they taste your dishes.

When you are asked to deliver a meal to a person with a long-term illness, a shiver of dread runs down your spine. You want to help, but you also know that this is not your area of expertise. In this situation, you would not hesitate to run to the Lord to ask for help.

That is the purpose of our weaknesses, whether they are physical, emotional, spiritual, or vocational. God wants you to run to Him; He desires your dependence because it reminds you of His loving care and sufficiency. The truth is, He wants you always to rely on His ability, and He lets you have weaknesses so you'll be sure to ask.

Father, help me learn to thank You for my weaknesses. They make me rely more on You.

Your Loving Shepherd

SCRIPTURE READING: John 10:1–15
KEY VERSE: John 10:15

As the Father knows Me, even so I know the Father; and I lay down My life for the sheep.

Though written in 1836, William Bradbury's hymn, "Savior, Like a Shepherd Lead Us," contains a dear and relevant truth for us today. Jesus is our loving Shepherd, and He takes care of our every need.

> Savior, like a Shepherd lead us, much we need Thy tender care;
> In Thy pleasant pastures feed us, for our use Thy folds prepare;
> Blessed Jesus, blessed Jesus, Thou hast bought us, Thine we are;
> Blessed Jesus, blessed Jesus, Thou hast bought us, Thine we are.
> Thou hast promised to receive us, poor and sinful though we be;
> Thou hast mercy to relieve us, grace to cleanse and power to free;
> Blessed Jesus, blessed Jesus, let us early turn to Thee;
> Blessed Jesus, blessed Jesus, let us early turn to Thee.

Many times we resist thinking of Jesus as our Shepherd until we find ourselves in the throes of trouble and despair. We may choose instead to meditate on His strength and power as our ruling Lord, or see Him as our merciful Savior who forgives our sins. Yet how many of us, when facing a great threat or trial, have turned to Psalm 23 and discovered amazing comfort and peace?

There is great security in Jesus. He is your intimate, loving Shepherd. Only in Him do we find the patience needed to protect and care for troubled and wandering sheep.

Heavenly Shepherd, thank You for protecting me. You are my intimate, loving Shepherd.

The Desires of Your Heart

SCRIPTURE READING: Psalm 25

KEY VERSES: Psalm 25:4–5

Show me Your ways, O LORD;
Teach me Your paths.
Lead me in Your truth and teach me,
For You are the God of my salvation;
On You I wait all the day.

Most of us are familiar with the scripture from Isaiah in which God said, "For My thoughts are not your thoughts, Nor are your ways My ways" (55:8). Yet many times we fail to see the goodness of this verse. God often takes us places we could never dream of going on our own. His vision is far beyond ours. His might and power open doors for us we thought were permanently closed.

God has a way of providing all we could ever hope for. The problem comes when we fail to trust Him in times of waiting. All of us have done this. We want something to take place so badly that we try to convince God to give us what we want now.

When we fail to see His immediate response, we often think He is not going to provide what we desire to receive. Jesus told His disciples to seek God first and then all the other desires of their hearts would be given to them.

Who plants desires in your heart? Many times God does, especially if you are walking closely with Him. These are the very things He wants to give you as a blessing from Himself. Don't worry about wrong motivations. God knows how to sift away selfish longings and replace them with healthy dreams and goals.

God's blessings are so satisfying, few have ever sought to return them. Therefore, wait for His way to be known, and the blessing you receive will fill your heart with boundless joy.

Father, help me to wait for Your way to be known.
Don't let me walk in my own way.

Try Him

SCRIPTURE READING: 1 Peter 1:3–7
KEY VERSE: 1 Peter 5:9

Resist him, steadfast in the faith, knowing that the same sufferings are experienced by your brotherhood in the world.

One of the ways Satan works to defeat you is through feelings of discouragement. He knows if he can cause you to doubt the goodness of God, there is a chance you will become fearful and give up. Often the Lord allows the enemy's arrows to get through His protective cover so that your faith is tried and strengthened.

Frustrations, feelings of inferiority, external pressures, and any number of difficulties can be delivered from the enemy's hand. What do you do when the going gets rough? Do you take your stand and resist the enemy the way Peter instructed us to do? Or do you become weak under the attack?

First of all, ask God to help you not to become discouraged in the midst of the battle. All of God's greatest saints had to learn how to handle heartaches and disappointments along with all kinds of evil. Reading about their victories and defeats will bring insight and hope to your life.

You will find that when you are at your weakest point, God is your greatest Source of help. Prayer is your most efficient tool for spiritual victory. Remember, it must be fueled by faith. You can trust God on all battle fronts because He is faithful. Whatever concerns you concerns Him. Trust Him. Try Him, and witness His power at work in your life.

I trust You, Lord. You are my greatest Source of help. Thank You for the privilege of prayer, which brings spiritual victory!

Beyond Betrayal

SCRIPTURE READING: Psalm 86
KEY VERSE: Psalm 86:2–4

Preserve my life, for I am holy;
You are my God;
Save Your servant who trusts in You!
Be merciful to me, O Lord,
For I cry to You all day long. Rejoice the soul of Your servant,
For to You, O LORD, I lift up my soul.

Most of us know what it feels like to watch someone we trust go down in defeat. Often, however, when this happens, we feel abandoned and a little taken advantage of.

It is critical to your spiritual health to stay focused on God, especially when you feel you have been betrayed by another. He knows that in our humanness we search for heroes. We like to put people up on pedestals that He never meant for them to stand upon. In doing so, we place expectations on them that they may be incapable of fulfilling.

The better way is to keep your eyes on Jesus. Make Him your only Hero. After all, He is the only One who is able to fulfill all the promises He has spoken.

It's okay to enjoy the goals and ambitions of others. We can and should applaud their accomplishments and encourage them in all good works. Just be careful that God approves your motivation to cheer and encourage. The Lord does not want you attributing more to an individual than He deems necessary.

Only God can meet all your needs. Ask Him to teach you how to be balanced in your relationships and in your view of others. Remember, each of us is a life under construction. Keep this in mind when others disappoint you.

Lord, You are my only Hero. Help me keep my eyes on You. You are the only One who can fulfill the promises I have received.

Constant Communion

SCRIPTURE READING: Psalm 63
KEY VERSE: Psalm 63:8

My soul follows close behind You;
Your right hand upholds me.

When we think about the good things in life, one thing overshadows all the rest, and that is fellowship with God. No one can take His place in our lives. As much as we love our family members and friends, the greatest friendship we will ever experience is with Jesus Christ.

He knows your heartache and your joys. He never tires of you but is always excited to hear your voice calling out to Him in prayer. He has promised good things for those who seek Him. If you want to find the key to the good things in life, discover the fellowship that God has waiting for you through Jesus Christ.

In *My Utmost for His Highest,* Oswald Chambers writes,

To be so much in contact with God that you never need to ask Him to show you His will, is to be nearing the final stage of your discipline in the life of faith. When you are rightly related to God, it is a life of freedom and liberty and delight; you are God's will, and all your commonsense decisions are His will for you unless He checks. You decide things in perfect delightful friendship with God, knowing that if your decisions are wrong He will always check; when He checks, stop at once.

Chambers describes life lived in constant communion with God. It is not the life of a reclusive servant, but the life of a child of God who is living in perfect fellowship with Jesus Christ.

How thankful I am, dear Lord, that You know my heartache and my joys. You never tire of me. You are always excited to hear my voice calling out to You.

Identifying Your Needs

SCRIPTURE READING: Philippians 4:11–19
KEY VERSE: Philippians 4:19

My God shall supply all your need according to His riches in glory by Christ Jesus.

Select someone you would say represents a person who "has it all," however you might define that condition. Maybe it is a friend or coworker or family member who seems to have everything that you desire. Did you stop to realize that this person has needs too?

It's true. The most "perfect" person in your eyes, the one who appears to have all he needs to be satisfied, still has needs. Everyone has areas of life that feel like aching voids, things missing from his being or experience that cause personal pain. These voids can be anything from a lack of peace to an insufficient bank account to a family laden with relationship problems.

What are your needs? As you make a list, distinguish the difference between a need and a desire. From God's perspective, a need is an essential ingredient for your physical, spiritual, and emotional well-being while a desire is simply something you want. There are some gray areas in this definition, of course, but God knows your legitimate needs and helps you weed out the items in your heart that disguise themselves as needs.

Some needs don't make themselves known all of the time, and in general needs change through the years. But you always have needs, and admitting that is not wrong. What you also have is God's promise: "My God shall supply all your needs according to His riches in glory in Christ Jesus" (Phil. 4:19 NASB).

God, help me to distinguish between legitimate needs and selfish desires. Thank You for Your promise to supply my legitimate needs.

Ask the Father

SCRIPTURE READING: Matthew 7:7–11

KEY VERSE: James 4:2

You lust and do not have. You murder and covet and cannot obtain. You fight and war. Yet you do not have because you do not ask.

In the human parent-child relationship, when a child needs or wants something, he asks his mom or dad. It would be silly for the child to assume that his parents automatically know all of his needs. For example, if the child said, "Dad, I was thirsty yesterday, and you didn't give me anything to drink," that parent would shake his head in amazement and say, "Well, son, you should have asked me."

In your relationship with God, of course, God already knows what you need before you indicate it. But even so, God wants you to enter into the experience of asking Him specifically. Jesus told us, "Ask, and it shall be given to you; seek, and you shall find; knock, and it shall be opened to you. For every one who asks receives, and he who seeks finds; and to him who knocks it shall be opened" (Matt. 7:7–8 NASB).

He did not mean that God will automatically hand you everything you request. He is too wise and loving a Father to do that: "If you then, being evil, know how to give good gifts to your children, how much more shall your Father who is in heaven give what is good to those who ask Him!" (Matt. 7:11 NASB).

God wants you to ask Him so you will learn the joys of a close relationship with Him. He wants you to feel His loving response and appreciate His care. What have you asked Him for today?

Teach me to ask, Lord. Teach me to keep seeking until I find and to keep knocking until the door is opened to me.

The Ultimate Friendship

SCRIPTURE READING: Luke 22:7–62
KEY VERSE: Romans 5:8

God demonstrates His own love toward us, in that while we were still sinners, Christ died for us.

It is perfect and necessary that God loved us while we were yet sinners. Only unconditional love could survive our flailing attempts to respond to His love.

What a Friend we have in Jesus, who bears all our sins and griefs! But we can be most awkward in embracing Him. We seek true love and friendship in anything from personal ads to gathering places when all we need to do is look to the right "address."

When He was a man, Christ saw His friends abandon Him. He returned to His hometown of Nazareth a minister, only to be completely rejected and threatened with death.

Immediately after the kindred moments of the Last Supper, the men closest to Jesus, the disciples, peeled away like lifeless skin.

Jesus prayed in anguish in Gethsemane. His watchmen slept. Jesus was arrested. His men stayed back, following from afar before scattering. Even beloved John only watched. Peter, bent on emotion in saying he'd never betray his Lord, betrayed Jesus three times.

One of the Twelve betrayed Christ into the hands of His murderers. Judas's love was fake even to the kiss. Only John is recorded as being there at Calvary's Cross.

There Jesus embraced us all, stretching wide His arms in ultimate friendship.

Lord, thank You for Your faithful friendship. You loved me while I was yet a sinner.

Remember Jonah

SCRIPTURE READING: Jonah 1:1–3
KEY VERSES: Psalm 139:7–8

Where can I go from Your Spirit?
Or where can I flee from Your presence?
If I ascend into heaven, You are there;
If I make my bed in hell, behold, You are there.

David knew what Jonah forgot. He asked, "Where can I flee from Your presence? If I ascend to heaven, You are there; if I make my bed in Sheol, behold, You are there" (Ps. 139:7–8 NASB). David understood that God is everywhere. There is no escaping His presence.

However, Jonah forgot that. Instead of doing what the Lord called him to do, he rebelled and became enmeshed in the thought of how God wanted him to go to Nineveh and preach repentance. Somehow he thought he could escape the presence and will of God.

There is little doubt about the wickedness of the Ninevites, but that was not the issue. Israel had become steeped in sin as well. The challenge for God's servant was one of obedience.

God is aware of the motives of your heart. Often a task that seems unfair is hard to complete. However, if God has called you to do it, there is no other avenue to take but obedience. After a detour into the belly of a great fish, Jonah unwillingly preached repentance to the Ninevites. As a result, they turned from their wickedness. Yet we never see God's joy breaking forth in Jonah's life. He was too angry at God.

When you are tempted to rebel against the Lord's will, remember the fate of Jonah, and set the course of your heart on obedience and trust in the Lord. There you will find great blessings.

Lord, when I am tempted to rebel against You, help me to remember
Jonah and set the course of my heart on trusting and obeying You.

What a Friend

SCRIPTURE READING: Psalm 119:65–72
KEY VERSE: Psalm 119:67

Before I was afflicted I went astray,
But now I keep Your word.

The words of the much-loved hymn, "What a Friend We Have in Jesus," sum up the essence of this passage:

What a friend we have in Jesus, all our sins and griefs to bear!
What a privilege to carry everything to God in prayer.
O what peace we often forfeit,
O what needless pain we bear,
All because we do not carry everything to God in prayer! (Joseph Scriven)

Have you ever been reluctant to talk to God about a pain in your life because you know the problem is related to a past sin of some kind? You feel ashamed, and somehow in the back of your mind you believe you deserve the consequences and therefore shouldn't ask God to relieve the pressure.

Yes, sin does bring with it a host of problems, and God does not promise to take away all consequences. In His mercy, He does remove the results much of the time. Sometimes, though, He wants you to learn through suffering, much as a child learns by being disciplined by his parents. Nevertheless, God does care about how you feel.

Part of the reason to allow the suffering to remain in your life is that you will learn to draw closer to Him. The Lord wants to heal your damaged emotions and recharge your spirit. Trust Him with that task, and you'll learn what He can do.

Lord, I want to draw closer to You. Heal my damaged emotions and recharge my broken spirit.

Feeding on the Word

SCRIPTURE READING: 1 Peter 2:1–6
KEY VERSE: 1 Peter 2:2

As newborn babes, desire the pure milk of the word, that you may grow thereby.

As any parent knows, a new baby has a limited menu. He drinks milk or a gentle formula that's just right for his developing digestive system. As he grows, he moves up to soft foods that have been specially mixed for easy swallowing. But it's only when a baby cuts his teeth that the real joy of eating begins.

God designed the believer's "appetite" for His Word to work in much the same way. As a young believer, you begin the nourishment process with the milk of Scripture, the elementary principles that lay the groundwork for deeper truths to come. Then as you mature in your relationship with Christ, you're ready to learn more.

A baby who doesn't progress to more substantial foods doesn't keep growing. Something is wrong. It would be unnatural and unhealthy for the baby to drink only milk for an extended period of time. If you don't move beyond the basics of faith, you soon become spiritually malnourished and cease to develop as God planned.

Are you growing in the Lord? Commit yourself to feeding on God's Word each day, trusting Him to work His principles into your heart as you obey His direction. The more of His truth you absorb, the more you'll grow to be like Christ.

Father, help me to commit myself to feeding on Your Word each day. I want to grow strong in Your precepts.

The Unpardonable Sin

SCRIPTURE READING: Romans 8:35–39
KEY VERSE: 1 John 4:9

In this the love of God was manifested toward us, that God has sent His only begotten Son into the world, that we might live through Him.

Many Christians worry needlessly about committing the unpardonable sin. Therefore, when it comes to this subject, we need to be very sober in our thinking. If you are a Christian and concerned that you have done something to cause God to turn from you, realize there is nothing strong enough to alter God's love toward you.

His love is infinite and does not change like the seasons of time. He has committed Himself to you, and the love He displayed at Calvary is eternal proof of this commitment. The very fact that you are concerned about your relationship with God is evidence that you love Him and need Him.

Christ's reference to the unpardonable sin is given to us to teach us what happens when a person refuses to accept Him as Savior and Lord. Jesus taught the only way a man or a woman experiences eternal salvation is by faith in the One whom God has sent.

When a person repeatedly denies Christ as Lord, he spiritually refuses God's wondrous gift of salvation and yields instead to Satan's lie. God is patient and long-suffering in His pursuit of mankind. However, He knows when man has said a final no to His love and forgiveness.

Take a moment today to renew your commitment to Him.

Dear heavenly Father, I renew my commitment to You. I declare my faith in Your Son, Jesus Christ. Take my life and use it for Your glory.

A Season of Waiting

SCRIPTURE READING: Genesis 16:1–6

KEY VERSE: Psalm 28:6

Blessed be the LORD,
Because He has heard the voice of my supplications!

He was in desperate need of a car. The one he had driven for ten years had finally broken down. God had always provided for his needs throughout his life. This time, however, he could not imagine how the provision would come.

Each time he prayed about the situation he felt the Lord saying the same thing: "Trust Me." But after weeks of hunting for rides to work and rearranging schedules for his family, he decided to go to a local car dealership. As he listened to the salesman, he could sense an uneasiness within himself.

He knew the Spirit of God was warning him to go home, but he tried to ignore it. He was tired of waiting, and he wanted action. Could he possibly disobey God and justify his actions?

That night as he closed the door to his home, he saw the worried look on his wife's face. "I couldn't do it," he said. "We'll have to trust God for a solution." She breathed a sigh of relief and said, "While you were gone, a man from the church called. He has a nice car he wants to give us."

God always provides what we need when we need it. However, sometimes that may require a season of waiting. Make sure you don't try to fill in any gaps along the way as Abraham did. God's reward is yours if you are willing to wait and trust Him to meet the need in His way.

Lord, I don't want to fill the gaps with my own plans. Make me willing to wait and trust You to meet my needs in Your way.

Wisdom for Every Decision

SCRIPTURE READING: 1 John 5:6–13
KEY VERSE: 1 John 5:9

If we receive the witness of men, the witness of God is greater; for this is the witness of God which He has testified of His Son.

He decided to take the promotion his company had offered. It meant a raise, a new position, and better retirement benefits. However, the manager he presently worked for became incensed and complained that the move would affect his department.

The employee immediately became confused. He knew the job was God's best for his life, yet his boss's guilt-laden words made the decision difficult.

John the Apostle wrote to a group of people who, like us, struggled with insecurities and fears. Their environment was unstable and the future unclear. Accusations and threats often brought up thoughts of violence and death. Their only hope was found in the truth given to them by God's Son.

John wrote, "If we receive the witness of men, the witness of God is greater" (1 John 5:9). There is conflict in our world, but God's presence and peace are greater. No one has to yield to false guilt or pressure from others.

Jesus has set you free. His Word is your eternal hope. He gave you His truth so you might experience freedom from bondage of guilt, fear, and insecurity. By applying Scripture to your life, you refuse to settle for anything less. Listen to God's voice, and you will have wisdom for every decision.

Lord, I want to be so intimate with You that I can hear Your voice and have divine wisdom for every decision.

Living out Your New Life

SCRIPTURE READING: Galatians 2:16–21

KEY VERSE: Galatians 2:20

I have been crucified with Christ; it is no longer I who live, but Christ lives in me; and the life which I now live in the flesh I live by faith in the Son of God, who loved me and gave Himself for me.

In Paul's day, people offered themselves to all kinds of sinful behavior. Prostitution and other forms of idolatry were common practices in pagan temples.

In an attempt to raise the spiritual consciousness of the early church, Paul insisted that believers retain a high standard of purity. They had received new life through Jesus Christ, but they needed to practice and live out this new life on a daily basis.

The church probably wondered, "How do we do this? Everywhere we turn, our eyes are met with forms of degradation." Sound familiar?

The only way we can maintain our purity is by an act of our wills, whereby we become living spiritual sacrifices to God.

Warren Wiersbe asserts, "God transforms our minds and makes us spiritually minded by using His Word. As you spend time meditating on God's Word, memorizing it, and making it a part of your inner man, God will gradually make your mind more spiritual."

When we desire God's will over the desires of the flesh, we deny self. We acknowledge that we have been crucified with Christ and we no longer live, but Jesus Christ now lives to the glory of God in us (Gal. 2:20).

Father, as I meditate on Your Word today, transform my mind and give me the mind of Christ.

Submission to God

SCRIPTURE READING: Philippians 2:1–11
KEY VERSE: Psalm 51:10

Create in me a clean heart, O God,
And renew a steadfast spirit within me.

In Beyond Ourselves, Catherine Marshall writes of spiritual renewal:

> One morning I was particularly discouraged. I was caught between all my blessings: A wonderful husband, three lovely children at home and a fourth in and out, a big new house, and my daily writing. I was, quite frankly, exhausted.
>
> So once more we took the situation to God . . . "Lord, we've tried everything we can think of. Every road has seemed a dead end . . . Tell us what it is."

God showed her that she was "dictating the terms" of her life: "A thought stabbed me. What if—for this period of my life—I was supposed to give up the writing? Immediately this possibility brought tears. Why should I have to relinquish something which I had from the beginning dedicated to God and something from which I also got such intense satisfaction?"

Resolutely she submitted her desires to God: "Though my emotions were in stark rebellion, I knew that sooner or later they would fall into line. When the relinquishment was complete, the breakthrough occurred."

The way to a renewed mind is the way of submission. When you submit your desires to Christ, He transforms your will and prepares you for a great blessing.

I submit to You, Lord. Transform my will and prepare me for Your blessings.

True Contentment

SCRIPTURE READING: Matthew 6:25–34
KEY VERSE: 1 Timothy 6:6

Godliness with contentment is great gain.

When he was younger, he dreamed of success; but as life progressed, he became bitter and withdrawn. A series of unfortunate incidents led to disillusionment—a college scholarship he could not complete; a marriage that, at best, was shaky; and children he longed to love but did not know how.

These were only signs of a deeper problem—a lack of true contentment and peace with God. Now when most people are approaching retirement, he is forced to work a job he hates so he can pay bills. He always thought contentment was something he could buy and own, but he was wrong.

Even author and philosopher C. S. Lewis sought the solace of contentment, which he labeled "joy." He had hoped to find it in a place or a state of mind, but instead he found it to be a Person, Jesus Christ.

Contentment comes to those who seek the things of God above the things of the world. It is the result of laying down earthly desires while cultivating a friendship with Christ.

As you think through your life, are you content? If nothing changed from this point, could you be satisfied with what God has given you? Remember, contentment abides where Jesus Christ is Lord of all. True contentment is need oriented, not want oriented.

Lord, help me to seek the things above instead of the things of the world. Help me to lay down my earthly desires and cultivate my friendship with You.

He Is Working Things Out

SCRIPTURE READING: Ephesians 2:1–10

KEY VERSE: Ephesians 2:8

By grace you have been saved through faith, and that not of yourselves; it is the gift of God.

While some err on the side of believing that God can't possibly love them because they are so unworthy, others lose sight of their spiritual helplessness. It's easy to forget how much Christ did for us on the cross. Catherine Marshall explains in her book, *Adventures in Prayer:*

The Scriptures spell out for us point by point how helpless we are in relation to our spiritual lives as well as our physical ones. We feel an impulse towards God. We think that we are reaching out for Him. Not so, Jesus told us, "No one is able to come to me unless he is drawn by the Father . . ."

With helplessness alone, one would be like a bird trying to fly with one wing. But when the other wing of God's adequacy is added to our helplessness, then the bird can soar triumphantly above and through problems that hitherto have defeated us . . .

First, be honest with God. Tell Him that you are aware of the fact that in His eyes you are helpless . . .

Second, take your heart's desire to God. You have accepted your helplessness. Now grip with equal strength of will your belief that God can do through you what you cannot. It may seem to you for a time that you are relying on emptiness . . .

Disregard these feelings, and quietly thank God that He is working things out.

Father, I am helpless. Here is my heart's desire. I believe You can do through me what I cannot do myself. I thank You that You are working things out in my life.

You Are Secure

SCRIPTURE READING: James 2:20–26

KEY VERSE: Jeremiah 29:11

I know the thoughts that I think toward you, says the LORD, thoughts of peace and not of evil, to give you a future and a hope.

John Wesley came to America with a sense of hope and determination, but he returned to England broken and discouraged. In his diary he confessed, "I went to America to convert the Indians; but Oh! who shall convert me?"

But God did not dismiss the cry of Wesley's heart. On the evening of May 24, 1738, during a church meeting, God poured His truth into John Wesley's heart, and Wesley trusted Jesus Christ as his personal Savior: "About a quarter before nine, I felt my heart strangely warmed. I felt I did trust in Christ, Christ alone, for salvation; and an assurance was given me that He had taken away my sins, even mine, and saved me from the law of sin and death."

For the first time, Wesley understood that it was not a matter of good works that saved him. Instead, his faith in Christ brought eternal change. Martin Luther's commentary on the book of Romans was the catalyst God used to turn Wesley's life around.

Up until the point of salvation, Wesley thought there was a way for him to work or achieve God's favor when all he really needed to do was to lay aside his working at salvation and trust in the matchless grace of God.

If you have accepted Christ as your Savior, there is no need for you to feel discouraged over your eternal destiny. God has a secure plan for your life, and He will never let you go.

Lord, how I thank You for the secure plan You have for my life and the fact that You will never let me go.

Your Inner Longings

SCRIPTURE READING: Matthew 9:9–13
KEY VERSE: Matthew 9:12

When Jesus heard that, He said to them, "Those who are well have no need of a physician, but those who are sick."

Throughout the Scriptures, people tried various things to satisfy their inner longings. The woman at the well was married several times. The rich young ruler was extremely wealthy. Yet a deep-seated emptiness occupied both lives.

There are others: Matthew was a crafty tax collector. Peter was a successful fisherman. Each worked to be something other than what God intended him to be. Yet even in their best moments, nothing satisfied the deeper hunger each had. Only Jesus could change their lives. Frustration, loneliness, heartache, and feelings of isolation are characteristics of a life lived outside God's will.

David Hazard commented on Augustine's life: "At the pinnacle of his career, while teaching philosophy to the sons of the powerful and wealthy in Milan, Augustine privately concluded that these philosophies were empty, vain. And though he wanted freedom from the wearying demands of his flesh he found he was trapped by them."

That was Augustine's turning point: "In the moment Augustine 'crossed over' the inner boundary—his human will—and consented to follow 'the Way' of Christ, his world was transformed . . . The living, real presence of Jesus became his inner fire, flaming out in all that Augustine would do or say."

God provides for our deep need of satisfaction. Let Him fan the flames of devotion in your heart.

Dear Lord, I am so thankful that You meet my inner needs. You satisfy the longings of my heart and soul. I thank You and praise You.

Object Lessons of Faith

SCRIPTURE READING: Exodus 14: 1-31

KEY VERSE: Exodus 14:13

Moses said to the people, "Do not be afraid. Stand still, and see the salvation of the LORD, which He will accomplish for you today. For the Egyptians whom you see today, you shall see again no more forever."

When your life is patterned after Jesus, you will not be easily drawn off course. Strength and stability are the results of close fellowship with the Savior. Faith in Him places you in a position to receive and enjoy the goodness of His hope and joy at every turn. Your faith and the study of His Word keep you from being misled by error or false doctrine.

Charles Spurgeon wrote,

Exodus 14:13 contains God's command to the believer when he is reduced to great straits and brought into extraordinary difficulties. He cannot retreat; he cannot go forward; he is shut up on the right hand and on the left. What is he now to do?

The Master's word to him is "stand still." It will be well for him if, at such times, he listens only to his Master's word, for other and evil advisers come with their suggestions. Despair whispers, "Lie down and die; give it all up." But God would have us put on a cheerful courage, and even in our worst times. Rejoice in His love and faithfulness.

What you believe sets the pattern of your faith. Do you believe that God will do what He promised? Doubt, discouragement, and fear are all object lessons whereby God tests the basis of your faith. If you are going through difficulty, don't despair. Set the focus of your heart on God, and He will drive away the cruelest tempter.

Dear heavenly Father, thank You for the object lessons of faith— doubt, discouragement, and fear. I choose to set my focus on You instead of these obstacles.

The Giver of Life

SCRIPTURE READING: Revelation 21:3–4

KEY VERSE: 1 Corinthians 13:12

Now we see in a mirror, dimly, but then face to face. Now I know in part, but then I shall know just as I also am known.

Paul shared this insight: "Now we see but a poor reflection; then we shall see face to face. Now I know in part; then I shall know fully, even as I am fully known" (1 Cor. 13:12 NIV). One day we will see Jesus, and all that we have suffered and enjoyed will pale in comparison to the truth and reality of His presence.

Often the reason we don't maximize the life we have is that we don't really know the One who gives life. We may have an idea or mental image of God, but the reality of His presence is not something we incorporate into our lives on a daily basis.

If we did, we would stop trying to solve our problems, and we would give Him the burdens of our hearts. We would not emphasize acquiring material possessions but trust Him to meet all our needs. We would be more interested in abiding in Him and allowing His presence to be evident through our actions.

Living with an eternal perspective begins by asking Jesus to saturate every area of your life with Himself. You don't have to wait until eternity to experience the intimate fellowship of God. Open your life up to Him fully and completely, and He will give you a blessed taste of eternity now.

Dear Lord, please saturate every area of my life with Yourself. I don't want to wait until eternity to experience intimate fellowship with You. I am ready for a divine encounter!

JULY

A Divine Encounter in Spiritual Growth

Measuring Your Growth

SCRIPTURE READING: Ephesians 4:11–16
KEY VERSE: Philippians 1:6

Being confident of this very thing, that He who has begun a good work in you will complete it until the day of Jesus Christ.

Some things are easy to measure—your height, your clothing size, your weight. But how do you measure spiritual growth? How can you determine how far you've come in your walk with the Lord?

God works in the lives of His children in different ways at different times. But as you pray, study the Bible, and worship regularly with other Christians, you should notice several changes.

Quick and genuine repentance. When the Holy Spirit convicts you of specific sin, you go immediately to Jesus to confess and turn away from it.

Rejoicing in trials. Spiritual battles become more intense, but you want to thank God for them.

Increasing desire to obey. Sin becomes less attractive; you find delight in following His commands.

Eagerness to share. As you discover His lovingkindness, you can't keep the joy to yourself. You tell others what He is doing in your life.

Are you becoming more like Jesus each day? No matter where you are in your relationship with Him, you can cling to this promise: "He who began a good work in you will perfect it until the day of Christ Jesus" (Phil. 1:6 NASB).

Lord, make me more like You. Complete the good work You have begun in me.

A Formula for Growth

SCRIPTURE READING: James 1:1–25

KEY VERSE: James 1:22

Be doers of the word, and not hearers only, deceiving yourselves.

James used the word *scattered* in James 1:1 to indicate the plight of early Christians living outside Palestine. God used Nero's persecution to scatter thousands of believers throughout Asia Minor so the gospel message would continue to grow and spread.

However, instead of carrying the Word of God to new converts, believers became spiritually bogged down by sin. Gossip, selfishness, and the pursuit of material gain caused deep division within the church. Almost overnight their focus had changed from the deeper things of God to envy and strife.

At the center of their problems was a lack of spiritual maturity. They had learned to talk the talk, but failed to walk the Christian walk of faith. We face this same problem. Too many go to church, give of their resources, and even read their Bibles, but fail to grow spiritually.

James admonished the early church to be more than mere hearers of the Word; he urged them to be doers of the Word. The formula for personal, spiritual growth is applying God's truth to every area of your life. Practice this, and the seed He plants within your heart will yield a great and mighty harvest.

Lord, I want to grow spiritually. Plant the seed of Your Word in my heart.

Committed to Growth

SCRIPTURE READING: 2 Peter 3:11–18

KEY VERSE: 2 Peter 3:18

Grow in the grace and knowledge of our Lord and Savior Jesus Christ. To Him be the glory both now and forever. Amen.

Many think tennis is a game of power and strength, but it is much more. It is also a game of strategy and endurance. Hours of practice and dedication are needed if one wants to become a better player.

The Christians whom Peter addressed in 2 Peter 3 had gained a great deal of spiritual knowledge over the years, but they stopped growing spiritually. They thought they knew all they needed to know. The spiritual danger was not the temptation to deny their faith, but to become complacent and drawn away by a lack of spiritual dedication.

Peter exhorted them to be on guard lest they be carried away by error. Spiritual growth is not meant for a season; it is to be a lifetime activity.

The measure of our spiritual growth is always found in Christ. The more time we spend with Him, the more we become like Him. Ask Him to help you make a commitment to Him and His Word. Dedication, endurance, and practice of the things of God are the winning combination for spiritual growth.

Lord, help me to make a commitment to You and Your Word. As I spend time in prayer and Your Word, make me more like You.

Moral Decline

SCRIPTURE READING: 1 Samuel 2:27–30
KEY VERSE: 1 Samuel 2:30

The LORD God of Israel says: "I said indeed that your house and the house of your father would walk before Me forever;" but now the LORD says: "Far be it from Me; for those who honor Me I will honor, and those who despise Me shall be lightly esteemed."

The moral decline of a nation can be traced back to its religious beliefs. Pagan societies have come and gone. Rome, at one time an invincible force, crumbled from within because of moral decay. Countless individuals with godly moral values think their opinions do not count for much. However, they are very wrong.

Gary Bauer, president of the Family Research Council, recently told how he had taken a trip to relax and "get away" from the furious pace of Washington, D.C. He traveled to Iowa where he met many citizens, all of whom had strong moral beliefs. They worked, attended church, and wanted the best for their children.

How does a nation—America or any other—become spiritually torn and tattered? It is simple; the people who are the very heart of any country's life give up and give in to mounting pressure to compromise what they know is right. In real life, a very small percentage of people want certain godless statutes installed. Yet if a nation's majority wavers in confusion, more than likely these issues will face little debate.

You must stand for what you believe. Be tenacious in prayer, asking God for His direction morally and spiritually. Don't settle for compromise; say no to issues that fail to reflect God's purity.

Father, forgive me for the times I ignore Your Word and Your principles. Help me to say no to issues that fail to reflect Your purity.

Divine Provision

SCRIPTURE READING: Hebrews 10:19–23

KEY VERSE: Hebrews 10:23

Let us hold fast the confession of our hope without wavering, for He who promised is faithful.

He had decided to buy the new car regardless of his financial state. He also tried to "forget" that his wife had just had a baby. He refused to consider a nice, affordable used car.

God is committed to meeting your needs. However, He is not committed to meeting all your wants. Several things work against God's desire to meet your needs:

Disobedience. When you disobey God, you face the consequences of your sin. Often that means waiting for the things He wants to build into your life.

Doubt. It defuses God's plan for you. It also signals a lack of faith in His ability to provide for you.

Manipulation. Trying to meet your needs your way leads to spiritual fraud. God sees through manipulation. He wants your life to be sincerely obedient before Him.

Wrong motivation. Motives that are not God–centered never yield lasting peace. Set your focus on God, not the things of this world.

Ignoring responsibilities. When you ignore your God-given responsibilities such as family, friends, and job, your fellowship with God becomes clouded, and you struggle spiritually.

Let Christ be your Divine Provider, and He will meet your needs perfectly.

Dear Lord, free me from disobedience, doubt, manipulation, wrong motivation, and ignoring my responsibilities.

A Time of Stillness

SCRIPTURE READING: Hebrews 10:35–39
KEY VERSE: Hebrews 10:35

Do not cast away your confidence, which has great reward.

Are you going through a time of stillness in your spiritual walk with God? Perhaps you have witnessed others leaving for the mission field or college, and you feel left behind. Maybe God has answered a prayer in a friend's life, and he has moved on to a promising new job or venture. Suddenly you are faced with a challenge. Looking at the situation from this perspective changes things completely.

Few of us would ever want to move ahead of God's will. We know that when we wait for His answers, we receive the very best He has to offer. Time spent waiting before God is not stagnant. Though we may feel as though there is little spiritual growth involved, there is plenty. God uses quiet seasons in life to strip us of the very things we love the most—ourselves and our own desires. Both keep us from recognizing God's goodness in all we know and experience.

You will never pass this way again. What you do today can never be repeated. You may say, "Thank goodness!" But ask yourself, *Even in this time of waiting and wondering, have I truly allowed God to be glorified in me?* Take advantage of this time that God has given you. Live in His peace, and remind all who meet you that He is ever faithful.

Dear Lord, help me to realize that You are at work always in my life, even in the quiet times when not much seems to be happening.

$\mathscr{A}$ $\mathscr{S}$piritual $\mathscr{I}$nventory

SCRIPTURE READING: Philippians 3:7–14
KEY VERSE: Philippians 3:7

What things were gain to me, these I have counted loss for Christ.

$\mathscr{I}$s there a room or closet in your home that you avoid because it's filled with stuff that needs to be cleaned out? Finally one day, you decide to tackle the task. As you move through the boxes, you have to make some decisions. Some things stay, and some things must go. Some items are garbage, and some are keepsakes.

Sorting through your belongings is a kind of prioritizing. You are forced to assign a value to the things you own and then treat them accordingly. In Philippians 3, Paul was conducting a kind of spiritual sorting: "Whatever things were gain to me, those things I have counted as loss for the sake of Christ. More than that, I count all things to be loss in view of the surpassing value of knowing Christ Jesus my Lord, for whom I have suffered the loss of all things, and count them but rubbish in order that I may gain Christ" (vv. 7–8 NASB).

Paul put a "trash" label on anything in his life that didn't count toward his relationship with the Lord. Along the way, he had lost much, from material possessions to public esteem. But Paul wasn't concerned. He knew that his "valuables," the blessings of knowing Christ as his Savior, were always with him.

Is there anything in your life that you value more than Christ? Maybe today is the time for a spiritual inventory.

Lord, I am taking a spiritual inventory today. Teach me Your values.

The Power of the Spirit

SCRIPTURE READING: Galatians 5:16–17
KEY VERSE: Acts 1:8

You shall receive power when the Holy Spirit has come upon you; and you shall be witnesses to Me in Jerusalem, and in all Judea and Samaria, and to the end of the earth.

As a believer, you are powerless apart from the presence of God living through the Holy Spirit within you. At His ascension, Jesus told His followers: "You shall receive power when the Holy Spirit has come upon you; and you shall be My witnesses both in Jerusalem, and in all Judea and Samaria, and even to the remotest part of the earth" (Acts 1:8 NASB).

It takes power to live the Christian life. God's power in us gives us the strength to victoriously face difficulties and challenges. It equips us with the same energy that Jesus had in His ministry.

Why, then, do we sometimes act and feel like failures? John the Apostle wrote, "Greater is He who is in you than he who is in the world" (1 John 4:4 NASB). When we yield to temptation, we feel defeated. Sin blocks the power of God in the life of a believer. We grieve His Spirit with our disobedience and in doing so become powerless in the eyes of the enemy. We are not strong enough within ourselves to say no to temptation. The power of God keeps us and protects us.

Sin and a lukewarm heart toward God leave you vulnerable to enemy attack. "Stay in Jerusalem" was Christ's command. Until you have received power from on high—clear instruction for living the Spirit-filled life—stay close to Jesus, your greatest Source of power and spiritual strength.

God, fill me with the power of Your Spirit. Endue me with Your divine strength.

Handling Your Weaknesses

SCRIPTURE READING: Romans 6:17–18

KEY VERSES: Romans 7:24–25

*O wretched man that I am! Who will deliver me from this body of death?
I thank God—through Jesus Christ our Lord! So then, with the mind I
myself serve the law of God, but with the flesh the law of sin.*

Your weaknesses are opportunities for God to display His strength and ability. Paul wrote to the people of the church in Rome, "Thanks be to God that though you were slaves of sin, you became obedient from the heart" (Rom. 6:17 NASB).

Often when we think of weaknesses, we think of how we have failed God and wonder how He could possibly continue to love and accept us. But outside of our salvation experience, God is not as concerned about change being instantaneous as He is about our hearts being turned toward Him in submission. He understands our weaknesses and vulnerabilities, and He is committed to working with us to teach us to obey and to live within the framework of His mercy and grace.

Once God's convicting hand touches certain habits and sins, you can immediately respond by turning and walking away from the temptations. God gives you the strength you need to do this.

The apostle Paul's struggle is a point of encouragement: "That which I am doing, I do not understand; for I am not practicing what I would like to do, but I am doing the very thing I hate" (Rom. 7:15 NASB).

For Paul there was victory, and the same is true for you. Jesus Christ is your hope and point of freedom from bondage (Rom. 7:24–25). He never gives up on you. Praise Him for His undivided love, mercy, and grace.

*Lord, I thank You that You never give up on me. Thank You for Your
undivided love, mercy, and grace.*

Spiritual Blindness

SCRIPTURE READING: John 9:1–12

KEY VERSE: John 9:1

As Jesus passed by, He saw a man who was blind from birth.

Remember the last time you learned something new about God? It was as if a door was opened to you that you had never passed through before. Up until that moment, you had experienced a certain degree of spiritual blindness; then God revealed His Word to you, and you received His truth into your heart and not just your mind.

That was what happened when Jesus healed the man born blind. Eyes that were unaccustomed to seeing the world's environment were suddenly given sight. The people asked, "Who sinned, this man, or his parents, that he should be born blind?" Jesus offered an explanation: "It was neither that this man sinned, nor his parents; but it was in order that the works of God might be displayed in him" (John 9:2–3 NASB).

Far too often, we rush to believe negative thoughts. The important lesson here is not whether or not sin was involved, but that God had opened this man's eyes. When you walk in spiritual darkness, God wants to give you spiritual sight. He is always in the process of bringing spiritual healing and fullness to your life.

The man born blind was destined for a miracle. From his birth, God had ordained the day of his healing. It is just as important to the Lord when you suddenly receive your eyesight in an area in which you were once spiritually blind.

Open my eyes, Lord. Heal my spiritual blindness.

Surrendered to God

SCRIPTURE READING: John 5:2–14
KEY VERSE: John 5:6

When Jesus saw him lying there, and knew that he already had been in that condition a long time, He said to him, "Do you want to be made well?"

Thomas à Kempis wrote, "If we are not surrendered to God, we will be at war with others." In reality, we can take this statement a step farther: "If we are not surrendered to God, we will be at war within ourselves." Internal peace and contentment signal that we are surrendered as much as is possible to the will of God for our lives.

Surrender is not an easy process. Because it involves self-will, it can be painful. However, it is essential to spiritual growth. Many times God will touch an area of your life that you love dearly, one that you feel meets some deep need.

He knows the things that captivate your attention and have the potential to draw you away from Himself. His love for you is so great that He wants you to know Him on an intimate level. But this rarely happens when you are caught up in the distractions of the world.

Sin enters the picture when you refuse to let go of the very things God has asked you to give up. Is there something within you that wants to say, "Lord, I love You, but please don't ask me to give that up"? Or "Father, I know that what I am doing is not in keeping with Your will for my life, but I just don't want to stop"?

If there is anything in your life that keeps you from being totally committed to the Lord, then God will reveal it. When He does, ask Him to give you the strength to let go of it.

Dear God, please reveal to me anything that keeps me from being totally committed to You. Then give me the strength to let go of it.

Saying No to Sin

SCRIPTURE READING: Galatians 6:7–9
KEY VERSE: Ephesians 2:1

You He made alive, who were dead in trespasses and sins.

When we say yes to sin, we grieve the heart of God. Therefore, whenever we become tangled in sin, our first response should be one of grief and remorse, not just over what we have done but over whom we have hurt.

When you are tempted to sin, ask yourself, *Who is the boss of my life?* If Jesus Christ is and you really want to grow spiritually, then the desire to become involved with things that do not reflect God's nature will fade over time.

Though each of us faces temptation periodically, saying no to sin should not be something we have to think over. Saying no comes easily when we realize that saying yes hurts Someone whose love we can't live without.

Have you ever thought of God in this way, as Someone who loves you more than all the rest? That is why Jesus came: to demonstrate God's personal love to mankind. His death at Calvary said it all. He bore our sins out of love and eternal devotion.

Oswald Chambers addressed the subject of the Cross:

The Cross did not happen to Jesus: He came on purpose for it. He is "the Lamb slain from the foundation of the world."

The center of salvation is the Cross of Jesus, and the reason it is so easy to obtain salvation is because it cost God so very much. The Cross is the point where God and sinful man merge with a crash and the way to life is opened, but the crash is on the heart of God.

Dear heavenly Father, help me to say no to sin and yes to You. You are the Boss of my life.

Where Sin Begins

SCRIPTURE READING: Ephesians 2:2–13
KEY VERSES: Ephesians 2:4–5

God, who is rich in mercy, because of His great love with which He loved us, even when we were dead in trespasses, made us alive together with Christ (by grace you have been saved).

In the book *Seeking the Face of God,* Gary Thomas discusses sin:

> Our quest to understand holiness begins with understanding the absurdity of sin . . . A performance-based Christian says, "I want to do this, but I know I shouldn't. I must either find a way to not do this or to not get caught." The relation-based Christian asks, "Who do I want to be in love with? My Lord or this sin?"
>
> Merely asking ourselves this question unmasks the ugliness of sin. Sin creates massive disturbances in our lives; holiness brings peace. When we look honestly at what each brings, we have to ask ourselves, why, indeed, this sin is even tempting us. Christianity, with its moral calling, may seem repressive to the world, but when we see sin as it really is (slow suicide), the moral calling of Christianity takes on a whole new light.

Sin offers nothing more than momentary satisfaction. It divides your fellowship with God. There is only one answer to sin, and that is a determined "No!" If you are struggling in a certain area, tell God exactly what you are feeling. Make sure you express yourself fully. Then pray that He will place a hedge of protection around your heart and mind.

All sin begins in the mind as temptation. Only when you act upon it does it become sin. Say no and turn away from all that keeps you from experiencing God's richest blessings.

Lord, help me to stop sin in my mind when it is still a temptation. I want to turn away from all that prevents me from experiencing Your richest blessing.

Blessed Assurance

SCRIPTURE READING: 1 John 3:18–24
KEY VERSE: 1 John 3:23

This is His commandment: that we should believe on the name of His Son Jesus Christ and love one another, as He gave us commandment.

It is easy to look across the church sanctuary and see someone whose salvation you would not question. Perhaps you also can identify someone you believe is struggling even more in his walk with Jesus than you are.

One of the enemy's traps is to get us to compare ourselves to others. It is a way that he deceives us into thinking we do not measure up.

At other times he gets us to think we're better than the next person so we become complacent in our faith. The only true measuring stick resting in a church pew is in the book rack. It is the Bible, the inerrant Word of God.

Listen to what God says about assurance of salvation: "For God so loved the world, that He gave His only begotten Son, that whoever believes in Him shall not perish, but have eternal life" (John 3:16 NASB); "Believe in the Lord Jesus, and you shall be saved" (Acts 16:31 NASB); and "This is His commandment, that we believe in the name of His Son Jesus Christ" (1 John 3:23 NASB).

The common thread in these Scriptures is that salvation comes only through belief in Jesus Christ as the Son of God. There is no other itinerary or requirement, no need for comparisons: "These things I have written to you who believe in the name of the Son of God, in order that you may know that you have eternal life" (1 John 5:13 NASB).

Father, thank You for the blessed assurance You have given me. Let me continually use the measuring stick of Your Word to check my spiritual growth.

Focus on Jesus

SCRIPTURE READING: Acts 16:22–32
KEY VERSE: Acts 16:25

At midnight Paul and Silas were praying and singing hymns to God, and the prisoners were listening to them.

If we are not careful, we can become guilty of allowing emotions to govern our lives. God instructs us to keep our focus on Jesus in order to grow spiritually. When we do this, the emotional ups and downs of this life will not shake or change our world.

In *Telling Yourself the Truth*, William Backus writes about joy:

Joy comes from your relationship to God and His unchanging faithfulness. You don't need to live in perfect circumstances to be happy. It's pleasant to be loved and appreciated, but not vital to your happiness.

The Bible tells how two men of God, Paul and Silas, were brought before Roman authorities at Philippi and beaten with rods and then thrown into jail . . . But did Paul and Silas moan and complain, "If it weren't for the cruelty of the unbelievers, we wouldn't be wounded and bleeding. We'd be happy!" No.

Paul and Silas had a strong belief that transcended circumstances, events, people, feelings; it even transcended pain. That belief was in the person, power, and presence of Jesus Christ. They believed their suffering wasn't as important as the message they carried . . .

They sang so loudly their voices were heard throughout the prison! And not only that, God . . . opened the prison doors for them. Their happiness came from the belief in Jesus Christ within them and not from circumstances around them.

Keep my focus on You, Jesus, instead of the circumstances of my life.

Godly Self-Acceptance

SCRIPTURE READING: Romans 5:1–11
KEY VERSE: Psalm 34:18

The LORD is near to those who have a broken heart,
And saves such as have a contrite spirit.

One of the greatest assets we can acquire is a sense of godly self-acceptance. Contentment, peace, and joy are the by-products of personal acceptance. When we learn to accept ourselves and view our lives the way God does, the need to strive in order to gain or achieve the praise of others disappears.

Always let your acceptance of yourself be rooted in Christ. Then you will never be disappointed. Feelings of loneliness can challenge a healthy self-worth, but you need not yield to the temptation to believe that you are anything less than what God has created you to be. When you feel lonely or left out, tell Him you are struggling, and ask Him to encourage your heart.

Focusing on the negative side of your situation leads to feelings of self-pity and doubt. But God has a better plan. His word of hope is simply this: "Call to Me, and I will answer you, and I will tell you great and mighty things, which you do not know" (Jer. 33:3 NASB).

God hears your prayers. He knows the cries of your heart and is filled with compassion concerning you.

The apostle Paul faced many trials in his lifetime. The secret of his faith and contentment was not in the company of others, but in Jesus Christ (Phil. 4:13). God is your Source of strength.

You are the Source of my strength, Lord. Help me view my life the way You do.

A Remedy for Sin

SCRIPTURE READING: 2 Samuel 11–12
KEY VERSE: Psalm 51:1

Have mercy upon me, O God,
According to Your lovingkindness;
According to the multitude of Your tender mercies,
Blot out my transgressions.

After God exposed David's sin with Bathsheba, David's heart was filled with remorse. His spirit was crushed by what he had done, and evidence of his sin and subsequent repentance is found in 2 Samuel 11–12.

At one point David's shame became so great, he cried out: "I have sinned against the Lord." Notice David did not deny his sin or excuse it. No. He owned up to what he had done and sought God's forgiveness.

When we confess our sin to the Lord, we are in essence agreeing with Him that what we have done is wrong and not in keeping with His moral standards. At that point we acknowledge our sin and decisively turn from it. That was what David did.

Sin has its consequences. Bathsheba became pregnant with David's baby, who later died. Not only did David have to endure the sorrow connected with his sin, but he also had to face the death of his son. Yet we never hear of David wallowing in guilt and shame. He sought God's forgiveness in humility and then set his heart on continuing to be the king God had called him to be.

When you sin, pray as David did. Know God's mercy keeps you. Confession and repentance are your hope. The moment you seek His forgiveness, He restores you. And it is there that you will find His love is unchanged by your failure.

I thank You, Lord, that Your love is unchanged by my failure. Thank You for providing a remedy for my sin.

The Blessing of Baptism

SCRIPTURE READING: John 3:1–16
KEY VERSE: John 3:16

For God so loved the world that He gave His only begotten Son, that whoever believes in Him should not perish but have everlasting life.

Many people struggle with the idea of baptism. Some want to argue that it is not necessary to be saved. Others argue over the method. Here is a good principle to live by: If Jesus did it, then He wants us to follow His lead.

Baptism by itself cannot save you. James and other gospel writers made that clear. The only way we come to God is by faith in His Son. On many occasions Jesus told those who came to Him that their faith prompted God to action. It is only by belief in Christ that we can experience salvation (John 3:16).

After salvation, our first priority should be to identify with Jesus Christ. Baptism is an outward sign of our commitment to God. It is a public statement of our faith and love toward God. Some may say, "Well, I don't need to make a public confession. My life is between me and the Lord."

Think for a moment how God publicly displayed His love and affection toward you at Calvary. Nothing could keep Christ from demonstrating His love for you on Calvary's Cross, and nothing should keep you from displaying your love for Him through baptism.

The moment the Ethiopian heard the gospel message, he was saved. His next desire was to be baptized. He asked, "What prevents me from being baptized?" Philip replied, "If you believe with all your heart, you may" (Acts 8:36–37 NASB).

Dear Lord, thank You for displaying Your love and affection toward me at Calvary. You have blessed my life!

Handling Habits

SCRIPTURE READING: Romans 8:14–17
KEY VERSE: Romans 8:17

And if children, then heirs—heirs of God and joint heirs with Christ, if indeed we suffer with Him, that we may also be glorified together.

E very believer has the power through the Holy Spirit to be set free from habits that bind. When we think of behaviors that bind us and keep us from being all that God designed us to be, we often rush to the obvious thought of bad habits. But any "bad" habit is only a result of a deeper unbelief. Usually people become involved with damaging activities because there are unmet basic needs in their lives.

These could be as basic as a need to be loved or accepted. Many of yesterday's children have faced rejection. As adults, they desperately seek ways to gain attention and be loved. Often these ways lead to destruction.

Each of us has a belief system that was built into us during childhood. It affects the way we view and respond to life. While a lack of positive affirmation in the childhood years can be a catalyst for low self-esteem and frustration, it does not have to lead to personal failure or a sense of hopelessness.

There is nothing eternal about our earthly grid system. The only thing that matters is what God says about our lives. And He has stated that He has a plan and a hope for each of us.

You can handle the habits in your life that bind you away from the truth of God by learning more about His personal love and devotion toward you. You are His child, a joint heir with Christ. Nothing bears more potential than this truth.

Lord, free me from every habit that would inhibit my spiritual growth.

Binding Behavior

SCRIPTURE READING: Psalm 119:33–40
KEY VERSE: Psalm 119:35

Make me walk in the path of Your commandments,
For I delight in it.

*H*ere's how to handle a binding behavior:

Identify the problem behavior. Be honest with yourself or ask a trusted friend to be honest with you. Denying there's a problem prevents you from experiencing true victory and hope.

Take responsibility for your behavior. No matter how small or large the behavior may seem, admit that it exists and you are responsible for its continued presence.

Trace it back to the source. Ask God to help you remember when you were programmed to feel or act a certain way. Low self-esteem, feelings of rejection, and helplessness all have beginning points. And all these behaviors lead to other habits that weaken your self-concept.

Forgive yourself and forgive others who have hurt you. Forgiveness does not mean the person who hurt you can walk away without being punished. Forgiveness is something you do for yourself so that you can experience freedom from bitterness and resentment. Harboring angry feelings can lead to physical and emotional health problems. God tells us that vengeance belongs to Him. Let the Lord have your hurt and pain, and He will take care of the situation.

Renew your mind with the truth of God's Word. You will discover that God loves you more than you can imagine. You also will receive needed strength and hope.

Lord, forgive me and help me to forgive others who have hurt me. Help me to take responsibility for my behavior and make things right.

Expect the Unexpected

SCRIPTURE READING: 2 Kings 3:10–18
KEY VERSE: 2 Kings 3:18

This is but a trivial thing in the sight of the LORD; He will also deliver the Moabites into your hand.

 o forward!
As we step out without any sign or sound—not a wave or splash wetting our feet as we take the first step—we shall see the sea divide and the pathway open through the very midst of the waters.

If we have seen the miraculous workings of God in some extraordinary providential deliverance, I am sure the thing that has impressed us most has been the quietness with which it was done, the absence of everything spectacular and sensational, and the utter sense of nothingness that came to us as we stood in the presence of this mighty God and felt how easy it was for Him to do it all without the faintest effort on His part or the slightest help on ours. It is not the part of faith to question, but to obey.

Are you craving a fresh encounter with God? Then expect the unexpected. God has the answer to your heart's deepest request.

A. B. Simpson identifies the great victory of faith:

Our unbelief is always wanting some outward sign. The religion of many is largely sensational, and they are not satisfied of its genuineness without manifestations, etc.; but the greatest triumph of faith is to be still and know that He is God.

The great victory of faith is to stand before some impassable Red Sea, and hear the Master say, "Stand still, and see the salvation of the Lord."

God, You are the answer to my heart's deepest requests. I expect the unexpected today.

Conversion Confusion

SCRIPTURE READING: 1 John 5:10–15
KEY VERSE: 1 John 5:12

He who has the Son has life; he who does not have the Son of God does not have life.

When John wrote of the "life" in today's key verse, he referred to eternal life. He narrowed its conditions to the simplest terms: the person who "has" the Son has eternal life. You cannot "have" the Son unless you ask for Him, unless you receive Him, can you?

God's people often question their salvation. This is needless worry amid Satan's psychological mind games. The enemy wants you to be so consumed with your doubts that you focus not on God but on yourself. You can become paralyzed either by fear (of God or of not measuring up) or by overload. A person who doubts his salvation often will try to work his way to righteousness or salvation, an impossible task similar to worldly religions bowing to something man-made.

John assured you that you can know you have eternal life. There is one way, and that is to trust in Jesus Christ as the Son of God who died on the Cross for your sins. You are trusting in a person, not an idea or philosophy. If you have recognized that you are a sinner and that Jesus is the Son of God, and if you have asked His forgiveness and His entrance into your heart, then you are saved.

God, thank You for Your life that flows into me and enables me to grow spiritually.

Advancing Through Adversity

SCRIPTURE READING: Genesis 37
KEY VERSE: Genesis 39:21

The LORD was with Joseph and showed him mercy, and He gave him favor in the sight of the keeper of the prison.

The story of Joseph isn't some fable that we read for entertainment and then pause long enough to consider the moral at the end of the story. It is the biblical account of a real man who endured real hardships. It is also a wonderful pattern after which we should model our responses in times of trial.

If you ever wonder why travail enters your life, take some time to read Joseph's story in chapters 37 through 50 of Genesis. Over many years he repeatedly faced heartache: his brothers threw him into a pit and sold him into slavery; Potiphar's wife framed him for rape; he was thrown into prison; he was forgotten by the butler he helped. Year after year, Joseph awoke daily to tribulation.

Yet nowhere does God's Word state that Joseph had done anything wrong. God wasn't punishing him. Instead, God advanced Joseph through his adversity. He used the pressure of trials to mold Joseph into the man who would lead and save an entire nation. Joseph never complained about his plight. He never blamed God or anyone else. He accepted his conditions and patiently trusted in the Lord.

Adversity is a part of life. Joseph was no more immune to it than you are. Yet isn't it comforting to know that Joseph's God is your God, and that through Christ, you can know Him in an even more personal way?

Dear heavenly Father, use the adversities of my life to mold me into what You want me to be.

Eternal Assurance

SCRIPTURE READING: John 6:35–46
KEY VERSE: John 14:6

Jesus said to him, "I am the way, the truth, and the life. No one comes to the Father except through Me."

Unbelievers often are stumped by the phrase "born again." To them, the salvation requirement of being born again is either so intimidating or so ludicrous that they are hesitant to discuss it. Even one of the noblest and most respected teachers of Jesus' day, Nicodemus, at first didn't understand the mandate.

When Jesus said that unless a man be born again he cannot see the kingdom of God, He was talking about a relationship. Entering into the kingdom of God is entering into a relationship with God. The way to enter that kingdom of God, or the rule of God, is to accept Jesus as Savior, asking His forgiveness of your sins, and agreeing that His substitutionary death on Calvary's Cross paid your sin debt in full. Then you are born into a new beginning.

There are many ways to appear religious and pious. Yet there is only one way to spend eternity in heaven. Jesus also said, "No one comes to the Father but through Me" (John 14:6 NASB). And He gave no command to "get some things straightened out first."

Unbelievers are in a condition of being lost. Conduct and behavior do not alter this condition. Only asking Jesus into your heart and trusting Him with your every step and your eternity will leave you with eternal assurance.

Precious Lord, I trust You with every step of my spiritual walk. Thank You for assurance of my eternal future.

Getting the Right Point of View

SCRIPTURE READING: Psalm 143

KEY VERSE: 1 Peter 1:13

Gird up the loins of your mind, be sober, and rest your hope fully upon the grace that is to be brought to you at the revelation of Jesus Christ.

When despair overtook David's life, he discovered the sure remedy: He needed to redirect his attention to the Lord. He felt his spirit failing within him, and in hurt and humility he would cry out to God.

Emotional and spiritual upheavals have a way of fragmenting the mind, sending your thoughts reeling in a thousand different directions as you try to quickly bring order to confusion. It's not easy to respond calmly, and sometimes carrying on with daily chores may seem a burden.

The Lord understands the way your heart and mind work. He designed you to be sensitive to your surroundings and to interact with other people, so it's no surprise to Him when a shock to your system causes heartache.

That is why He gives these specific directions for responding to trials: "Prepare your minds for action, keep sober in spirit, fix your hope completely on the grace to be brought to you at the revelation of Jesus Christ" (1 Peter 1:13 NASB).

Getting the right view of His love-filled plan for your life is the way to push through the numbness of spirit that often accompanies severe circumstances. You can then say with David, "For your name's sake, O LORD, preserve my life . . . bring me out of trouble" (Ps. 143:11 NIV).

Help me to grow in the midst of trouble, O Lord. For Your name's sake, preserve me and bring me out of trouble.

The Divine Potter

SCRIPTURE READING: Jeremiah 18:1–6
KEY VERSE: Hebrews 13:5

Let your conduct be without covetousness, and be content with such things as you have. For He Himself has said, "I will never leave you nor forsake you."

According to Romans 8:29, God predestined believers to become conformed to the image of His Son. The question then is, how do you become conformed to the image of Jesus?

The analogy in Jeremiah is that God is the Potter and we are the clay. God is taking our raw clay and molding us into the servants He wishes us to be. The process takes time. Actually because of the promise that God will never leave us or forsake us, we know that God will never abandon this potter's wheel.

A potter cannot be precise unless the lump of clay is in the center of the wheel. For us, this means we must be at the center of God's will. We must surrender to His lordship and trust that whatever He envisions for us is perfect.

Have you ever watched a potter work? To achieve a preconceived shape, the potter will place pressure at different points on the clay, and he'll speed up or slow down the wheel to get just the right result.

God uses life's pressures to mold us. He has a perfect shape in mind for us, and He knows how to use each circumstance to derive the greatest benefit for us. That is why so many saints say they cherish certain trials they endured, even if they once felt they were spinning out of control.

They believe Ephesians 2:10. They believe they are His workmanship.

You are the Potter, Lord, and I am the clay. Mold me into a vessel fit for Your purposes.

Rejecting Rejection

SCRIPTURE READING: Psalm 30

KEY VERSE: Psalm 30:1

I will extol You, O LORD, for You have lifted me up,
And have not let my foes rejoice over me.

A pause in front of the mirror. And then another. Endless shopping because nothing fits or looks just right. Laboring over the morning hairdo because that one curl just won't behave. Lingering over the ironing board because the pleat just isn't pleated enough. Cleaning a room to the last detail. Doting over the inconsequential appearance of an automobile.

Are you a slave to perfectionism? Being consumed with perfection really is nothing more than being consumed with other people's opinions. This usually stems from a lack of self-confidence born from a fear of rejection.

If you are basing your sense of self-worth on the opinions or acceptance of others, your focus is horizontal. It should be vertical. You should focus only on how God sees you, and His Word assures you that He made you in His image, He redeemed you with His Son, and He loves you and accepts you without condition.

Most often, feelings of rejection are self-generated. It is what we perceive others are thinking, when in reality they are probably too preoccupied with themselves to consider us. So it boils down to a choice: We can choose to feel rejected and listen to the enemy's lies, or we can choose to stand on God's promises and in faith walk in the assurance of who we are in Him. Since we can choose, it becomes a matter of obedience.

Dear God, please give me vertical focus. Help me to focus on who I am in You.

Compromising Convictions

SCRIPTURE READING: Daniel 1:8; 3:16–18

KEY VERSE: Psalm 26:1

Vindicate me, O LORD,
For I have walked in my integrity.
I have also trusted in the LORD;
I shall not slip.

When Daniel refused to defile himself by eating the king's food, he held fast to a conviction he deemed worthy enough for death. Convictions always challenge our level of commitment.

Daniel viewed continuing his relationship with God far more important than satisfying the king's whims. Once he took his stand, God provided a solution to the situation, and Daniel was allowed to eat what was in keeping with God's commandments.

Pleasing God, not men, was the most important issue to Daniel. Loving the Lord and keeping His commandments were his utmost desires. It wasn't a matter of preference but a matter of godly conviction.

Preferences are based on feelings. They change erratically and are often abandoned for the sake of immediate gratification. However, a conviction is based on God's principles and deals with life from an eternal perspective.

Satan's ultimate goal is to move you from a point of conviction to a point of preference. Once he has done that, he changes your view from God's best to what satisfies the flesh. Be wary of compromising your convictions, for you belong to the King of kings and the Lord of lords.

Dear Lord, help me to stand firm in my convictions despite the temptation to compromise.

Your Mental Energy

SCRIPTURE READING: Ephesians 5:15–17
KEY VERSE: Ephesians 5:7

Do not be partakers with them.

James Thurber's short story, "The Secret Life of Walter Mitty," is about a man who is caught perpetually in his world of daydreams. The simplest activity becomes to him like a mission out of a movie, and his mind is never on the task at hand.

Although the story is humorous, it points out a problem that can be very serious. Spending endless hours in a fantasy world is time-consuming and time-wasting because it removes the daydreamer from the real world in which God wants him to live and operate.

Does that mean it's not OK to dream? No. God created each of us with powerful imaginations and creative impulses that He wants to use. The issue is the amount of time and the objective involved. It's a matter of stewardship of your time. Any hobby or activity that removes your focus and priority from the Lord is spiritually harmful and a poor use of the time that God has given you.

Ecclesiastes 5:7 (NASB) tells us very simply: "In many dreams and in many words there is emptiness. Rather fear God." Where do you spend your mental energy?

Over the years, empty pursuits can take their toll. Proverbs 28:19 (NIV) explains, "He who works his land will have abundant food, but the one who chases fantasies will have his fill of poverty."

Dear heavenly Father, help me channel my mental energy to Your pursuits and purposes.

Free Indeed

SCRIPTURE READING: Galatians 5:1–3

KEY VERSE: Galatians 5:1

Stand fast therefore in the liberty by which Christ has made us free, and do not be entangled again with a yoke of bondage.

In the first verse of Galatians 5 (NASB), the apostle Paul wrote, "It was for freedom that Christ set us free; therefore keep standing firm and do not be subject again to a yoke of slavery." What was Paul talking about?

Many times the things that bind us do not seem harmful at first glance. In this particular entry in God's Word, we find that the Galatian believers were simply doing what tradition and the Law of Moses had taught them to do: Be circumcised as an outward sign of their allegiance and devotion to God. Yet their wrong theology quickly became a stumbling block to their spiritual growth.

Paul told them, "I testify again to every man who receives circumcision, that he is under obligation to keep the whole Law" (v. 3 NASB). The "whole Law" carried with it a tremendous burden. In fact, the requirements were so great that no one could keep them, which was the point of Christ's coming.

What we could not do for ourselves, Jesus did for us. He is the Fulfillment of the law and our Doorway to eternal freedom and rest.

When you come to a point in your life where you find yourself striving to earn God's approval, think of Paul's admonition to you: "It was for freedom that Christ set us free." Never abuse the freedom the Lord has given you. But likewise, never dismiss the fact that when the Son sets you free, you are free indeed!

Thank You for freedom, Lord. Help me never to abuse the freedom You have given me.

The Priority Struggle

SCRIPTURE READING: Matthew 6:31–34
KEY VERSE: Matthew 6:33

Seek first the kingdom of God and His righteousness, and all these things shall be added to you.

Any one of us for a number of reasons may stray in our devotion to God. It takes sheer discipline to remain faithful, especially when trouble hits. However, we can achieve this, no matter what the circumstances, when our hearts are focused on Him.

When your priorities get off center, it is easy to feel disillusioned and complacent. Before you know it, you have allowed a shift to take place in the things you hold dear. Some of the signs that priorities are out of line are the presence of sin, fear, compulsiveness, indifference, and self-involvement.

How can you keep your priorities straight? Begin by asking God to make you sensitive to the areas of your life that He wants to prioritize. Let Him arrange your days and your future. He always brings new experiences and ideas to mind. When you try to manage life apart from the Savior's wisdom, fearfulness and worry are always present. You can trust Jesus to keep you balanced and on target. He knows what He has planned for you, and if you will follow His lead, you will be surprised at the joy and peace He brings your way.

Learn to give yourself away to others. That was a top priority to Jesus, and it should be for you as well. When the Spirit of God rules your life, your pathway will be sure and pleasant.

Father, rule my life by Your Spirit. Make my pathway sure and pleasant.

AUGUST

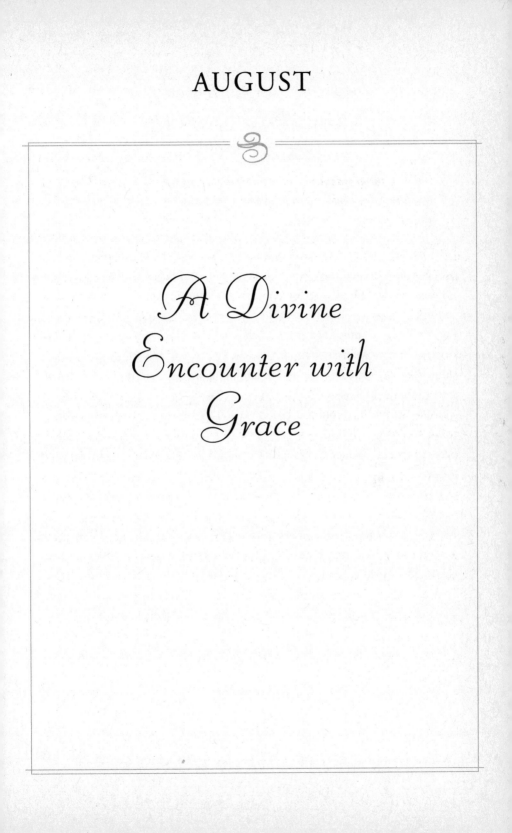

A Divine Encounter with Grace

The Infusion of God's Grace

SCRIPTURE READING: Ephesians 2:8–10
KEY VERSE: Romans 6:4

We were buried with Him through baptism into death, that just as Christ was raised from the dead by the glory of the Father, even so we also should walk in newness of life.

*Y*ou cannot come to Jesus apart from the grace of God. If you could save yourself, then there would be no need for a Savior. But God's pattern for salvation includes the infusion of His grace in the lives of those who come to Him.

Grace is all-important to the believer. It is God's personal touch, His handprint of intimacy in your life. It is the evidence of His advent and the one thing that keeps you founded in His abiding love. His grace breathes potential into all that you do and say.

The apostle Paul told us: "(By grace you have been saved), and raised . . . up with Him . . . in order that in the ages to come He might show the surpassing riches of His grace in kindness toward us in Christ Jesus" (Eph. 2:5–7 NASB).

He reminded us that we have been buried with Jesus through baptism into death, so that as Christ was raised from the dead through the glory of the Father, we, too, might walk in newness of life (Rom. 6:4). The mission of grace did not end at the Cross. It overflows into every area of our lives, filling us with hope and the blessed assurance that we are loved with an eternal love. Thus, God has called us to be distributors of His grace to others. Just as it has been given to you, let grace motivate you to give it away to someone today.

God, thank You for Your grace that fills me. Help me to give it away to someone today.

A Proper Perspective

SCRIPTURE READING: Luke 15:11–32
KEY VERSE: John 1:12

As many as received Him, to them He gave the right to become children of God, even to those who believe in His name.

You've probably heard and read Jesus' parable of the prodigal son many times, and the emphasis of the lesson is usually on the wayward brother. No matter how badly he had behaved, no matter how much he did not deserve his father's forgiveness, he received it anyway.

The one often overlooked is the other brother, grumbling in the corner while the party is in full swing. Many of us, if we're honest, secretly identify with him. It just doesn't seem fair. There he was, faithful and obedient all those years, and the "bad seed" got showered with attention just because he did something good for once.

Jesus was pointing out that both brothers were accepted into the same grace. The "good" brother did not realize it, but he was surrounded by the same unconditional love: "My child, you have always been with me, and all that is mine is yours" (Luke 15:31 NASB). The steady brother had simply lost this perspective and become mired in a hidden attitude of self-righteousness and pride.

You can rejoice when someone trapped in sin is welcomed into the Father's arms. Remember, you were no better when He embraced you with forgiveness. It should remind you of your own homecoming and fill you with an eagerness to share the delights of belonging to the Father.

God, I am so thankful that You are my Father and I can never lose Your eternal love.

Just Come

SCRIPTURE READING: John 3:1–7
KEY VERSE: John 3:13

No one has ascended to heaven but He who came down from heaven, that is, the Son of Man who is in heaven.

icodemus was a Pharisee, well respected for his knowledge of the Scriptures. Yet he had never heard the principles of God taught the way Jesus presented them. Up until the time he met Jesus, the entirety of his life was consumed with maintaining the traditions of the Jewish Law.

While Nicodemus witnessed the miracles of Christ, he had a hard time accepting the teachings of Jesus because of the religious liberties He seemed to take, from a Jewish viewpoint. Finally, when he could stand it no longer, Nicodemus went to Jesus. Many people try to make an issue over the fact that he went to the Lord under the covering of night instead of the light of day. However, the Savior is never concerned about how or when we come to Him, only that we come.

In the retiring moments of the evening, Nicodemus was free to ask his questions without the comments or interjections of other onlookers. Christ's full attention was his, and the moment quickly turned timely and informative. "How can a man be born when he is old?" asked Nicodemus. "He cannot enter a second time into his mother's womb and be born, can he?" (John 3:4 NASB).

From the Savior's point of view, the question was irresistible as Jesus revealed the Father's glorious intent toward mankind. Do you know the Savior in a personal way? Has He come into your life with the saving power of God? He is not concerned about how or when you come, only that you come.

Lord, I come! Envelop me in Your grace.

The Resurrected Lord

SCRIPTURE READING: John 3:15–17

KEY VERSE: Romans 5:8

But God demonstrates His own love toward us, in that while we were still sinners, Christ died for us.

Nicodemus had all that life could offer. Or at least he had enough to make him happy—that was, until Jesus appeared on the scene. He might have known something was missing in his life, but God's presence through the life of His Son let him know for sure that something was amiss.

Maybe you have a good job, a loving family, and a nice home, but like Nicodemus, you feel that there has to be more to life. The good news is that there is much more to your existence than what you see and feel around you. There is an eternity waiting for you.

Nicodemus was probably a likable fellow. He had studied the Scriptures thoroughly and knew Messiah would come to Israel. His desire to talk with Jesus was admirable. Though he came to the Lord under night's covering, at least he came asking questions and seeking truth.

In the end, Nicodemus was one of the only two men to give our Lord a proper burial. And Nicodemus supplied the spices used in our Lord's burial. However, the greater gift had already been given.

Jesus did this when He gave His life for Nicodemus and you. He became the atonement for Nicodemus's sin. This is what Jesus does for you today. Will you accept Him as your Savior? If you have, will you now allow Him to be your living, resurrected Lord?

Jesus, You are my living, resurrected Lord. I praise You!

The Discipline of Grace

SCRIPTURE READING: Romans 5:6–8

KEY VERSE: Colossians 2:13

You, being dead in your trespasses and the uncircumcision of your flesh, He has made alive together with Him, having forgiven you all trespasses.

In the *Disciplines of Grace*, Jerry Bridges acknowledges our need for divine grace:

Some days we may be more acutely conscious of our sinfulness and hence more aware of our need of His grace, but there is never a day when we can stand before Him on our own two feet of performance, when we are worthy enough to deserve His blessing.

At the same time, the good news of the gospel is that God's grace is available on our worst days. That is true because Christ Jesus fully satisfied the claims of God's justice and fully paid the penalty of a broken law when He died on the cross in our place. Because of that the Apostle Paul could write, "He forgave us all our sins" (Colossians 2:13).

Does the fact that God has forgiven us all our sins mean that He no longer cares whether we obey or disobey? Not at all. The Scripture speaks of our grieving the Holy Spirit through our sins (Ephesians 4:30).

And Paul prayed that we "may please God in every way" (Colossians 1:10). We grieve God, and we please God.

Clearly, He cares about our conduct and will discipline us when we refuse to repent of conscious sin. But God is no longer our Judge.

Through Christ, He is now our Heavenly Father who disciplines us only out of love and only for our good.

Lord, thank You for the discipline of grace, which makes me want to please You in every way.

Your Greatest Shield

SCRIPTURE READING: John 8:43–45
KEY VERSES: 1 Peter 5:8–9

Be sober, be vigilant; because your adversary the devil walks about like a roaring lion, seeking whom he may devour. Resist him, steadfast in the faith, knowing that the same sufferings are experienced by your brotherhood in the world.

There are times when God will allow you to see difficulty as it approaches. When this happens, you can prepare for the battle through prayer and the study of His Word. Other times trouble strikes without warning. His Word offers insight into how He wants us to handle the battle.

Many of the problems we face are direct assaults sent by Satan with one thought in mind: destroy, discourage, disable God's child. Throughout God's Word, we are cautioned to be on the alert against the schemes of the devil (1 Peter 5:8–9).

Peter knew what he was talking about when he cautioned the early church. He understood what it was like to be the target of the enemy's deception, and he was passing on the wisdom he had learned to others.

Every believer will face the same battle at one time or another. While Paul's thorn in the flesh (2 Cor. 12:7) was believed to be physical in nature, it also was a direct result of the enemy's attack. Satan sought to buffet him to the point of spiritual retreat.

Make no mistake about it: If Satan sought to undo Paul with discouragement, he will do the same to us. That is why Paul told us to put on the whole armor of God (Eph. 6:10–18). Claim what God has provided you. This is your greatest shield and protection: His Word and the fact that you belong to Him.

Dear heavenly Father, thank You for Your grace and power, which prepare me for battle.

Handing over Your Burdens

SCRIPTURE READING: Isaiah 53

KEY VERSE: Matthew 11:29

Take My yoke upon you and learn from Me, for I am gentle and lowly in heart, and you will find rest for your souls.

Have you ever been on a hike and had to carry a backpack? Even if there weren't many supplies inside, those few extra pounds probably took their toll on your energy. When you stopped for a rest and slid off straps from your shoulders, that moment of unburdening was delicious.

You may be carrying spiritual burdens right now and not know you are bearing extra "pounds." Unconfessed sin, unnecessary guilt, anxiety, fear, depression—these are just a few of the loads you could be laboring under. God didn't design you to function this way. That is why He sent a caring, gentle, loving Savior to take care of these problems for you through His forgiveness and grace.

"Surely our griefs He Himself bore, And our sorrows He carried; Yet we ourselves esteemed Him stricken, Smitten of God, and afflicted. But He was pierced through for our transgressions, He was crushed for our iniquities; The chastening for our well-being fell upon Him, And by His scourging we are healed. All of us like sheep have gone astray, Each of us has turned to his own way; But the LORD has caused the iniquity of us all To fall on Him" (Isa. 53:4–6 NASB).

Jesus wants you to lean on Him and hand over your burdens, all of them. When you do, you'll experience a lightness of spirit that knows no bounds.

Lord, thank You for taking care of all my problems through Your forgiveness and grace. I am handing over my burdens to You—all of them!

You Can Do Nothing

SCRIPTURE READING: 2 Corinthians 12:1–10
KEY VERSE: 2 Corinthians 12:1

*It is doubtless not profitable for me to boast. I will come to visions and reve-
lations of the Lord.*

You've worked so hard for years trying to build your life into what you
felt it should be. Still, somehow, after all that effort, there are areas of
your life that are out of control and a source of private pain.

In her book, *The Confident Woman,* Anabel Gillham explains her
struggle with weakness:

For me, my dream was that my prince would come and we would melt into
an inseparable oneness and maybe even live "happily ever after." A lovely
fairy tale. I tried so hard to make it come true.

But according to John 15:5, Jesus said, "Apart from Me, you can do
nothing." Nothing: not any thing; that which does not exist; a nonentity—
a thing, event, or remark of no account; absence of all magnitude or quantity; a zero. Nothing? That's a sobering thought.

I want to argue with God. I want to say, "But, Lord, there are some
things I can do quite well!" That's not the point. This is the basic plan, the
rudimentary principle of His original intent: If I am incapable of doing a
thing—if I can, indeed, do nothing—how much help do I need to get my
life straightened out? To recreate my marriage? To face each pressure filled
moment? To do anything? You're right. I don't need someone to help me; I
need someone to do it all for me. It would be 42 long years before I realized
this truth.

Lord, thank You for Your grace that is manifested in my life.

Sustaining Peace

SCRIPTURE READING: John 14

KEY VERSE: John 14:27

Peace I leave with you, My peace I give to you; not as the world gives do I give to you. Let not your heart be troubled, neither let it be afraid.

Nothing this world has to offer can satisfy your deep inner need for peace. Our world is not made for peace and contentment. In the Garden of Eden, there was peace because there was unblemished fellowship with the Lord, and the love that existed between man and God was untarnished. However, sin changed this situation.

Peace never comes as a result of our circumstances. It is the overflowing evidence of an intimate relationship with the Lord Jesus Christ. Those who followed Jesus were certain of one thing: They would face strife in this world, but God's peace would sustain them.

Some even gave up their lives because of their faith in Jesus. Yet even there, at the executioner's hands, they were enmeshed in the peace of God. Does this mean that they never felt anxious or battled fear? No, but we do find an early church determined and focused on the outcome of their faith and not on their circumstances.

They were, as the author of Hebrews wrote, aliens or strangers in this world (Heb. 11:13). But to God's glory, they were citizens of heaven.

Does the outcome of your faith tell the same story? If not, open your heart to Jesus. Tell Him about the fears that plague your soul, and accept His ever-present sense of peace, a gift of His grace, which is sure to guard your heart and mind.

Dear Lord, thank You for Your peace, Your sustaining gift of grace to me.

A Slave to Sin

SCRIPTURE READING: Romans 6:8–14

KEY VERSE: Romans 6:14

Sin shall not have dominion over you, for you are not under law but under grace.

The story is told of a prince who left the safety of his father's castle to seek adventures in the wide world. He left his riches behind and began to live as an unfortunate peasant. He dressed in rags, got food where he could, and endured many hardships. He lived so long that way, he almost forgot that he had once lived like a prince and could not even remember where the palace was.

Eventually after much searching, his father found him and brought him home. The boy had been a prince the whole time; he had simply chosen not to live like one.

The prince's actions seem irrational, don't they? But that's exactly what we as believers do when we push aside the grace of God and choose to live in the spiritual poverty of bondage to sin: "Now if we have died with Christ, we believe that we shall also live with Him, knowing that Christ, having been raised from the dead, is never to die again; death no longer is master over Him . . . Even so consider yourselves to be dead to sin, but alive to God in Christ Jesus" (Rom. 6:8–9, 11 NASB).

Are you living as an heir to the riches of God's glorious grace, or are you living as a slave to sin, as though you had never been redeemed? You do have a choice: "Sin shall not be master over you, for you are not under law but under grace" (Rom. 6:14 NASB).

Dear Father, I choose the riches of Your grace. I am no longer a slave to sin.

God's Eternal Purpose

SCRIPTURE READING: John 4
KEY VERSE: John 4:23

The hour is coming, and now is, when the true worshipers will worship the Father in spirit and truth; for the Father is seeking such to worship Him.

Salvation is God's eternal purpose for your life. God has saved you by His grace. There is nothing you can do to save yourself. Good works and well-thought-out deeds will not purchase a place for you in heaven. Those who have learned this truth have great peace because they know salvation has nothing to do with themselves and all to do with God's Son.

Those who become anxious in their relationship with the Lord often believe they can somehow disappoint Him, thus receiving eternal punishment. In talking with the woman at the well, Jesus made a remarkably freeing statement: "An hour is coming, and now is, when the true worshipers shall worship the Father in spirit and truth; for such people the Father seeks to be His worshipers" (John 4:23 NASB).

There was nothing this woman could do to change her past. She was a sinner. Yet when Jesus came to her, He did not place before her a list of conditions by which she would be saved. The only requirement was faith in Him as God's Son and her living Lord.

When you accept Christ as your Savior, He sends His Holy Spirit as a deposit of His grace. The Christian life is much more than a patchwork of unstable hopes and restless dreams. You can be sure of your eternal future. There are no erasure marks in heaven, no names in the Lamb's Book of Life with a line crossed through them.

Lord, thank You for the grace that assures my eternal destiny.

The Issue of Grace

SCRIPTURE READING: Romans 8:1–6

KEY VERSE: Romans 5:21

. . . so that as sin reigned in death, even so grace might reign through righteousness to eternal life through Jesus Christ our Lord.

A great concern of the early church was the issue of grace. Believers were constantly being presented with varying views that, if followed, could easily lead them astray. In Galatians, the apostle Paul warned against abandoning grace and following a legalistic doctrine: "It was for freedom that Christ set us free; therefore . . . do not be subject again to a yoke of slavery" (Gal. 5:1 NASB).

Most early believers came out of a Jewish background that was strongly rooted in works and tradition. Jewish believers could not quite grasp the idea of grace that proclaimed Christ's death as the basis of salvation. Gentile believers were seen as followers of Christ, but there was a strong movement underway to require them to adhere to Jewish tradition.

Amazingly many within the church still struggle with this issue today. Some think if they live solely by grace, they will wander away from God. Thus, they strive to stay close by performing certain religious deeds. The opposite reaction is to take grace to the extreme and live any way you please under the guise that you are saved and on your way to heaven.

We are called to be holy people who worship only the Lord. Take the grace of God seriously. Do nothing to harm your relationship with Him. Let go of any legalistic attitudes, and enjoy the freedom that is yours as a child of God.

Dear Lord, I don't want to do anything to harm my relationship with You. Cleanse me of any legalistic attitudes. I want to enjoy the freedom that is mine as Your child.

Living by Grace

SCRIPTURE READING: Ephesians 1:1–6

KEY VERSES: Colossians 1:5–6

Because of the hope which is laid up for you in heaven, of which you heard before in the word of the truth of the gospel, which has come to you, as it has also in all the world, and is bringing forth fruit, as it is also among you since the day you heard and knew the grace of God in truth.

W. E. Vines observed that grace stresses "freeness and universality, its spontaneous character, as in the case of God's redemptive mercy, and the pleasure or joy He designs for the recipient."

Henry Thiessen in *Lectures in Systematic Theology* explains, "The grace of God is God's goodness manifested toward the ill-deserving." In other words, grace is God actively bestowing His love and mercy toward those who do not deserve it.

God offers grace freely to those who are called by His name. It is not something He is forced to do; He chooses to do it because of His unconditional love for us. No wonder Paul was quick to stress living by grace rather than living by works. He knew there was nothing we could do in and of ourselves to merit God's favor.

Instead of striving to please God through completing a list of dos and don'ts, Paul exhorted believers to seek to know Christ through a personal relationship. God's grace is not limited to the salvation experience. Because we are believers, our lives are saturated by His grace. There is never a moment when the grace of God is shut off from us.

No matter what your circumstance, the God of all grace is with you. Don't be afraid to call out to Him. His grace is sufficient to heal, encourage, and wipe away every tear. Today tell Him how much you love Him and long to have a closer relationship with Him.

Lord, I am so thankful that as a believer my life is saturated by Your grace. I love You and long for a closer relationship with You.

A Second Chance

SCRIPTURE READING: Romans 5:1–6
KEY VERSE: Romans 5:8

God demonstrates His own love toward us, in that while we were still sinners, Christ died for us.

One of the most encouraging things you can receive from God is the hope that comes from being given a second chance. This is especially important when you have yielded to temptation or feel that you have fallen short of His plan and purpose for your life. The truth is that God never limits the opportunity for forgiveness.

Second chances encourage us to go on and not to give up even when the whispers of the world around us seem to say the opposite. After his denial of Christ, Peter was in need of a second chance, and Jesus, through His grace, provided it (John 21:15–17).

How many of us have longed for God's cleansing touch when we become trapped by our wrongful actions? The only cure for sin or failure of any kind is God's grace applied to our lives. This changes the stumbling sinner into a person living victoriously for Jesus Christ.

Even before you knew Him, Jesus knew and loved you. His love saved you, and His love will keep you throughout eternity: "God demonstrates His own love toward us, in that while we were yet sinners, Christ died for us" (Rom. 5:8 NASB).

Are you struggling with the idea of grace and how it applies to your life? Realize that God loves you. He stands beside you and is pleased to call you His own. This grace is yours.

Dear heavenly Father, thank You for Your love that saved me and gave me a second chance.

Forgiveness Is Not Cheap

SCRIPTURE READING: John 8:1–11
KEY VERSE: John 8:11

She said, "No one, Lord." And Jesus said to her, "Neither do I condemn you; go and sin no more."

No one knows what Jesus wrote in the sand the morning the woman caught in adultery was brought to Him. Some say He wrote the Ten Commandments. Others think He wrote the word *forgiven*. Regardless of the written message, the principle was clear: Grace would abound.

We can't earn God's grace. It is a gift He gives to all who come to Him seeking His forgiveness. Scantily clothed and lying at the Savior's feet, this woman probably thought her fate was sealed. The punishment for adultery was death by stoning, a stark reminder that sin is neither kind nor respectful of those it takes captive.

Yet suddenly and unpredictably Jesus offered this woman a second chance. Warren Wiersbe commented, "For Jesus to forgive this woman meant that He had to one day die for her sins. Forgiveness is free but it is not cheap."

Jesus was not soft on sin. "Nor is Christ's gracious forgiveness an excuse to sin," continued Wiersbe. "'Go and sin no more!' was our Lord's counsel . . . Certainly the experience of gracious forgiveness would motivate the penitent sinner to live a holy and obedient life to the glory of God."

We need God's grace because we have fallen short of His plan. Forgiven and blessed by His matchless grace are those who call Him Savior and Lord.

Savior, thank You for forgiving me and blessing me by Your matchless grace. You are the Lord of my life.

Living in God's Grace

SCRIPTURE READING: Psalm 84
KEY VERSE: Psalm 84:11

The LORD God is a sun and shield;
The LORD will give grace and glory;
No good thing will He withhold
From those who walk uprightly.

Many Christians have no trouble confessing their salvation through faith in God's grace, but many Christians at the same time do not understand that they are to live in God's grace.

Romans 5:1–2 (NASB) states: "Having been justified by faith, we have peace with God through our Lord Jesus Christ, through whom also we have obtained our introduction by faith into this grace in which we stand; and we exult in hope of the glory of God."

Notice that believers "stand" in God's grace, meaning it remains with us in our daily walk. It was a gift in the beginning, when you accepted Christ, and it is a lasting gift to you every day. You can add nothing to His grace. Since it is a gift, you owe God nothing. Besides, you could never repay Him for the death of His Son or for loving you enough to justify you into His fellowship. Grace is God's kindness and graciousness toward humanity regardless of our worthiness and the fact that no one deserves it.

Trying to repay God by doing good works or by drawing an imaginary line, however noble the intention, is an ill-conceived idea. Accept God's grace as evidence of His love for you because that is exactly what it is: unconditional, undeserved love. All He wants is your love in return. Works and obedience naturally follow as sweet by-products.

Oh, God, thank You for the grace You extended to me, even though I didn't deserve it. I love You!

The Peace of God

SCRIPTURE READING: Psalm 4
KEY VERSE: Psalm 4:8

I will both lie down in peace, and sleep;
For You alone, O LORD, make me dwell in safety.

Trying circumstances often are the biggest inhibitors of experiencing a life of liberty in Christ. It is easy to get distracted from God's promises of love and hope through His unfailing grace when under the same roof you live with a troubled teen or an unbelieving spouse. Or perhaps you quietly battle depression, poor health, or even oppression at work.

If you are facing a seemingly overwhelming difficulty, rely on what you know to be true. It was through unconditional love for us that God sacrificed His only Son while we were yet sinners. We never warranted His mere glimpse, much less the death of Jesus. Such love and forgiveness, immeasurable the moment you accepted Christ, remain every bit as vast now.

The love of God does not depend on your circumstances, your health, or your ability to feel His love. Try heightening your trust in God instead of heightening your anxiety, and "by faith" stand in God's grace. Accentuate God's many blessings and constantly remember Him.

You can enjoy the peace of God when you walk in His Spirit, obey Him, absorb His Word, and trust His grace. You, too, can reach the point at which you exult in your tribulations to bring perseverance, to bring proven character, to bring hope eternal.

Thank You, Father, for Your love and kindness toward me today. I praise You.

The Measure of God's Grace

SCRIPTURE READING: Romans 5:20–6:6
KEY VERSE: Romans 6:6

*Knowing this, that our old man was crucified with Him, that the body
of sin might be done away with, that we should no longer be slaves of sin.*

Imagine the most beautiful waterfall you've ever seen. Now, in your mind,
stand at its base and hold a thimble under the crashing water. This illus-
trates the measure of God's grace in your life, covering your sin. You can no
more contain a waterfall in a thimble than you can contain God's love and forgiveness for you.

If you have accepted Christ as your Savior, then you have accepted His
atoning work on the Cross. God set no limits on the effects of Jesus' sacrifice,
so why should you? If you are wracked with guilt over sin, whether it happened
long ago or is ongoing, and you can't seem to escape its snare, remember you
cannot out-sin God's grace.

While God will judge sin and will discipline a wayward believer, He also
will forgive any transgression. And if you do it again tomorrow, He'll forgive
you. This is not a license to sin but an invitation to accept God's grace humbly
and repent into an obedient walk with Jesus.

The believer's goal should be to greet God's grace and forgiveness with
genuine thanksgiving and contrition. We could never produce one achievement that would warrant our Lord's grace, and we could never produce
enough failures for Him to take it away.

When you hold that thimble under Christ's Cross and catch one drop of
His blood, you have enough.

I humbly accept Your grace, Lord. I revel in its sufficiency.

An Extravagant Request

SCRIPTURE READING: Acts 20:16–24

KEY VERSE: Acts 20:24

None of these things move me; nor do I count my life dear to myself, so that I may finish my race with joy, and the ministry which I received from the Lord Jesus, to testify to the gospel of the grace of God.

The apostle Paul, formerly one of the most vehement enemies of the early Christian church, was so transformed by the grace of God that he was consumed with making sure others learned of His grace. Facing even death, Paul went to Jerusalem, though his best friends pleaded with him to stay away.

How many of us have so surrendered to Christ that we are ready to submit totally to the leading of the Holy Spirit? Sometimes we grapple even to recognize His gentle whisper. If only we could be as Paul, so sensitive to the Spirit of God that we would be driven by Him!

In his modern paraphrase of the New Testament, *The Message*, Eugene Peterson updates Paul's language in his farewell to his friends:

I feel compelled to go to Jerusalem. I'm completely in the dark about what will happen when I get there. I do know that it won't be any picnic, for the Holy Spirit has let me know repeatedly and clearly that there are hard times and imprisonment ahead. But that matters little. What matters most to me is to finish what God started: the job the Master Jesus gave me of letting everyone I meet know all about this incredibly extravagant generosity of God.

Paul wasn't consumed with convicting people of their inevitable sin; he concentrated on grace: that incredibly extravagant generosity of God.

Thank You for Your generosity, dear God. Make me increasingly sensitive to Your Spirit.

The Greatest Gift

SCRIPTURE READING: Romans 3:21–27
KEY VERSE: Mark 10:45

The Son of Man did not come to be served, but to serve, and to give His life a ransom for many.

Within a few books in the middle of the New Testament, the apostle Paul posed a revealing question-and-answer session. Through two passages, he explained how a holy and just God reconciled sinful man to Himself.

In Ephesians 1:4–5 (NASB), Paul wrote, "He chose us in Him before the foundation of the world, that we would be holy and blameless before Him. In love He predestined us to adoption as sons through Jesus Christ to Himself, according to the kind intention of His will."

To make us righteous in God's sight, though we were hardly holy and blameless, God adopted us through Jesus Christ. But how?

Turn to Colossians 1:22 (NASB): "He has now reconciled you in His fleshly body through death, in order to present you before Him holy and blameless and beyond reproach."

Because of Jesus' substitutionary death on the Cross, believers are now holy and blameless. It was through, and only through, the death of Jesus that God orchestrated your proper standing in relationship to Him. God sacrificed His own Son so you could become one of His children.

Jesus' sacrifice is the greatest gift ever given. It is God's grace at its zenith, the one moment on which mankind hinges. It is a free gift from God's heart, and all He asks is that you believe with all your heart.

Jesus, thank You for giving me the greatest gift—the gift of Your grace.

Equal to Every Emergency

SCRIPTURE READING: 2 Corinthians 4:1–6
KEY VERSES: Galatians 3:26–27

You are all sons of God through faith in Christ Jesus. For as many of you as were baptized into Christ have put on Christ.

The gospel of Christ—the plan of salvation, the redemption, the sanctification, and the glorification of man—finds no greater expression than in the word *grace.*

Where there is no grace—unmerited favor bestowed with no anticipation of return—there is no gospel of Christ. You begin the Christian life by grace and continue in grace for eternity. You can never make yourself more presentable to God. His grace, given to the believer through Christ, His Word, and His Spirit, bestows His acceptance and unending favor upon you.

Such grace is a fathomless reservoir of unfailing love, available to all who call on the name of Christ. Kenneth Wuest writes in his *Word Studies in the Greek New Testament*: "There is enough grace to give every saint constant victory over sin, and then some more. There is enough grace to meet and cope with all the sorrows, heartaches, difficulties, temptations, testings, and trials of human existence, and more added to that. God's salvation is shock proof, unbreakable, all sufficient. It is equal to every emergency."

Lord, thank You for the expression of Your love and grace through a salvation that is shockproof, unbreakable, and all-sufficient.

Spiritual Treasure

SCRIPTURE READING: Matthew 6:19–21
KEY VERSE: Mark 10:21

*Jesus, looking at him, loved him, and said to him, "One thing you lack:
Go your way, sell whatever you have and give to the poor, and you will
have treasure in heaven; and come, take up the cross, and follow Me."*

If you have an attic, you have probably had the experience of a clean-out-
the-attic day. Maybe it's raining outside, and since you can't think of a
reason to put off the task any longer, you begin working. You turn on the light,
brush the dust off some lids, and start opening boxes. Each discovery leads to
a memory, and it's not long until you're not really cleaning out anymore.

Two things impress you: the passing of years and the impermanence of
material goods. Your mother's old tablecloth is discolored and moth-eaten; the
stack of papers from school is yellow and brittle. No matter how much you
may try to preserve these items, time takes its toll.

That is why it is so crucial for the real valuables of your life to be made of
material not subject to decay. Jesus said, "Do not lay up for yourselves treasures on earth, where moth and rust destroy and where thieves break in and
steal; but lay up for yourselves treasures in heaven, where neither moth nor rust
destroys and where thieves do not break in and steal. For where your treasure
is, there your heart will be also" (Matt. 6:19–21).

Of course, Jesus was speaking of spiritual treasure, the kind you accumu-
late as you allow Him to work through your life through the power of the Holy
Spirit. Which kind of treasure are you saving for?

*Dear Lord, please work in my life through Your power and grace. I
want to lay up spiritual treasures in heaven.*

Yielding to His Purpose

SCRIPTURE READING: 1 Timothy 1:12–17
KEY VERSE: 1 Timothy 1:15

This is a faithful saying and worthy of all acceptance, that Christ Jesus came into the world to save sinners, of whom I am chief.

Sometimes to see the grace of God at work in your life, you have to step back and yield to His purposes. In her book *Adventures in Prayer,* Catherine Marshall tells this story of Mrs. Nathaniel Hawthorne, wife of the famous American author:

In 1861 Una, the Hawthornes' eldest daughter, was dying of a virulent form of malaria. The attending physician, Dr. Franco, had warned . . . that unless the young girl's fever abated before morning, she would die.

Moreover, Una had been delirious for several days, had recognized no one. As the night deepened, the girl lay so still that she seemed to be in the anteroom of death . . . "I cannot bear this loss," Mrs. Hawthorne thought. Then suddenly, unaccountably, another thought took over. "Why should I doubt the goodness of God? Let Him take Una, if He sees best. More than that: I can give her to Him! I do give her to You, Lord. I won't fight against You anymore."

Then an even stranger thing happened. Having made this great sacrifice, Mrs. Hawthorne expected to feel sadder. Instead she felt lighter, happier than at any time . . . Some minutes later, she walked back to the girl's bedside, felt her daughter's forehead. It was moist and cool . . . Una was sleeping naturally. And the mother rushed into the next room to tell her husband that a miracle had happened.

Lord, let Your grace work in my life. I yield to Your purposes.

Unmerited Favor

SCRIPTURE READING: Hebrews 4:11–16
KEY VERSE: Hebrews 4:16

Let us therefore come boldly to the throne of grace, that we may obtain mercy and find grace to help in time of need.

Jesus chose to save you. He also wants to deliver you from sin and the temptation that accompanies it. However, you must grasp the idea He has set before you in the key verse today.

Most of us have heard Christian leaders explain how grace is God's unmerited favor directed toward those who love Him. He knows our hearts, sees our burdens, and wants to release us from the weight of trial. Yet He also knows we must be willing to relinquish all self-control of the situation.

Grace comes when you realize you cannot do something in your own strength. For example, you cannot save yourself. Only God can do this. There are other things you face that need an application of His grace. You may be dealing with a sense of fear, rebellion, or even confusion. You have tried trusting God, but nothing seems to work for long.

Have you ever wondered why God allows this to continue? Grace is the answer, and His mercy seeks to draw you closer to Himself. God does not tempt you to falter, but He certainly uses the tool of temptation to teach you how to submit and trust Him for all things.

As His child, you can come before His throne seeking hope and deliverance for every area of your life. Go confessing your love and need, and He will gather you in His arms of grace.

Lord, use the tool of temptation to teach me how to submit and trust You for all things. I love You and need You. Gather me in Your arms of grace.

Grace Is at Work

SCRIPTURE READING: Romans 4
KEY VERSE: Romans 4:8

Blessed is the man to whom the LORD shall not impute sin.

Most New Testament believers were familiar with the Law of Moses, especially if they were Jewish. However, the idea of grace posed a problem. The new believers were accustomed to abiding by many rules and regulations with the hopes of one day earning a place in God's kingdom. They offered sacrifices, ate certain foods, and kept certain rituals in order to remain in a place of righteousness before God.

But God's grace does not demand any of these things. Instead, it frees us from the penalty of sin and offers us a place of eternal life without us doing anything outside of our belief in Jesus Christ.

Yet many today still look for a way to earn their way into heaven. For some reason, our humanity wants to resist any thought of dying to self-love. However, God's grace leads us to do just that. If we are to accept His gracious gift, we must accept its conditions. Jesus Christ must become our life and breath.

The idea of grace might have seemed too simple to many in the New Testament church. They longed to continue in their traditions. In doing so, they failed to experience the freedom that God's grace brings.

Grace is not something you can do. It is something only God can do for you. Freely He gives His love, hope, and comfort. Ask Him to teach you more about His grace at work in your life.

Thank You, Lord, for grace at work in my life. Thank You that grace frees me from the penalty of sin and offers me eternal life.

Spiritual Focus

SCRIPTURE READING: Philippians 3:7–14
KEY VERSE: Philippians 4:4

Rejoice in the Lord always. Again I will say, rejoice!

*I*f you wear glasses or contact lenses, you know how blurry and fuzzy the world can be when you're not wearing them. A simple task like getting ready in the morning is difficult, maybe impossible, if you've misplaced them somewhere. And it would be ridiculous to think about going through the day without them.

What many don't realize, however, is that trying to operate without spiritual focus is detrimental as well. Your daily circumstances are anything but simple, and it's easy to get lost in a fog of confusion, misaligned priorities, and feelings of being overwhelmed. Before you know it, you're moving in a direction you do not want to go, but you don't know how to slow down and allow God to give you His direction.

When you realize that your spiritual life is out of focus, you need to slow down and spend serious time in prayer and study of His Word. All other goals and activities fall into place when you see Jesus as He is, as your Lord and Savior and dearest Friend. Through His love and grace, He wants to clear the fog away and sharpen your spiritual vision with His eternal perspectives.

Paul declared in Philippians 3:8 (NASB): "I count all things to be loss in view of the surpassing value of knowing Christ Jesus my Lord, for whom I have suffered the loss of all things, and count them but rubbish in order that I may gain Christ."

Jesus, help me to see You as You are, and keep my focus fixed there.

The Bondage of Sin

SCRIPTURE READING: John 8:31–36

KEY VERSE: John 8:32

You shall know the truth, and the truth shall make you free.

The prisoner had languished behind bars for more than two decades. Over the years, though, he had repented of his crimes and wanted to reenter society. The parole board took his years of obedient service into strong consideration during the review of his case. When the order was handed down to release him, the guards walked the corridor to his cell, keys jangling. They turned the lock, swung the door open, and said, "You're free to go. Pick up your things at the desk."

But the prisoner just stood there as if confused. They explained what happened, but still he didn't move. In fact, he decided to live in his cell for the rest of his life. He had the opportunity to live as a free and unfettered man, but he chose captivity. Does this story sound strange? Of course, it does. What rational person would want to stay in jail?

But that's what a believer does when he chooses to remain in bondage to a sin. It's as though you are standing behind bars, right next to an open door. Jesus wants you to turn to Him for freedom, but you have to decide that His liberation is better than the temporary thrills that sin seems to offer.

Lord, thank You for Your grace that frees me from the bondage of sin. I receive it with thanksgiving!

Rest in His Care

SCRIPTURE READING: Luke 15:1–7
KEY VERSE: Luke 19:10

The Son of Man has come to seek and to save that which was lost.

The Pharisees were appalled that Jesus associated with sinners. They publicly grumbled about Jesus' actions to show their disgust for what they called loose, disreputable behavior. Sometimes He even ate meals with sinners and social outcasts.

Jesus responded immediately. He wanted them to understand that His real mission is to save lost mankind, all who recognize that they are separated from God by their sin and believe that He pays the price for them. Jesus wanted the Pharisees and scribes to know how much each lost soul means to Him, how much He is willing to do to restore the person to fellowship with God.

Jesus, the true Shepherd, compared His love for sinners to a shepherd boy searching for one lost sheep. This shepherd boy left his other ninety-nine sheep safe in the fold to seek the missing one. The shepherd was personally responsible for each sheep in his care. If something happened to one of them, he had to give an account to the owner of the flock. Imagine this boy's relief and joy when he finally carried the wandering one home.

Jesus has this same love for you. He wants you to know your infinite value, to come to Him and rest in His care.

Thank You for Your love, Lord. I rest in Your care today.

A Rebellious Heart

SCRIPTURE READING: Psalm 55:1-6

KEY VERSE: Psalm 55:1

Give ear to my prayer, O God, and do not hide Yourself from my supplication.

He has a wife and three children whom he adores. He spends time with them whenever he can, going fun places and listening to their hurts and needs. His business ethics are unimpeachable; he is known by all as a fair man who goes the extra mile when nobody asks him to. And his charity work for the local hospital helped build a much-needed burn treatment center.

Would you ever guess that this man has a rebellious heart? He does. It's not easy to see by judging from external appearances. Even though he outwardly obeys the law and is concerned for the well-being of others, he is dead in his spirit to the things of God and doesn't care what God says about his life.

Every person is born with a spirit that is disobedient to God. It is literally "bent away" from the Lord and set on its own course. According to Ephesians 2:1 (NASB), "You were dead in your trespasses and sins." People who continue to go their own way, ignoring the way to God through Jesus Christ, will perish and be lost forever.

Are you camouflaging a rebellious heart? Have you asked Jesus to correct your sinful condition? Jesus is the only One who, through His grace, can make your heart right, inside and out.

Lord, through Your grace, please make my heart right inside and out.

Avoiding a Hardened Heart

SCRIPTURE READING: Hebrews 3:7–19
KEY VERSE: Hebrews 3:12

Beware, brethren, lest there be in any of you an evil heart of unbelief in departing from the living God.

Unbelievers are not the only ones who can have hardened hearts. The Israelites in the wilderness were the children of God, and yet they persisted in closing their hearts to God's leadership through those trying years. Whenever circumstances did not go their way, they grumbled. When they did not understand what God was doing, they doubted Him. When they felt that God wasn't doing the best thing for them, they worshiped other gods. No wonder God allowed them to be tested so severely at times.

Refusing to trust the Lord or refusing to obey is a signal of inner rebellion and a prideful spirit. Can you identify times in your life when you felt that your way was best? Maybe you didn't disobey a specific command of God, but you carefully avoided praying about a certain topic. Deep within, you knew that God's answer on that topic was probably no, and that was not what you wanted to hear.

Closing your ears leads to closing your heart. If you sense that God is tugging at your heart about an issue, don't put Him off. Set aside a season of prayer before Him in His Word. He will deal with any waywardness of spirit. He desires your love and devotion so much that He doesn't want you giving your heart away to something else. Through His grace, God will tenderize your heart again if you ask Him.

Tenderize my heart again, dear Lord. Make me pliable to Your will.

Grace for Every Weakness

SCRIPTURE READING: Ephesians 6:10–12
KEY VERSE: 1 John 4:4

*You are of God, little children, and have overcome them, because He who
is in you is greater than he who is in the world.*

World War II marked the beginning of the modern spy age.
Governments entrenched themselves in intelligence and counter-
intelligence games, seeking to learn all they could of the opposing countries'
military plans.

Powerful military leaders such as Rommel, Patton, and Bradley were
intensely examined by their foes. Scrutiny was not limited to their military
knowledge, but to all facets of their lives, professional and personal. The reason? To find a weak point that the opposition could use to undermine and
defeat the leaders' objectives.

This same tactic has been used since the beginning of time in the spiritual
realm. Satan cannot change the believer's eternal destiny, so he attempts to
destroy our witness and walk. Satan seeks out our weaknesses, areas where we
are vulnerable. He does not waste much time tempting us in areas where we
experience little difficulty.

It is times like these when 1 John 4:4 enables us to feel victorious. Satan is
not omniscient. He is limited in his powers and abilities. However, there is no
limit to God's ability to thwart Satan's objectives and provide overcoming grace
for every weakness.

*Dear heavenly Father, thank You for grace that helps me overcome
every weakness.*

SEPTEMBER

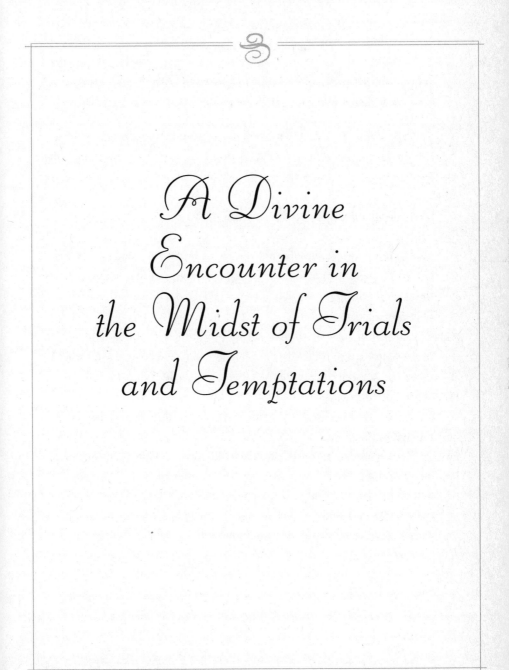

*A Divine
Encounter in
the Midst of Trials
and Temptations*

Moving out of Your Comfort Zone

SCRIPTURE READING: 1 Peter 1:17–21
KEY VERSE: Romans 8:32

He who did not spare His own Son, but delivered Him up for us all, how shall He not with Him also freely give us all things?

Trials are God's way of moving you out of your comfort zone and to new and exciting challenges. Instead of adopting a negative view of difficulty, resolve to understand that God will bring good out of your trouble (Rom. 8:32).

Oswald Chambers offers direction for you:

Are you painfully disturbed just now, distracted by the waves and billows of God's providential permission, and having, as it were, turned over the boulders of your belief, are you still finding no well of peace or joy or comfort; is all barren?

Then look up and receive the undisturbedness of the Lord Jesus. Reflected peace is the proof that you are right with God because you are at liberty to turn your mind to Him. If you are not right with God, you can never turn your mind anywhere but on yourself. If you allow anything to hide the face of Jesus Christ from you, you are either disturbed or you have a false security.

. . . He will be a gracious benediction of peace in and through you . . . We get disturbed because we have not been considering Him. When one confers with Jesus Christ, the perplexity goes, because He has no perplexity, and our only concern is to abide in Him. Lay it all out before Him, and in the face of difficulty, bereavement and sorrow, hear Him say, "Let not your heart be troubled."

Dear heavenly Father, help me view trials as Your way of moving me out of my comfort zone and to new and exciting challenges.

How Power Is Perfected

SCRIPTURE READING: 2 Corinthians 12:7–10

KEY VERSE: 2 Corinthians 12:9

He said to me, "My grace is sufficient for you, for My strength is made perfect in weakness." Therefore most gladly I will rather boast in my infirmities, that the power of Christ may rest upon me.

God often uses our weaknesses to strengthen and refine us spiritually. The apostle Paul experienced this truth through a trial that he called "a thorn in the flesh."

We don't know the nature of his infirmity, but we do know the reason it was given. Within Paul's life was a temptation to become prideful over all he had learned and received spiritually.

God used a physical weakness to sharpen Paul's spiritual focus. Three times the apostle beseeched God to remove his suffering, and three times God told him: "My grace is sufficient for you, for power is perfected in weakness" (2 Cor. 12:9 NASB).

Our weakest moments are opportunities for God to reveal His greatest truths to our hearts. His objective in allowing these times is never to destroy us but to bring us to a wondrous point of total dependence on Him.

God used the negative circumstance of Paul's life to achieve the greatest results, glorification of Jesus Christ. Learn to respond prayerfully to times of weakness. Ask God to show you the purpose for what you are facing and give you His wisdom and strength to handle the situation according to His will for your life.

Lord, show me the purpose of what I am facing, and give me Your wisdom and strength to handle the situation according to Your will for my life.

An Anchor for Life's Storms

SCRIPTURE READING: 1 Peter 2:20–24
KEY VERSE: 1 Peter 2:20

For what credit is it if, when you are beaten for your faults, you take it patiently? But when you do good and suffer for it, if you take it patiently, this is commendable before God.

Some of us remember life in the 1950s. World War II had ended, and there was a sense of optimism. For some it was a time of rebuilding. Winston Churchill had led England through the most difficult period of its existence.

Doggedly he had proclaimed: "We shall not flag or fail. We shall go on to the end. We shall fight in France, we shall fight on the seas and oceans, we shall fight with growing confidence and growing strength in the air, we shall defend our island, whatever the cost may be, we shall fight on the beaches, we shall fight on the landing grounds, we shall fight in the fields and in the streets, we shall fight in the hills; we shall never surrender." England prevailed, and so did peace.

What is your anchor in stormy times? For those who went through the war, it may have been in a sense of determination and the will to survive as a nation or even as an individual. However, there is an even deeper lesson here, one that assures us of victory.

Jesus is the Anchor of our souls. Just as Churchill rallied his country to victory, we must rally ourselves at the foot of Jesus' Cross. There must be within our lives a determination to follow Jesus above all else. Our world has changed drastically over the last decades. Yet Christ remains eternally the same. And even in this unsettling time of trial and tribulation, He is our strong hope and victory!

You are my Anchor, O Lord. Hold me steady in the midst of life's storms.

A Rough Row

SCRIPTURE READING: Romans 8:20–25

KEY VERSE: Acts 14:22

Strengthening the souls of the disciples, exhorting them to continue in the faith, and saying, "We must through many tribulations enter the kingdom of God."

Someone has described the Christian life as headed into a storm, in a storm, or coming out of a storm. The question for the believer is not if trials will come, but what to do when they do come. Jesus said we would enter the kingdom of God through many tribulations (Acts 14:22). Paraphrased in today's language, Jesus might say we have a rough row to hoe before we enter God's presence.

Accepting the blunt reality of trial and hardship is the first step to dealing with adversity. The Christian is no more immune to cancer or hurricanes than the non-Christian. The ruin of the Fall and the entrance of sin into the universe adversely affect both man and creation (Rom. 8:22).

We must realize that the primary purpose of adversity is to expose our weakness and drive us to fresh trust and dependence on Jesus Christ. Jesus wants us to trust Him with each burden, each problem, each setback.

He knows that as we trust Him, we will advance in our adversity. In our weakness, we can discover His strength. The winds of financial misfortune, illness, divorce, or death may be too much for us to handle, but nothing is too complicated or burdensome for God.

Dear Lord, please help me to realize that the primary purpose of adversity is to expose my weakness and drive me to fresh trust and dependence upon You.

A Catalyst of Future Blessing

SCRIPTURE READING: Psalm 61

KEY VERSE: Isaiah 30:15

Thus says the LORD GOD, the Holy One of Israel:
"In returning and rest you shall be saved;
In quietness and confidence shall be your strength."

God allows storms to touch our lives only when there is a need. Just as He waters and purges the land, He uses the storms of life to water and purify our souls.

When a storm erupts, we may frantically try to solve the situation or understand what we have done wrong. Did we say something that hurt another? Was sin involved and we failed to confess it? Or did we forget to spend time alone with God in prayer?

The prophet Isaiah wrote that our strength comes from trust in God (30:15). When life gets rough and feels as though everything will come apart, stop rushing and wondering, and run to Jesus. He is the Anchor of your soul, the One who is strong and faithful and has promised never to abandon you.

He will never turn His back on you. Even if trouble comes as a result of a sin or transgression, He remains faithful to you. He has never given up on anyone, and He will not start with you. You are His beloved, and He has a plan for your life. So you can begin again today.

He knows the intensity of the winds that whip at your heart. Let these winds become a catalyst of future blessing. Ask the Lord to show you how to respond to the pain you are feeling, then make a commitment to be quiet and still in your spirit. Walk closely with Him, and know that He will renew your hope.

Dear heavenly Father, let the winds of life become a catalyst of future blessing. Show me how to respond to the pain I am feeling. Help me to be quiet and still in my spirit and walk closely with You through the storm.

Help for Troubled Times

SCRIPTURE READING: Matthew 14:22–34
KEY VERSE: Matthew 14:27

Immediately Jesus spoke to them, saying, "Be of good cheer! It is I; do not be afraid."

Jesus did not come to His disciples during the first, second, or third watch the night the storm swept over the Sea of Galilee. Instead, He waited until the fourth watch, approximately 3:00 A.M., when the waves were at their fiercest and the wind at its strongest.

The afternoon before, He had miraculously fed five thousand people with five loaves of bread and two sun-dried fish. The people had witnessed a miracle but missed the underlying lesson of Christ's deity. Christ immediately withdrew to the hillside to be alone with the Father while sending the disciples ahead of Him across the sea. Then the storm hit.

Storms often come even when we have been obedient. The disciples never questioned Jesus' judgment in directing them to set sail without Him. The feeding of the five thousand was meant to illustrate that Christ was their complete sufficiency. However, the lesson needed underscoring; and Jesus allowed the winds and the waves to do just that.

Is there a storm raging in your life, maybe one that is not of your own doing? Has the cry just gone out for the beginning of the fourth watch, and you feel as though all hope is gone? Take courage! Jesus will not leave you alone in the storm but will come to you. He is your present help for troubled times.

Don't leave me alone in the storm, Lord. Come to me and be my help in troubled times.

The Light of God's Love

SCRIPTURE READING: Psalm 27
KEY VERSE: Psalm 27:1

The LORD is my light and my salvation;
Whom shall I fear?
The LORD is the strength of my life;
Of whom shall I be afraid?

The Tybee lighthouse near Savannah, Georgia, has seen many storms. Hurricane-force winds have threatened its existence. Gale-driven rains have bludgeoned its walls, and yet it survives. Even when floodwaters cover the roadway that leads out to the island on which it stands, the lighthouse remains a beacon of hope.

David declared, "The LORD is my light and my salvation; Whom shall I fear? The LORD is the defense of my life; Whom shall I dread? . . . Though a host encamp against me, My heart will not fear; Though war arise against me, In spite of this I shall be confident. One thing I have asked from the LORD, that I shall seek; That I may dwell in the house of the LORD all the days of my life, To behold the beauty of the LORD, And to meditate in His temple. For in the day of trouble He will conceal me in His tabernacle; In the secret place of His tent He will hide me; He will lift me up on a rock" (Ps. 27:1, 3–5 NASB).

More than once, King David found himself in a hopeless situation. He would have given up were it not for his hope in God. Instead of becoming angry and bitter, he chose to cling to the goodness of God even in harrowing circumstances. The storms of life will drive you to the light of God's love and care, or they will force you to retreat in sorrow.

Father, let the storms of life drive me to the light of Your love and care.
I don't want to retreat in sorrow.

How God Makes Soldiers

SCRIPTURE READING: Psalm 18
KEY VERSE: Psalm 18:34

He teaches my hands to make war,
So that my arms can bend a bow of bronze.

David wrote, "He trains my hands for battle, So that my arms can bend a bow of bronze" (Ps. 18:34 NASB). When we read these words, our minds rush to the thought of a man with very strong biceps bending a bronze instrument as if it were a toy. However, we fail to recognize that to have this type of strength, we must be trained by the storms of life.

God answered David's prayer, but not without sacrifice and learning. Rarely does the Lord provide strength without proper preparation. Even in times of emergency when we sense His closeness and undergirding power, we can usually look back and exclaim, "He was preparing me all along."

The storms of life come in many forms; some are emotional in nature while others are physical and problematic. No matter how serious they appear, they are tools in God's loving hands. They buffet our lives with pain and sorrow, yet in the end, they yield a worth more valuable than gold.

Charles Spurgeon described what happens to you: "When God puts a burden upon you He puts His own arm underneath . . . The Lord always trains His soldiers, not by letting them lie on feather-beds . . . He makes them ford through streams, and swim through rivers, and climb mountains, and walk many a long march with heavy knapsacks of sorrow on their backs. This is the way in which He makes them soldiers."

Make me a soldier, Lord. Use adversity to train me.

Under Assault

SCRIPTURE READING: 1 Samuel 27:1–6

KEY VERSE: 1 Peter 3:14

Even if you should suffer for righteousness' sake, you are blessed. "And do not be afraid of their threats, nor be troubled."

One of the reasons God allows trials to come into our lives is to prepare us for future spiritual battles. God anointed David to be king over Israel, yet He allowed him to be banished and hunted like a common criminal. Instead of ruling Israel, David once was even constrained to the land of the Philistines at Ziklag (1 Sam. 27:1–6).

Adversity and suffering met him at every turn. Yet those were the very ingredients that God used to prepare David for kingship. Adversity became his tutor and suffering his guide. In the midst of trial, David developed the spiritual and physical disciplines that made him Israel's greatest king.

God never trains us for battle in regions of ease, comfort, and pleasure. Instead, He sends us to places like Ziklag where disappointment tempts our souls. In these environments we must learn to trust and follow only Him.

How long have the winds of adversity clawed at your life? Months? Years? God has not forgotten you. He is in the process of preparing you for future blessing. Therefore, stand firm in the hope and knowledge of His salvation.

Thank You, Lord, that You are preparing me for future blessing. Help me stand firm in the hope and knowledge of Your salvation.

God Sees Victory

SCRIPTURE READING: Psalm 138
KEY VERSE: Psalm 138:7

Though I walk in the midst of trouble, You will revive me;
You will stretch out Your hand
Against the wrath of my enemies,
And Your right hand will save me.

F. B. Meyer discusses God's guidance:

God guides us, often by circumstances. At one moment the way may seem utterly blocked; and then shortly afterward some trivial incident occurs, which might not seem much to others, but which to the keen eye of faith speaks volumes . . .

They are not haphazard results of chance, but the opening up of circumstances in the direction in which we would walk. And they begin to multiply as we advance toward our goal, just as the lights do as we near a populous town, when darting through the land by night express.

In times of trial, cling to the hope God has given you. Each of us has many candles of hope tucked away in the resources of memory. When David was on the run and hiding from King Saul, one of the ways he found encouragement was to think back to the times God had proven faithful in the past. He found hope and strength in the memory of the Lord's goodness.

Cloistered away deep within David's heart were the promises of God. Among them was a single promise that said one day he would sit on Israel's throne. Circumstances and the envy of others did not change God's plan for His servant. In the quotation, Meyer reminds us that at any moment God may open a previously locked door of blessing. Presently we may see sorrow and tragedy, but God sees victory.

Lord, I am so excited that at any moment You may open a previously locked door of blessing. Help me to be ready to walk through it.

Times of Testing

SCRIPTURE READING: Mark 4:35–41

KEY VERSE: Psalm 107:29

He calms the storm,
So that its waves are still.

Jesus made it clear to His disciples that they would go to the other side of the Sea of Galilee. However, when the storm clouds gathered and winds approached gale force, the disciples lost all vision about where they were going and who had sent them there. The growing swells of the sea and the darkness of the night led them to believe death was a certainty.

The storm must have been tremendous to frighten the seasoned fishermen. Yet Jesus was not taken off guard nor was His deity challenged by its severity. When the disciples woke Him, they were amazed at His ability to command the wind and sea to stop their raging.

Their eyes had been focused on their physical circumstances and not on the One who had the power to rescue them. Jesus could have told them the storm was coming, but He chose to wait and allow them to react to what seemed an impossible situation. Their faith had to be tested, and they had to learn that Christ was their only Source of help in time of trouble.

Many times, life's afflictions are not the result of sin. The disciples did nothing to cause the storm. In fact, they were very much in the will of God. If the climate of your life is stormy, ask the Lord to reveal the reason for the tempest. In times of testing, God is preparing you for greater service.

Dear Lord, You are my only Source of aid in times of trouble. I call on You for help.

Pruning the Branches

SCRIPTURE READING: John 15:1–8
KEY VERSES: John 15:1–2

I am the true vine, and My Father is the vinedresser. Every branch in Me
that does not bear fruit He takes away; and every branch that bears fruit
He prunes, that it may bear more fruit.

Roses take the right amount of fertilizer and sunlight to produce beautiful buds. The location of the plant and type of soil are also important. However, another element is essential to producing healthy rose bushes, and that is pruning. The rule, according to one grower, is to "prune until you see good wood."

Along with the obvious dead wood, growers cut away any small shoots they know won't produce buds. When the plant is the most vulnerable from battling winter freezes and icy temperatures, the pruner takes his shears and trims away everything that threatens to limit its growth and flowering.

So it is with us. Jesus said, "I am the true vine, and My Father is the vinedresser. Every branch in Me that does not bear fruit, He takes away; and every branch that bears fruit, He prunes it, that it may bear more fruit" (John 15:1–2 NASB).

God cuts away the dross in our lives until He sees "good wood." Without pruning, we would never bear the sweet fragrance of Christ. It is in the cutting that God strips us of ourselves and shapes us to His image.

Don't become discouraged at His pruning touch. God is constantly at work in the lives of those He plans to use greatly.

O God, even in the midst of difficulties I know that You are at work
in my life. I praise You!

A Way Out

SCRIPTURE READING: Hebrews 4:14–16
KEY VERSE: 1 John 2:1

My little children, these things I write to you, that you may not sin. And if anyone sins, we have an Advocate with the Father, Jesus Christ the righteous.

Often we quote these verses from Hebrews but fail to consider their deeper meaning. The writer of Hebrews discovered a truth that revolutionized the way we view temptation. He stated that we now have a Great High Priest who is able to sympathize with all our struggles.

Jewish believers were accustomed to going to the temple to worship. It was there that they approached the priest, who made a sacrifice for their transgressions. Whatever the law required, whether two doves or something else, they would bring as an offering to God. The priest then would sacrifice the animal(s) on behalf of the individual. The animal's blood became the symbol of atonement.

As the Lamb of God, Jesus became the eternal sacrifice for mankind's sin. In the Father's eyes, Jesus' blood shed at Calvary was sufficient payment for your sin, not just part of it but all of it. He is your Advocate before God's throne of grace (1 John 2:1). He is able to personally identify with the temptation you face. Although He did not yield to sin, He certainly faced its power.

Temptation is not sin. It is the step before it. The important factor here is that Jesus, being tempted in all ways, did not yield Himself. He knows the intense pressure created by temptation, but He also knows there is a way out. Whatever your struggle, Jesus is aware of it, and He will set you free.

Lord, You know the intense pressure created by temptation. You also know the way out. Show me the way.

Power of the Cross

SCRIPTURE READING: Luke 22:14–20
KEY VERSE: Luke 22:20

Likewise He also took the cup after supper, saying, "This cup is the new covenant in My blood, which is shed for you."

Today's passage is taken from the section concerning the Lord's Supper, when Jesus establishes a new covenant with all believers. The old covenant was with Abraham and his heirs, who became the nation of Israel. In the lamplight of the Upper Room, Jesus provided His disciples with a rare look into the future. Lifting the cup of wine, He said, "This cup which is poured out for you is the new covenant in My blood" (Luke 22:20 NASB).

While Jesus' actions and words appear to contradict the Law of Moses and the covenant God established with Abraham, they are really parallel in theological thought. God requires payment for sin. Therefore, there must be a covering substantial enough to remove the stain of sin in our lives.

God recognized the sacrificing of sheep and goats as an atonement for sin, but there was no eternality to this system. Jesus brought change and eternal hope to mankind. His life and death opened the way to salvation and freedom from the bondage of sin. On the Cross, a new covenant was established, and the need for repetitive sacrifice was taken away.

Christ's death broke sin's power over your life. You can now say no to temptation before it takes hold of you. But should you stumble, turn quickly to Him who loves you, and seek His restoration. As you confess your weaknesses, He is faithful to forgive and restore.

Father, thank You that sin's power is broken over my life, enabling me to say no to temptation before it takes hold of me. Thank You that when I do stumble, You are faithful to forgive and restore.

Training to Win

SCRIPTURE READING: 1 Corinthians 9:24–26
KEY VERSE: Psalm 84:11

The LORD God is a sun and shield;
The LORD will give grace and glory;
No good thing will He withhold
From those who walk uprightly.

Many people make a tremendous mistake by assuming that trial and difficulty are results of something they have done wrong. They have forgotten Paul's analogy of the athlete who must prepare himself mentally and physically to compete and win the prize. Even in Paul's day, an athletic competition was a big event. The only way an athlete became stronger was through training, and that meant having his strength tested.

Training to win is not a light and easy task. It requires hard work, discipline, and the ability to withstand all kinds of pressure. Paul asked, "Do you not know that those who run in a race all run, but only one receives the prize? Run in such a way that you may win. And everyone who competes in the games exercises self-control in all things. They then do it to receive a perishable wreath, but we an imperishable. Therefore I run in such a way, as not without aim" (1 Cor. 9:24–26 NASB).

Trials are God's tools to test your faith in His ability. When you fail to learn a certain spiritual principle, don't be surprised if He allows another trial to arise. He is teaching you how to trust in His strength and not your own. Learning how to handle the valley times of life readies you for the many blessings God has prepared for you.

Lord, thank You that every trial I experience leads to a blessing. Use the valleys of my life to prepare me for the blessings You have planned for me.

The Blessings of Brokenness

SCRIPTURE READING: John 12:24–26
KEY VERSE: Psalm 119:107

I am afflicted very much;
Revive me, O LORD, according to Your word.

There is one way to God's blessing, but often it leads us through the valley of brokenness. Do not pray to be broken in order to receive God's goodness. Instead, pray to be made like Jesus Christ. Brokenness is something God initiates. Therefore, don't waste time looking for its coming. It can sweep into your life at a time of intense need when you are asking God to bring insight and blessing.

At first, you may feel confused and even bewildered at its appearing. After all, isn't it the blessing of God you look forward to gaining? But if you could see brokenness the way God views it, you would find that to be broken of God is really a spiritual honor given in preparation for a blessing.

Brokenness empties you of the chaff that prevents you from hearing His voice and responding to His will. Like wheat being winnowed and then crushed in preparation for the making of bread, your life is tested and stripped of impurities so all that remains is the sweet aroma akin to His beloved Son.

Charles Spurgeon noted of our troubles: "Our troubles have always brought us blessings, and they always will. They are the dark chariots of bright grace . . . These clouds will empty themselves before long, and every tender herb will be gladder for the shower. Our God may drench us with grief, but He will refresh us with mercy."

Dear heavenly Father, thank You for the blessings that brokenness brings.

The Process of Brokenness

SCRIPTURE READING: Exodus 2:11–16; 3:1–4
KEY VERSE: Psalm 139:17

How precious also are Your thoughts to me, O God!
How great is the sum of them!

Moses was not fit for service in God's kingdom the instant he became aware of his heritage. He knew the suffering of God's people, but he was not ready to identify with them by becoming their leader. The story in Exodus 2 tells that when he was a baby, his mother set him adrift in a basket made of pitch and tar. Pharaoh's daughter pulled him from the water and raised him in royalty. Later, as a young man, he was forced to confront his destiny.

It was a tremendous trial having all the pleasures of palace life eliminated, but Moses discovered something worth much more than earthly treasure. After years of living as an outcast, he was given an opportunity to step into the presence of the living God.

The Bible tells us: "The angel of the LORD appeared to him in a blazing fire from the midst of a bush . . . yet the bush was not consumed. So Moses said, 'I must turn aside now and see this marvelous sight'" (Ex. 3:2–3 NASB).

Brokenness is a process, and Moses was on a divine course. The moment he turned aside to "see" the burning bush was the very moment the Lord called out to him. Moses would not have noticed any call before that one.

God knows when you have been broken in such a way that you are willing to respond to Him. Are you broken and weary? Lift up your eyes and behold the marvelous sight of God's burning love for you.

Lord, help me to recognize that the process of brokenness is at work in the circumstances of my life. Help me to recognize Your love and concern for me in every situation and to respond in a positive way.

A Gateway to Blessing

SCRIPTURE READING: Psalm 25
KEY VERSE: Psalm 25:10

All the paths of the LORD are mercy and truth,
To such as keep His covenant and His testimonies.

There are two ways you can respond to brokenness: with a desire to do God's will and endure a time of testing, or with rebellion against God's surgical hand in your life.

The first is a gateway to blessing. The second leads to what many call "being placed on the shelf by God." When we refuse to allow the Lord to have the whole of our lives, we deny Him access to our hearts, wills, and emotions. In essence, we fold our arms and proclaim we know more about who we are and what we need than He does.

Even in brokenness, God will bring a sense of resurrection hope. Though we struggle and hurt, it is only for a season; then comes the blessing. Amy Carmichael explains,

"All the paths of the Lord are lovingkindness." (Psalm 25:10) All does not mean "all but these paths we are in now" or "nearly all, but perhaps not just this specially difficult painful one."

All must mean all. So your path with its unexplained sorrow, and mine with its unexplained sharp flints and briers, and both with their unexplained perplexity of guidance, their sheer mystery, are just lovingkindness, nothing less. I am resting my heart on that word. It bears one up on eagle's wings; it gives courage and song and sweetness too, that sweetness of spirit which it is death to lose even for only half an hour.

Dear Lord, help me to rest my heart upon Your Word. Let it bear me up on eagle's wings and give me courage and sweetness of spirit.

A Season of Brokenness

SCRIPTURE READING: Jeremiah 29:11–14

KEY VERSE: Jeremiah 29:13

You will seek Me and find Me, when you search for Me with all your heart.

During a season of brokenness, you need to tell yourself the truth about your circumstances and your position in Christ. You are a child of God, and He loves you with an eternal love. He is in ultimate control of all difficulty and uses it to guide you into a greater spiritual maturity. When hardship comes, you must recall that God has allowed it for a purpose.

There is never a time you are outside His reach of love. No trial is stronger than His ability to save and protect you. The Bible confirms that God does not initiate sorrowful circumstances, but He certainly uses them to foil the enemy's plan to derail and ruin your life.

You may be facing a series of physical, emotional, or spiritual tests not because you have sinned but because you love God greatly. Only you know whether something has come between you and the Savior. If you have allowed sin to enter your life, confess it immediately, and then continue in your quest for a life that reflects the love and grace of Jesus Christ.

Satan has a chief goal in mind for the believer, and that is to trick you into giving up. Realize he will stop at nothing to achieve his desire. Never forget that God is stronger than any assault Satan can muster. The Lord uses the wiles of the enemy to train you for kingdom existence. Through adversity, God will draw you closer to Himself.

Lord, I am so thankful that I am never outside Your love. No trial is stronger than Your ability to save and protect me.

Strengthen Your Grasp

SCRIPTURE READING: 1 Corinthians 9:24–27
KEY VERSE: 1 Corinthians 9:24

Do you not know that those who run in a race all run, but one receives the prize? Run in such a way that you may obtain it.

In times of brokenness, you may notice that you are having trouble keeping your perspective. Trial, heartache, and disappointment can water the thoughts of weariness and discouragement.

There is nothing wrong with asking God to encourage your heart, especially if you are having trouble keeping your spiritual focus. Paul found solace in God's friendship and the love of others. At the end of his life and during a time of tremendous emotional stress, he wrote asking Timothy to come to him.

Jeremiah, Elijah, and David faced similar periods of brokenness that threatened their spiritual and emotional well-being. However, they were able to keep their spiritual focus by practicing the presence of God. They found victory and hope in worshiping and praising Him even if trouble abounded on every side.

When we face times of difficulty, the greatest temptation is to give up. Paul used an analogy of a runner to show us how to handle brokenness when it comes: "Do you not know that those who run in a race all run, but only one receives the prize? Run in such a way that you may win" (1 Cor. 9:24 NASB).

When you keep your heart locked on the goodness of God, you become like an athlete in training. A higher call is waiting, and you must be prepared for the challenge. Strengthen your spiritual grasp, and God will grant you a mighty victory.

Lord, help me to keep my priorities in times of trouble. Strengthen my spiritual grasp, and grant me a mighty victory.

Hear His Call

SCRIPTURE READING: John 20

KEY VERSE: John 20:16

Jesus said to her, "Mary!" She turned and said to Him, "Rabboni!" (which is to say, Teacher).

Jesus' death brought an unspeakable amount of brokenness to the lives of the disciples. During His earthly ministry, they witnessed the Lord doing many wondrous things. They saw Him raise the dead, heal the sick, and proclaim the unconditional love of God. A strong sense of security came just from being in His presence.

All their needs were met, including the need of fellowship. Imagine what it was like to be with Jesus by a campfire as He talked and shared the truths of God's Word. No one who knew Jesus wanted to believe that one day He would no longer be with them.

When He was arrested, their world broke apart. Anxiety and dread overtook them. They barricaded themselves in the Upper Room and hid from the authorities out of fear that they might be next to die.

However, God did not leave them broken and disillusioned. From the first moment of His resurrection, He sent word to His disciples (John 20:17). He was no longer dead. He had risen, just as He said He would do.

If you are facing a time of intense brokenness, ask the Lord to speak to your heart. At the tomb, Mary cried. Her broken heart could withstand no more pain, and Jesus knew this. From death's gate, He stepped through life's veil and called out to her (John 20:16). Let Him do this for you even now.

Oh, Lord, speak to my heart in this season of brokenness. Step through the veil and touch me in the midst of my pain.

The End of Brokenness

SCRIPTURE READING: James 1:22–25
KEY VERSE: James 1:25

He who looks into the perfect law of liberty and continues in it, and is not a forgetful hearer but a doer of the work, this one will be blessed in what he does.

One of the amazing results of brokenness is refreshment. If you allow brokenness to have its way in your life, ultimately you will experience greater inner peace and refreshment for your soul. This may be hard to imagine, especially when you find yourself in the throes of spiritual or emotional unrest.

God uses times of brokenness to bring you to the end of yourself. When this happens, your dependence shifts from self-seeking to seeking God and His will. The surest way through brokenness is found in surrender to and dependence on Jesus Christ. The more you resist God's intervention, the more difficult things become.

God created you and knows what it takes for you to fully glorify Him. He also wants to bless you, but blockages in your life keep Him from doing so. This is not a dark thought. Throughout life, God is at work shaping, molding, and sanding off the rough edges of our lives. If God is interested in your becoming all that He means for you to become, don't look at it negatively. Rejoice that He is at work in your heart.

In *The Imitation of Christ*, Thomas à Kempis wrote, "True quietness of heart . . . is gotten by resisting our passions, not by obeying them." At the end of brokenness, there is abundant life springing forth from a heart overflowing with God's love.

Lord, I surrender to You. Shape me, mold me, and sand off the rough edges of my life.

Stay on Course

SCRIPTURE READING: 2 Corinthians 1:3–7
KEY VERSE: 2 Corinthians 1:5

As the sufferings of Christ abound in us, so our consolation also abounds through Christ.

Have you ever wondered why God allows certain circumstances to come into your life? Most of us have, especially when trials come or we face feelings of inadequacy or fear. We look heavenward and whisper, "God, why did this happen? Why am I having to face this?"

It is always better to voice your complaint to the Lord than to hide it deep within your heart. God knows your frustrations, and He will listen to what you have to say. Remember, He always deals with you in love. Even in difficult times, God is at work to bring good into your life.

He uses life's trials to teach you how to trust and depend on Him in a greater way. Times of emotional darkness are His training grounds. It is in the disappointments and misunderstandings of life that God stretches your muscles of faith.

When you hurt, He promises to comfort you. He does this so you also will learn how to comfort others struggling with similar pain. Only those who have experienced doubt, discouragement, fear, loneliness, and other emotional trials are adequately equipped to minister to others who are hurting. This is just one of the results of facing adversity. Therefore, when it comes, refuse to be drawn off course. Keep your focus on Christ, and He will guide you through troubled times victoriously.

Father, I refuse to be drawn off course by life's trials. Help me keep my focus on You. Guide me through troubled times victoriously.

Good Out of Evil

SCRIPTURE READING: 2 Corinthians 5:15–17
KEY VERSE: Romans 8:28

We know that all things work together for good to those who love God, to those who are the called according to His purpose.

God uses the trials we face to teach us more about Himself. Even when we create the havoc by disobeying Him, God can bring good out of evil (Rom. 8:28). However, we must be willing to submit to His plan and let go of the things that draw us away from His fellowship.

Sin is a dark tempest. It will divide the mind and cause you to think and do things that are not in keeping with who you are in Christ. Jesus has given you a new life. The apostle Paul reminded us that "the old things passed away" (2 Cor. 5:17 NASB). He was talking about your former lifestyle before you were saved.

Yielding to temptation brings sorrow, friction in relationships, and spiritual deadness. Therefore, when God sounds a warning, heed His call. Don't be drawn away. Stand your ground, and rely on His sovereign care to lead you.

Not every valley experience is the result of sin. Sometimes God allows us to go through great difficulty so that our faith in Him is strengthened:

Sometimes God sends severe blasts of trial upon His children to develop their graces. Just as torches burn most brightly when swung to and fro; just as the juniper plant smells sweetest when flung into the flames; so the richest qualities of a Christian often come out under the north wind of suffering and adversity. (*Streams in the Desert*, by Mrs. Charles E. Cowman)

Father, please direct my path and bring good out of evil.

The Greater Good

SCRIPTURE READING: Isaiah 50:8–11
KEY VERSES: Lamentations 3:21–22

This I recall to my mind,
Therefore I have hope.
Through the LORD's mercies we are not consumed,
Because His compassions fail not.

After a disagreement with his supervisor, an employee admits to spending an entire evening thinking about how he could get back at his boss. However, God's greater plan did not include him losing his mental cool and jeopardizing what the Lord had given him to do. Each of us has a responsibility to obey God.

Trouble, trial, and injustice can tempt you to be disobedient. When this happens, you can respond one of two ways. You can take matters into your own hands, and as the prophet Isaiah recorded, you will receive no help from God: "All you who light fires and provide yourselves with flaming torches, go, walk in the light of your fires and of the torches you have set ablaze. This is what you shall receive from my hand: You will lie down in torment" (Isa. 50:11 NIV). Or you can experience the greater good by trusting God to save and protect you.

God wants you to depend on Him. Not just for the big things, but for the everyday trials as well. When was the last time you faced a situation that appeared too great for you to handle? Were you determined to go through on your own steam? If you were, you missed the wonder of God's deliverance. There is a tremendous hope to be gained in this life, but you must lay down your rights and allow God to be your very life in order to experience it.

Lord, help me to lay down my rights and allow You to be my life. I seek the greater good!

Uncontrollable Circumstances

SCRIPTURE READING: Psalm 40:1–8

KEY VERSE: Psalm 40:2

He also brought me up out of a horrible pit,
Out of the miry clay,
And set my feet upon a rock,
And established my steps.

How do you respond to the times your circumstances seem out of control? Many find themselves caught up in a fast and furious pace without thinking about what they are doing.

Each of us faces moments when life requires a change of plans. Sudden and unplanned interruptions or crises have the potential to send us reeling toward disaster. However, as a believer, you do not have to submit to mind-boggling actions.

Jesus kept a rigorous schedule that was often accented by what seemed to be emergencies or unscheduled delays. Yet never once was He taken off guard nor did He become fractious over the needs and desires others placed on Him.

Jesus never rushed or hurried anywhere. He was never surprised by His circumstances. He had a mission and purpose, and He never became frantic over whether it would become a reality. He knew it would because He was kept by the power of God.

You can gain your greatest sense of control by knowing that God's hand of providence guides your life. There is never a time, a trial, or a temptation when you are outside His presence. He is able to grant victory over the most unreasonable situation. Allow Him to be your strength in whatever you are facing. The prophet Isaiah wrote, "In quietness and trust is your strength" (30:15 NASB). True victory is found here.

Father, help me to remain quiet and confident when circumstances seem out of control, knowing that they are actually under Your divine control.

Proving God's Promises

SCRIPTURE READING: 2 Timothy 2:11–13
KEY VERSE: Malachi 3:10

"Bring all the tithes into the storehouse, That there may be food in My house, And prove Me now in this," Says the LORD of hosts, "If I will not open for you the windows of heaven And pour out for you such blessing That there will not be room enough to receive it."

God uses our trials to mold and shape us into images of His love and grace. To face heartache and suffering victoriously, we must believe there is hope. This is where faith comes into play. God wants to bless you. But you must learn to trust Him with every issue of life; then the blessings will come abundantly.

A. B. Simpson wrote of trials:

When God tests you, it is a good time for you to test Him by putting His promises to the proof, and claiming from Him just as much as your trials have rendered necessary.

There are two ways of getting out of a trial. One is to simply try to get rid of the trial, and be thankful when it is over. The other is to recognize the trial as a challenge from God to claim a larger blessing than we have ever had, and to hail it with delight as an opportunity of obtaining a larger measure of Divine grace. Thus even the adversary becomes an auxiliary, and the things that seem to be against us turn out to be for the furtherance of our way. Surely, this is to be more than conquerors through Him who loves us.

Don't shy away from proving the promises of God. God always answers prayer. And the greatest joy you will ever receive comes when you discover His personal devotion to you.

Dear Lord, help me to recognize trials as challenges from You to claim a larger blessing than I have ever had. Help me to delight in them as opportunities for securing a larger measure of Your grace.

The Testing of Faith

SCRIPTURE READING: Matthew 14:22–33
KEY VERSE: Matthew 14:27

Immediately Jesus spoke to them, saying, "Be of good cheer! It is I; do not be afraid."

You do not know the real depth of your faith until it is put to the test. You cannot know how you will react to stormy gales when your world is canopied by blue skies and white puffy clouds. The testing of your faith as a believer is crucial to your walk with the Lord. If you trust Him, then you have nothing to fear. Even in darkness, when your soul cries out, there will be a sense of faith that goes beyond the immediate trial.

Learn to be quiet in your heart and mind. Ask Him to teach you how to walk beside the still waters of His truth and love. When trouble comes, our minds are often consumed with thoughts of fear and needing to do something. But when you practice walking with your Savior on a daily basis, the storms of life subside.

Dear heavenly Father, teach me how to walk beside the still waters of Your truth and love.

The Storms of Life

SCRIPTURE READING: Philippians 4:4–9
KEY VERSE: Philippians 4:7

The peace of God, which surpasses all understanding, will guard your hearts and minds through Christ Jesus.

Here are some things you can know about the storms of life:

God knows exactly where you are emotionally and mentally when trouble hits. He understands your frustration and need to ask why a certain event has taken place. He never condemns your feelings. Instead, He provides wisdom for all you face.

He will not leave you comfortless. That was a promise Jesus made to His disciples before His death. Today, it is one of our greatest sources of encouragement. Jesus does not leave us on our own to deal with heartache and trials. He has given us the Holy Spirit to comfort and support us when we are too weak to continue. When feelings of anxiety rise, practice growing still before the Lord. Think on His goodness and how He never fails you.

At times, God does allow the pressures of life to build so that we can learn how to deal with them from a position of faith and not fear. Philippians 4:6–7 (NASB) is a promise you can claim: "Be anxious for nothing, but in everything by prayer and supplication with thanksgiving let your requests be made known to God. And the peace of God, which surpasses all comprehension, will guard your hearts and your minds in Christ Jesus."

Are you ready to listen for God's voice? He avails Himself to all who seek His face. Therefore watch, listen, and pray. Then you will discover the mind and hope of God.

Father, I am so glad You know where I am emotionally and mentally when trouble hits. You understand my frustration and my need to question. Thank You for not condemning me for my feelings, and for providing wisdom for all I face.

The Trials of Life

SCRIPTURE READING: 1 Peter 1:13–16
KEY VERSE: 1 Peter 1:16

Because it is written, "Be holy, for I am holy."

You are handling the trials of life victoriously when you . . .

Remove any hindrances to your spiritual walk with the Lord. Sin causes a separation in your fellowship with the Lord. Wrong attitudes and thinking get you spiritually off track. Ask the Lord to set a guard around your mind so the focus of your life will be centered only on Him.

Resolve to remain balanced in your judgment. In times of trouble, doing this can be especially difficult. When an emergency arises, you want to spring to action. If possible, remain steady and watchful, listening for God's directive voice. He is aware of your need.

Refuse to take the easy, quick way out of a situation. Instead, be committed to His plan. If He has placed you in a certain job or relationship, be willing to remain until He leads you elsewhere.

Recognize that your only true hope is in Christ. God has a purpose for the trials you face. His main desire is for you to seek His encouragement above that of friends and family. One reason He allows you to experience difficulty is so that you can develop a dependency on Him.

Resist the temptation to return to your former lifestyle. When you step back to where you were before you were saved, you compromise your relationship with Jesus Christ. God loves you, but He will not tolerate sin.

Lord, remove any hindrances in my spiritual walk. Help me to remain balanced, to refuse to take the easy way out of situations, and not to return to my former lifestyle.

OCTOBER

A Divine
Encounter in
Personal Ministry

People God Picks

SCRIPTURE READING: 2 Corinthians 2:12–17

KEY VERSE: 2 Corinthians 2:14

Thanks be to God who always leads us in triumph in Christ, and through us diffuses the fragrance of His knowledge in every place.

God rarely picks people who are extremely qualified to do His work. Rather, He often chooses those who, from the world's perspective, are weak and less than qualified, yet have deep hunger to know Him.

The reason God takes this route is simple. As long as we claim a certain degree of self-adequacy, our dependence on God is hampered, and we are tempted to think that we have something of value to offer Him. The only things we can offer the Lord are our hearts and humble awareness of His greatness and power.

You may reason that the apostle Paul was an adequate messenger of the gospel. He was, but not on his own. It wasn't until he met Jesus Christ on the Damascus road that he was faced with the severity of his inadequacy. In accepting Christ as Savior and Lord, Paul positioned himself for great potential.

If you are tempted to think, *God is certainly fortunate to have me in this position; look at all I can do for Him,* more than likely you are headed for trouble. It is true that God created us with certain abilities and talents, but never to make us strong or adequate in our own eyes.

God is your strength. And He alone deserves all the glory and honor from every good thing you do. Give Him praise for your life today.

Dear God, You are my strength. You deserve the glory and honor from every good thing I do.

Stimulated to Action

SCRIPTURE READING: Acts 17:22–31

KEY VERSE: Acts 17:16

Now while Paul waited for them at Athens, his spirit was provoked within him when he saw that the city was given over to idols.

In Acts 17:16, we read that as Paul waited for the arrival of Silas and Timothy in Athens, he became "provoked" at what he saw. The city was filled with images of idols. Men had erected statues and monuments to gods that did not exist—the evidence of an inner need to worship something or someone greater than themselves.

Being "provoked" as the apostle Paul was did not mean being angry as we know it. Here the word *provoked* means "stimulated to action." At the sight of the spiritual ignorance of the Athenians, Paul was provoked to speak the truth concerning Christ and His messiahship.

Because Paul, a scholar in his own right, knew that words delivered in anger are rarely worth considering, he challenged the Athenian philosophers to a debate. He was amazed at their attempt to worship every god imaginable, even to the point that they made sure they did not leave one out.

Warren Wiersbe comments on Paul's effort: "Paul's message is a masterpiece of communication. He started where the people were by referring to their altar dedicated to an unknown god. Having aroused their interest, he then explained who that God is and what He is like. He concluded the message with a personal application that left each council member facing a moral decision, and some of them decided for Jesus Christ."

Dear Lord, stimulate me to action in behalf of lost souls. Provoke me to respond.

Tools for Growth

SCRIPTURE READING: 1 Peter 5:6–10
KEY VERSE: 1 Peter 5:10

But may the God of all grace, who called us to His eternal glory by Christ Jesus, after you have suffered a while, perfect, establish, strengthen, and settle you.

Imagine being forced to leave your home and live in a land far from those you love. Some of us find this hard to visualize, while others have experienced this very trauma. In recent years, we have witnessed entire ethnic groups being forced to flee their homelands for fear of annihilation.

That was the same dilemma facing the early church in Jerusalem. Nero, the Roman emperor at the time, blamed the Christians for a fire that burned a large portion of Rome. Believing Jerusalem was the hub of Christian activity, Nero sought to disperse the early church and crush it by forcing its members to leave the city.

Nero's persecution of Christians was both relentless and hideous. Yet he could not stop the early church from growing. In fact, though they were forced underground, the church grew at a rapid rate. Today we see this same thing taking place in China and other parts of the world where there is severe persecution. Trial and persecution cause those who suffer to run to God.

Peter reminded the early church that the outcome of their faith would produce results. No matter what you are facing, you can trust that God stands beside you, and He will take your difficulties and persecution and bring a tremendous sense of victory out of each one. Let Him show you how to use life's difficulties as tools for tremendous spiritual growth and witness to others.

Lord, please teach me how to use life's difficulties as tools for spiritual growth and witness to others.

Reactions to the Cross

SCRIPTURE READING: Luke 12:51–53
KEY VERSE: 1 Corinthians 1:8

*Who will also confirm you to the end, that you may be blameless in the
day of our Lord Jesus Christ.*

Have you ever noticed how people in general like to discuss issues from
an "open-minded" perspective? Some even pride themselves in their
ability to consider many viewpoints without being judgmental. But somehow, should the topic of conversation turn to Jesus Christ or His death on the
Cross, tempers flare and lines are drawn. Suddenly, some very "open-minded"
people become angry and closed. The mere mention of His name can call up
responses such as, "Don't try to push your religion on me."

Such reactions are not new. Paul explains in 1 Corinthians 1:18–20 (NASB):
"For the word of the cross is to those who are perishing foolishness, but to us
who are being saved it is the power of God. For it is written, 'I WILL DESTROY
THE WISDOM OF THE WISE, AND THE CLEVERNESS OF THE CLEVER I
WILL SET ASIDE.' Where is the wise man? Where is the scribe? Where is the
debater of this age? Has not God made foolish the wisdom of the world?"

Jesus Himself warned in Luke 12:51–52 (NASB): "Do you suppose that I
came to grant peace on earth? I tell you, no, but rather division; for from now
on five members in one household will be divided, three against two, and two
against three."

Don't be surprised by negative reactions to the Cross. Only those who
cling to it for salvation can see the wisdom of God expressed through Christ.

*Lord, help me to share Your Word regardless of negative reactions of
others. Help me to guide others to see Your wisdom expressed through
Christ.*

Jesus in Your Heart

SCRIPTURE READING: Galatians 2:20–3:3
KEY VERSE: Galatians 5:24

And those who are Christ's have crucified the flesh with its passions and desires.

Children have a way of putting profound truth in very simple terms. Dr. D. James Kennedy shares this story in his book, *New Every Morning:*

A five-year-old Christian boy was very ill, so ill that he required open-heart surgery. After a successful operation, the doctor checked on the little boy in his hospital room.

With bright and eager eyes, the little boy asked, "Doctor, was He there?" The doctor asked, "Was who where?" The young lad replied, "Was He there? Did you see Jesus in my heart?" At that, the doctor suppressed a smile and replied, "Yes, son, He is there."

The question for you as an adult is this: Can people see Jesus in your heart by the way you live? If you're trying to generate a Christian image through your efforts, then you're headed for failure and burnout. All that others will see is stress and a lack of peace.

But when you grasp the truths of Galatians 2:20 (NASB), you learn to let the light of Christ shine through you: "I have been crucified with Christ; and it is no longer I who live, but Christ lives in me; and the life which I now live in the flesh I live by faith in the Son of God, who loved me, and gave Himself up for me."

Jesus wants you to let go of self-effort and abide in His love, turning your struggles over to Him. Then you can be sure others will see Him when they look at your heart.

Lord, help me let go of self-effort and abide in Your love. I turn my struggles over to You. Let others see You when they look at me.

God Works Through You

SCRIPTURE READING: 1 Corinthians 1:1–5
KEY VERSE: 1 Corinthians 1:4

I thank my God always concerning you for the grace of God which was given to you by Christ Jesus.

If you've ever heard a gifted speaker deliver a message, you know how convincing the words can be. You find yourself hanging on every sentence, maybe even taking notes as fast as you can write. Somehow, the way he or she communicates makes the difference in how much you listen.

Maybe you feel inadequate talking about your faith in Christ because you are not a dynamic speaker. You hold back, even when a perfect opportunity presents itself, just because you are self-conscious. But God never intended for you to rely on your own abilities as a witness.

The apostle Paul wrote, "When I came to you, brethren, I did not come with superiority of speech or of wisdom, proclaiming to you the testimony of God. For I determined to know nothing among you except Jesus Christ, and Him crucified . . . And my message and my preaching were not in persuasive words of wisdom, but in demonstration of the Spirit and of power" (1 Cor. 2:1–2, 4 NASB).

We know from other passages that Paul was an excellent public debater, but that is not his point here. He deliberately approached the Corinthians with an attitude of humble simplicity, in weakness, so that God would do the work through him. Regardless of your abilities, God wants to pour His power into your life to enable you to do His work.

Precious Lord, pour Your power into my life. Enable me to do Your work.

Investing in Eternity

SCRIPTURE READING: Colossians 3:1–4
KEY VERSE: Colossians 3:2

Set your mind on things above, not on things on the earth.

Have you ever seen the devastating effects of an earthquake? Maybe you are even a survivor of an earthquake. The terror of such an experience is overwhelming: The ground shakes, and structures bend, warp, explode, and fall. Things that seemed so permanent are heaps of rubble. Towers that seemed solid and substantial are on the ground. It is a sobering reminder of the impermanence of earthly things.

That's why it is so critical to set your focus on the things that don't change, the things that cannot be destroyed. Paul urged, "If then you have been raised up with Christ, keep seeking the things above, where Christ is, seated at the right hand of God. Set your mind on the things above, not on the things that are on earth. For you have died and your life is hidden with Christ in God. When Christ, who is our life, is revealed, then you also will be revealed with Him in glory" (Col. 3:1–4 NASB).

Your identity in Christ places your true citizenship in heaven. In a real sense, you don't belong here, where things pass away and change continually. It's been said that the only two things that are eternal are God's Word and people. When you invest your time in the eternal, your time is not wasted. And best of all, one day you'll see the investments of your life come to fruition in heaven.

Lord, I want to invest my time in eternal things. I want to see the investments of my life come to fruition in heaven.

A Demanding Decision

SCRIPTURE READING: John 6:53–58
KEY VERSE: John 6:65

And He said, "Therefore I have said to you that no one can come to Me unless it has been granted to him by My Father."

Each of us has questions we would like to ask God, and He welcomes each one. Nicodemus, a Pharisee, had never heard anything to equal the teachings of Jesus. Questions filled his mind even though he was a known scholar of the Law of Moses. Nicodemus's confusion rested in the fact that he had not yet received the real truth of God.

You may wonder if you will be able to discern God's message when it comes. But because of the presence and ministry of the Holy Spirit in our world, confusion is not likely. God woos each of us. He knows what it takes to draw you to Himself. While the ultimate decision to follow Christ is yours to make, God has an unmistakable way of making Himself known to the human heart.

When Nicodemus first heard Jesus, he did not have the spiritual aptitude to understand the deeper truths of God. Still, his heart's desire was to know truth. Like many today, Nicodemus could sing the hymns, but the words had little meaning beyond Jewish tradition.

After His death, Nicodemus was one of only two men who claimed Christ's body for burial. He did that at great personal risk. More than likely, after his display of devotion to Jesus, Nicodemus lost his position as a teacher of the law. Living in devotion to Christ demands a decision. Nicodemus made his.

If you have already made your decision, ask God to give you a desire to help others make theirs.

Lord, give me the desire to help others make a decision for You.

An Act of God's Will

SCRIPTURE READING Matthew 28:19–20
KEY VERSE: John 6:27

Do not labor for the food which perishes, but for the food which endures to everlasting life, which the Son of Man will give you, because God the Father has set His seal on Him.

Remember how you felt the last time you helped someone? Maybe you helped a stranded motorist. Maybe you joined a neighbor for a home repair job or took on a task that was burdensome and you were glad to eventually complete it.

Whatever the circumstance, you probably were warmed by the fact that you had performed an act of goodwill. But what about doing an act of the Father's will? Often our deeds are only for temporal benefit. Have you ever considered extending your efforts to eternity?

Our best labor is to accept and honor the words Jesus spoke as He prepared to return to heaven. He commanded us to make disciples of all the nations.

This means whether at home or abroad we are to share the gospel of Jesus Christ. We can't all ship off to a distant land, but we can put our arms around a hurting family member, friend, coworker, or stranger and say, "You know, Jesus loves you, and so do I. I'll pray for you. Is there anything else I can do?"

Jesus commanded all believers to take Him and His Word seriously in our approach with others. When you honor His command, you will honor God. The result of your love and obedience is an inexpressible appreciation of the fruit of the Spirit. People notice when we share the love of Christ.

Give me a heart of compassion, Lord. Help me to reach out to people in need.

Light to the Lost

SCRIPTURE READING: 2 Corinthians 4:3–6
KEY VERSE: John 6:40

And this is the will of Him who sent Me, that everyone who sees the Son and believes in Him may have everlasting life; and I will raise him up at the last day.

Many Christians who work in secular jobs often are encouraged to be "candles in darkness." It is a deep darkness, wrought by the evil ruler of this world and the spiritual blindness of those he has deceived.

A man may have functioning physical eyes, but in spiritual matters he cannot see the hand in front of his face, especially when the hand belongs to Jesus. This is where the Christian can at least provide a good example.

Spiritually blind people often have no idea they are perishing. They are fulfilling selfish desires and motives, believing the only necessary authority springs from themselves. Self-reliant people inevitably develop pride, a sin God especially despises, and pride can build an almost impenetrable shell.

But there likely will come a time when the self-sufficient life of a spiritually blind person bottoms out. When he has nowhere else to turn, when he is completely desperate and searching for answers, God may turn your candle into a flame-thrower. The example you have provided, the testimony you have repeatedly given, the Scripture you have recited, the love you have shown—all are light to a lost person. And since it is the light of Jesus, it is a bright light indeed. While you're praying for spiritually blind people, be sure to offer the light of Christ to them.

Lord, make me a candle in the darkness. Use me to open the eyes of those around me who are spiritually blind.

Closed Doors

SCRIPTURE READING: Acts 16:5–10
KEY VERSE: Revelation 3:8

I know your works. See, I have set before you an open door, and no one can shut it; for you have a little strength, have kept My word, and have not denied My name.

You have heard the cliché, "When God closes a door, He opens a window." However, many times this does not hold true. God may close a door to something we desire greatly because He has something better in mind. And His best is much greater than an open window.

Still, when you confront a closed door, the natural response is to ask, "Why, Lord?" Yet in Acts 16 when God closed a door of ministry, the apostle Paul never questioned God's reasoning or timing. He might have wondered what was happening, but he never expressed anything but total trust in God's wisdom (Acts 16:7–8). Paul and his party of missionaries responded in obedience to Christ.

When you confront a closed door, turn to the Lord, and ask for His guidance and blessing. No matter how difficult it seems, surrender your personal desires concerning the entire matter.

God had a plan in mind for Paul's ministry, but at that moment it did not include Bithynia. A few days later the spiritual door was opened for him to go into Macedonia, which was an even greater field of service.

God's delays are often preludes to great blessing. His denials are sent for our protection, and the times He requires us to wait are moments He uses to build our faith. Be willing to wait for His timing in your life and ministry, and you will not be disappointed.

Teach me to wait, Lord. Your timing is always perfect!

Your Great-Commission Role

SCRIPTURE READING: Mark 16:15–20

KEY VERSE: Mark 16:15

And He said to them, "Go into all the world and preach the gospel to every creature."

Have you ever considered your role in the Great Commission? Before He ascended to the Father, Jesus commanded His disciples to, "Go into all the world and preach the gospel to all creation" (Mark 16:15 NASB).

With such a broad-reaching command, we somehow tend to think its implications are limited. We often read over this passage and think it applies only to certain chosen servants. Surely Jesus means someone else. Jesus knows whom He's picked out to fly overseas.

We've all had similar thoughts. But the Great Commission is not exclusionary. His assignment isn't only for preachers and missionaries. He intends for all of us to fulfill His commandment wherever we are. You can obey Him while standing at your backyard fence. Or at a social gathering. Or at the mall. Or by getting on your knees or opening your wallet.

God knows your particular situation and how you can best fulfill His commission. Perhaps He wants you to pray for a particular missionary family. Perhaps He wants you to witness to a sibling, neighbor, or friend. Ask God to make clear your Great-Commission role, and be willing to break free from your comfort zone if needed. God may not ask for your presence in a faraway land, but He may want you to pray for someone or give financially.

God, please show me my role in the Great Commission. I am willing to break free from my comfort zone to touch the lives of others.

A Bowl of Hot Soup

SCRIPTURE READING: James 2:14–20

KEY VERSE: James 2:20

But do you want to know, O foolish man, that faith without works is dead?

While believers realize good works do not bring salvation, we all sometimes act as if we don't realize salvation should bring good works. You were saved by grace through Christ's sacrifice on the Cross. You didn't work for it and could not have earned it if you tried. However, you can offer expressions of gratitude to God with your conduct and character. Scholar Warren Wiersbe shares a wonderful example:

A pastor friend told about a Christian lady who often visited a retirement home near her house. One day she noticed a lonely man sitting, staring at his dinner tray. In a kindly manner she asked, "Is something wrong?"

"Is something wrong!" replied the man in a heavy accent. "Yes, something is wrong! I am a Jew, and I cannot eat this food!"

"What would you like to have?" she asked.

"I would like a bowl of hot soup!"

She went home and prepared the soup and, after getting permission from the office, took it to the man. In succeeding weeks, she often visited him and brought him the kind of food he enjoyed and eventually she led him to faith in Christ. Yes, preparing soup can be a spiritual sacrifice, a good work to the glory of God.

Good works often leave someone indebted enough to lend you his ears.

Lord, show me ways to do good to those in need around me.

The Greatest Opportunity

SCRIPTURE READING: Acts 9:1–31
KEY VERSE: Acts 9:15

*But the Lord said to him, "Go, for he is a chosen vessel of Mine to bear
My name before Gentiles, kings, and the children of Israel . . . "*

God knows exactly when a person is open to receiving the gospel message.
Most of us are familiar with the artwork that shows Jesus at the door of
a cottage knocking. A closer look at the painting reveals that there is no door
handle on the outside where Jesus is standing. It is our responsibility to open
the door from the inside once we hear His knock on the door of our hearts.

The apostle Paul studied under one of the greatest theologians of his time.
Yet all he learned was based on tradition and the Law of Moses. Saul (Paul) was
completely unaware of God's plan to save mankind by grace and not works.
Up until his Damascus road experience, Paul had not heard the gospel message with his heart.

Alongside the Roman roadway, Paul came in contact with the risen Lord
and gave his life to the Savior. Jesus calls to each of us, but He will not press
us. Many think they can wait until another time to receive Jesus as their Savior,
but only God knows if we will be given another opportunity.

While God loves all men and women, He has placed a serious stipulation
on who will be with Him in heaven. Only those who profess Jesus Christ as
their Savior will stand before His throne in eternity.

And just think: God has given you the great opportunity to guide others
to receive Him and receive eternal life.

Thank You for the opportunity to guide others to receive You.

Discovering Your Life Message

SCRIPTURE READING: Psalm 119:1–8

KEY VERSE: Psalm 119:57

You are my portion, O LORD;
I have said that I would keep Your words.

God builds a life message in a variety of ways. Never seek to have the same message that another believer has. Though you may gain many insightful lessons from those who are strong in their faith, your life is unique and special before God. He has a message for you that no one else can share.

That is why it is imperative to ask Him to give you a love for His Word. Studying His Word and committing yourself to prayer are sure ways to learn more about Him and develop spiritually. In times of meditation and worship, He reveals His desire and will in a mighty way. Nothing can so train you for life like the time you spend alone with Jesus.

This is where He can motivate you toward certain goals and aspirations. Many people long to know God's will for their lives. They feel as though they do not have a life message, but God has one for them. The heavenly Father doesn't overlook anyone.

The key to discovering your life message is spending time alone with Him. Doing this takes real discipline and determination. Realize there remains a battle for your thoughts, and the enemy to your soul is continually seeking to throw you off and discourage you. Stay on course, and you will soon have an effective life message to share with others.

Father, keep me on course with Your will and Your Word. Give me a life message that will touch the lives of others.

The Mystery of Salvation

SCRIPTURE READING: Ephesians 3:1–10
KEY VERSE: Ephesians 3:10

To the intent that now the manifold wisdom of God might be made known by the church to the principalities and powers in the heavenly places . . .

A major point in church history came as the result of Paul's letter to the Ephesians in which he wrote of "the mystery" of salvation. In New Testament times, a mystery was not something eerie or evil. It was a spiritual truth that God had hidden until the proper time of revelation.

The mystery Paul mentioned is the salvation of Gentile believers through faith in Jesus Christ. Until that point, salvation had been viewed as being given first to the Jews and then only to Gentiles who yielded themselves to the Mosaic Law.

However, Christ's death on Calvary's Cross changed this. No longer was there a social or an ethical status to be reached. Jesus' death was sufficient payment for our sins. The only requirement for the Gentiles and Jews was faith in Christ. That was, and is today, salvation's only stipulation.

Faith in Jesus Christ is the only way to know and experience the fullness of God. We become heirs to His kingdom the moment we give our lives to Christ. There are many who need to know the personal reality of God's love. Become a beacon of His truth by asking Him to bring those across your path who are in need of a Savior.

Dear heavenly Father, make me a beacon of Your truth. Bring those across my path who are in need of a Savior.

How to Treat Unbelievers

SCRIPTURE READING: Colossians 4:5–6
KEY VERSE: Matthew 5:16

Let your light so shine before men, that they may see your good works and glorify your Father in heaven.

Many people have become Christians due to the influence of a Christian friend or coworker. If you ask them what was the predominant characteristic of the individual who attracted them to Christ, most would allude to a keen, unworldly sense of love and acceptance.

Treating the unbeliever in a biblical fashion is not an easy chore for some Christians. We operate on such different standards and think on such contrasting wavelengths that compatibility can be quite difficult. Despite such differences, God often uses ordinary Christians as His instruments to proclaim the gospel of Christ.

The non-Christian is just like you before you were saved, dead in sin and separated from God. The love of God can be clearly communicated to the unbeliever through upright conduct, positive conversation, and a servant spirit.

Don't judge those around you who are not Christians. Focus instead on releasing the love of Christ through your daily lifestyle.

Everybody needs the Lord—even people who seemingly resist all overtures. The love and grace of God expressed through your words and deeds can be amazingly used by Him in a most wonderful way.

Lord, help me to express Your love and grace through kind words and deeds today.

Sharing God's Love

SCRIPTURE READING: 2 Timothy 2
KEY VERSE: 2 Timothy 2:15

Be diligent to present yourself approved to God, a worker who does not need to be ashamed, rightly dividing the word of truth.

*N*ever choose to be a worker for God," advises Oswald Chambers, "but when once God has put His call on you, woe be to you if you turn to the right hand or to the left. We are not here to work for God because we have chosen to do so, but because God has apprehended us."

What has God apprehended you to do? Perhaps you are a schoolteacher, a construction worker, a builder, or a professional working in a city with a large corporation. No one else can do what He has given you to do.

His call to you is the same call He gave the early church: Share the love and forgiveness of Jesus Christ with a lost and dying world. This is the truth you received, and it is the same truth that countless individuals are longing to hear.

Ask Him to make you sensitive to the needs of others. Many times, people do not know how to share the hurts hidden deep within their hearts. Only God's love can draw these hurts to the surface where healing can take place.

Jesus met people at the point of their greatest need, and He wants you to do the same. Be willing to go to those who are friendless, lonely, hurting, and in need of compassion and a listening heart. This is His call to each of us: "Share My love, My forgiveness, and My grace so that others will know the love of My Father."

Father, help me to share Your love, Your forgiveness, and Your grace so that others will come to know Your love.

Praying for the Lost

SCRIPTURE READING: Acts 24:10–27
KEY VERSE: Acts 24:25

Now as he reasoned about righteousness, self-control, and the judgment to come, Felix was afraid and answered, "Go away for now; when I have a convenient time I will call for you."

In Acts 24, Paul stood before Felix with a clear conscience. He had professed the gospel message without violating the moral and judicial laws of his day. Yet he was arrested and accused of stirring up dissension and being "a ringleader of the sect of the Nazarenes" (v. 5). Knowing Paul's citizenship rights, the governor had little recourse except to be lenient in his judgment of the apostle.

God is creative in His approach to mankind's need for salvation. Paul did not compromise his convictions; he preached the gospel of Christ openly in the temple and later under house arrest to the guards who were chained to his side. Sensitivity to the leading of the Holy Spirit achieves far more in the area of witnessing than we ever could accomplish in our own strength.

As a result of Paul's obedience to Christ and then to the authorities over him, Felix began visiting Paul and inquiring about the Way (terminology used by early Christians to describe their life in Christ). Although it appears that Felix never accepted Jesus as his Savior, he was given a divine opportunity to do so through the testimony of the apostle Paul. What a privilege it is to witness to and pray for our government officials. Even though they have tremendous authority, they are not above God in their decisions; they need your prayers.

Father, I thank You for the opportunity to witness to and pray for government officials.

Sharing Hope in Hard Times

SCRIPTURE READING: Philippians 1:19–24
KEY VERSE: Philippians 1:20

According to my earnest expectation and hope that in nothing I shall be ashamed, but that with all boldness, as always, so now also Christ will be magnified in my body, whether by life or by death.

Upon entering a city, Paul immediately went into the local temple, synagogue, or meeting place to present the gospel message to the Jews. However, his words were often met with anger and rejection. But God did not allow Paul to suffer disgrace.

He had given the Jewish people a promise: He would send the Messiah to them for their redemption. Over the years their hearts had hardened. In piety they worshiped God but refused His offer of redemption. Going through the motions of worship cannot save anyone.

Israel missed God's greatest gift of love when they rejected the Lord Jesus Christ. The years they spent in suffering were meant to draw them closer to God. Yet even this bitter fate did not move them to heartfelt worship.

When you live above the hardness of your circumstances as Paul did, God will protect and keep you. He will also preserve the message of hope He has commanded you to take to a lost and dying world. Don't let others' criticism keep you from obeying God. When you feel discouraged, go to Him. Ask Him to plant Scripture in your heart, so you may experience His hope in desperate times and share that hope with others.

Lord, use me for Your kingdom purposes. Plant Your Word in my heart so I can share hope with others.

Willing to Go

These things I have written to you who believe in the name of the Son of God, that you may know that you have eternal life, and that you may continue to believe in the name of the Son of God.

In her book, *Tramp for the Lord,* Corrie Ten Boom writes of a time when God called her to go beyond what seemed humanly reasonable. She had just finished speaking at a church in Denmark when two nurses approached her and asked her to go to their apartment for tea. When she arrived at the apartment, she realized she would have to walk up ten flights of stairs to get to her destination:

> "Oh Lord, I do not think I can make it." But the nurses wanted me to come up so badly that I consented to try . . .
>
> We finally reached the apartment . . . I knew that a blessing of some kind was waiting for us . . . I opened the Bible and pointed out the verses about salvation. A mother of one of the nurses listened intently . . . I prayed, then the two nurses prayed and finally the mother folded her hands and said, "Lord Jesus, I know already much about You. I have read much in the Bible, but now I pray You to come into my heart . . . Make me a child of God. Amen."

Corrie turned and looked at one nurse's father, and he, too, expressed a desire to accept Jesus as his Savior. Corrie writes, "Suddenly the room was filled with great rejoicing and I realized the angels had come down and were standing around, singing praises unto God."

Are you willing to go wherever God calls you to go? His blessings wait for you there.

Lord, forgive me for the times I fail You. Make me willing to go anywhere at Your command.

The Quilt

SCRIPTURE READING: 1 Peter 4:7–10
KEY VERSE: Colossians 3:17

And whatever you do in word or deed, do all in the name of the Lord Jesus, giving thanks to God the Father through Him.

Not only do you possess spiritual gifts, but you also have innate abilities that God transforms for use according to His purposes when you let Him do so. No matter who you are—old, young, rich, poor, or somewhere in between—God wants to use you to bless the lives of others.

In his book, *The Quilt,* T. Davis Bunn tells the fictional story of an elderly grandmother named Mary, who invests her life and energies into enriching those around her for the Lord. Now she is very old, with hands twisted by arthritis. Even though she is ready to be with the Lord anytime He calls her, she cannot shake the burning feeling that God wants her to do one more thing.

When she shares with her family and friends that she feels this last big work should be the making of a giant quilt, they are incredulous. How can a woman her age with useless hands do such a thing? Then Mary unfolds her real plan. She would oversee the making of the quilt and provide the pattern and materials. Any lady who wanted to help could come to her home and quietly assist, but everyone had to promise one thing: With every stitch she had to say a prayer of thanksgiving.

There was no way to measure the spiritual transformations in the lives of these women. The quilt became a living testimony of God at work.

Dear Lord, use me to bless the lives of others through my spiritual gifts and abilities.

Always Ready to Answer

SCRIPTURE READING: 1 Peter 3:13–18
KEY VERSE: 1 Peter 3:15

But sanctify the Lord God in your hearts, and always be ready to give a defense to everyone who asks you a reason for the hope that is in you, with meekness and fear.

Mr. Doe really stood out at his company. When other coworkers were complaining, he quietly went about his business with a smile. He did not abuse company property or time, and he always had a moment to spare to listen to a problem or give encouragement. His team leader could always count on him to finish a task, and everyone could tell by the way he spoke on the phone to his family that he had excellent relationships at home.

That is why one day Mr. Smith walked into his office just before closing time and said, "You know, there's something about you that's different. It's not just how you do things; it's your attitude. You don't get your feathers ruffled. How do you keep it all under control?"

Mr. Doe asked Mr. Smith if he would like to have a quick dinner with him and hear his answer. Mr. Smith was so intrigued by this man that he said yes, and that night he was open to hearing whatever Mr. Doe had to say about spiritual matters.

That is the way God intends for us to operate as believers. "Always be prepared to give an answer to everyone who asks you to give the reason for the hope that you have" (1 Peter 3:15 NIV). You don't have to seek a listening ear. God will bring open ears to you as He leads, and He will give you the words to say under the guidance of the Holy Spirit.

Dear Lord, open the ears of those around me so I can share Your Word with them.

Salt of the World

SCRIPTURE READING: Matthew 5:13–16
KEY VERSE: Matthew 5:13

You are the salt of the earth; but if the salt loses its flavor, how shall it be seasoned? It is then good for nothing but to be thrown out and trampled under foot by men.

Many people on special diets need to limit or even eliminate their intake of salt. To compensate, they search for other ways to spice up their food, from sauces to herb mixes, because some things just taste too bland without it. Salt is used for flavor and as an excellent preservative; no wonder salt remains an important ingredient even today.

It is no surprise, then, that Jesus compared those who belong to Him with salt: "You are the salt of the earth; but if the salt has become tasteless, how can it be made salty again? It is no longer good for anything, except to be thrown out and trampled under foot by men" (v. 13 NASB).

You are to be the good, Christlike "flavor" in your world. Just as salt without any taste would be useless in its intended functions, so is a believer who refuses to yield his or her life to Christ. He does not lose his salvation, of course, but he does not keep his ability to flavor his world for the Lord.

Salt is also used as a healing agent. Have you ever exposed an open wound to salt water, in the ocean, for example? It hurts badly, but it usually feels and looks much better afterward. Very often when a believer demonstrates love to a nonbeliever, that love rubs into the open heart wound of the hurting person, causing initial pain. Over time, though, that exposure may bring healing in Jesus.

Dear heavenly Father, make me like salt in this world—a healing agent to those who are hurting.

Building Bridges to Others

SCRIPTURE READING: Matthew 25:31–46
KEY VERSE: Matthew 25:45

Then He will answer them, saying, "Assuredly, I say to you, inasmuch as you did not do it to one of the least of these, you did not do it to Me."

He invited a coworker to go backpacking with his church group. He knew the man wasn't saved, but that didn't matter. He was building a bridge of friendship. He knew once the relationship was established, God would provide an opportunity to share the gospel message.

She waited for God's timing before asking her neighbor to visit her church. For months the women had exchanged recipes and stories about their children. Even though the neighbor did not attend church regularly, she began to show interest in spiritual things. A year later she prayed to receive Christ as her Savior.

Many times God will allow you to tell of His saving grace immediately. Other times He may want you to wait before leading another down salvation's path. It's important to remember that God is in control of each situation. Waiting offers great opportunities for the construction of relational bridges by which His love and acceptance can travel.

Think of Jesus and the many ways He related to people. At one point the Pharisees tried to insult Him by calling Him a friend to tax collectors, but it didn't work. Matthew was a former tax collector and could testify to Jesus' love and acceptance of all.

Lord, help me to build bridges to others. Make me sensitive to Your timing.

A Vessel of Love

SCRIPTURE READING: 1 Timothy 2:1–8
KEY VERSE: 2 Timothy 4:2

Preach the word! Be ready in season and out of season. Convince, rebuke, exhort, with all longsuffering and teaching.

Paul's foremost desire was that all men and women would come to know Jesus Christ as Savior and Lord. From the first day he taught the truth of the gospel until his death in Rome, Paul was driven by one message: the salvation of the Cross. He was consumed by God's love, and he wanted others to experience it in a personal and abiding way.

Paul had a tremendous ability to communicate clearly across social, philosophical, and economic lines. He met people on their own turf and presented the gospel shamelessly. He was fearless in his approach to the gospel message because his own life had been radically changed. Once a persecutor of Christians, he became a missionary for Jesus Christ.

He wasn't repulsed by sinful men; he was drawn to them out of compassion, as Christ was to the people of His day. For Paul, each encounter was an opportunity to tell someone about Jesus Christ and the forgiveness that was his if only the person would believe in God's Son.

We live in a world besieged by sin and darkness where people lack identity and hope. Ask God to help you understand the desperate needs of our society and its people and to use you as a vessel of His love.

Dear God, please give me an understanding of the desperate needs of society, and then use me as a vessel of Your love.

The Light of Life

SCRIPTURE READING: John 1:1–13
KEY VERSE: Ephesians 5:8

For you were once darkness, but now you are light in the Lord. Walk as children of light . . .

Lamps were among the most valued possessions in Israelite homes. Light was a symbol of life, and a good lamp provided light for every household function. In fact, an Israelite woman checked her lamp all through the night, adding more oil or fixing the wick, to make sure the light stayed strong and sent the message "all is well."

Jesus wants our lives to be like a good lamp, sending out the daily signal that all is well in our relationship with Him. When people see you, they should see the light of Christ and give glory to God.

Can those around you see Jesus in the way you behave and the way you talk? Does your life communicate His positive truth, or do you send negative statements of criticism or discouragement? Do your actions make someone want to know more about your Lord?

Perhaps the statement your life is making right now is not what it should be. Maybe you are discouraged by inconsistency or feelings of inadequacy. Remember that Jesus gives you the strength and wisdom you need because He is the Light of life. God promises to continue building His truth into your life day by day so that your character and conduct reflect His distinguishing presence.

Lord, let others see Your light in me and give glory to You. Let my character and conduct reflect Your presence.

Sharing Your Story

SCRIPTURE READING: Acts 22:3–15
KEY VERSE: Acts 22:10

So I said, "What shall I do, Lord?" And the Lord said to me, "Arise and go into Damascus, and there you will be told all things which are appointed for you to do."

Do you remember what your life was like before you asked Jesus to be your Savior? You might have looked "good" on the outside, yet struggled with strong urges on the inside. How did you feel when the burden of all the guilt was lifted away? It was wonderful, wasn't it? That is your testimony.

A testimony is not just a superdramatic story told by someone who committed high-profile sins and then came to the Lord. This kind of conversion experience, like Paul's on the road to Damascus, may be the kind with which you are most familiar. You may even feel inferior or insecure about your story, secretly believing that it is not interesting enough.

Once you believe in the inefficacy of your story, you are more hesitant to tell it and could even come to question the validity of your salvation experience. What a sad condition. If only you could grasp that the grace that Jesus gave to you is the same grace He pours on all His people.

As an aid to remembering the tremendous work Christ has done and is continuing to do, make a list of transformations that you noticed in your heart and behavior. Then pause to give Him thanks for each one, and ask the Lord for an opportunity to share with someone who needs to hear exactly your story.

Lord, thank You for the changes You have made in my life. Give me the opportunity to share with someone who needs to hear my story.

Actions Speak Louder Than Words

SCRIPTURE READING: Psalm 19

KEY VERSE: Psalm 19:14

Let the words of my mouth and the meditation of my heart
Be acceptable in Your sight,
O LORD, my strength and my Redeemer.

If you could not speak a word, what would your life say to others? Would anyone know something is different about you, that you are a Christian?

We are constantly communicating something. The way we walk into a room tells a great deal about how we feel about ourselves. The way we listen to others communicates whether we are interested or bored.

Nonverbal communication is powerful. Jesus was and is an excellent nonverbal communicator, not just because He understood the heart of man, but because He took time to listen to the hurts and needs of those around Him. He touched people with His hands as well as His heart. He encouraged them with an eternal message of hope. Actions do speak louder than words.

Communicating God's forgiveness and love was the cornerstone of Christ's ministry on earth, and it is yours as well. The Great Commission has been given to each and every one of us.

You are called to be His messenger, encourager, and proclaimer. Maybe not all at once and maybe not to a foreign country, but certainly when the need arises, you are to share His love and forgiveness to a hurting and dying world. Therefore, pray that God's love will be the first and last thing others see in you.

Lord, may Your love be the first and last thing others see in me.

Let Your Light Shine

SCRIPTURE READING: Colossians 3:12–17
KEY VERSE: Colossians 3:12

Therefore, as the elect of God, holy and beloved, put on tender mercies, kindness, humbleness of mind, meekness, longsuffering . . .

Jesus told the people: "Let your light shine before men in such a way that they may see your good works, and glorify your Father who is in heaven" (Matt. 5:16 NASB).

Following this theme, Paul wrote, "Those who have been chosen of God, holy and beloved, put on a heart of compassion, kindness, humility, gentleness . . . " (Col. 3:12 NASB).

The "good works" we do in Christ never consist of worldly honors and material gains. On our own, we can never achieve the level of spirituality Christ spoke of. But thanks to His presence in us, this is attainable. We honor God by allowing the Holy Spirit to reflect Christ's life in us.

The Light of your life should be Jesus Christ. A heart of compassion, a look of kindness and true humility, or a gentle spirit cannot be forced. It is an overflow of the Holy Spirit's presence in the life of a believer.

Can we block His activity? Yes. Sin, legalism, complacency, and lack of repentance block God's work in and through us.

When God sees you, He sees the very core of your being. Allow Him to work through you to reveal His nature so that when people see you, they will see Jesus, and lives will be changed.

Dear God, work through me to reveal Your nature so that when people see me, they will see You.

A Living Message

SCRIPTURE READING: Philippians 1:1–6
KEY VERSE: Philippians 1:6

Being confident of this very thing, that He who has begun a good work in you will complete it until the day of Jesus Christ.

As the saying goes, "There is only one you." You are a living message for Christ in a one-of-a-kind way that no one else can duplicate. Message building is a lifelong process, and the Lord wants you to participate actively in developing His purpose for you in many ways:

Read and study the Scriptures. Time in God's Word is essential for growth. As you learn who God is and what He has done, He unfolds His truth in a personal way through the Holy Spirit and gives you wisdom and understanding for everyday life.

Realize God's ultimate goal. While His specific plans for you are custom made, His goal for every believer is the same—to conform us to the likeness of His Son—so your words and actions are reflections of Jesus' character.

Review God's pattern of operation. Ask, "How has He gotten my attention before? What is He teaching me in this present situation?" Read and study the many character portraits in the Scriptures.

Reach out to serve others. Meeting the needs of others and becoming involved in their lives challenge you to trust the Lord to provide the resources. Your faith will grow as He uses you to bless others.

Dear Lord Jesus, make me a living message of Your love.

NOVEMBER

A Divine Encounter in Times of Adversity

Cease Striving

SCRIPTURE READING: Psalm 46

KEY VERSES: Psalm 46:1–2

God is our refuge and strength, A very present help in trouble. Therefore we will not fear, Even though the earth be removed, And though the mountains be carried into the midst of the sea.

ome, behold the works of the LORD, Who has wrought desolations in the earth. He makes wars to cease to the end of the earth; He breaks the bow and cuts the spear in two; He burns the chariots with fire. 'Cease striving and know that I am God; I will be exalted among the nations, I will be exalted in the earth.' The LORD of hosts is with us; The God of Jacob is our stronghold" (Ps. 46:8–11 NASB).

The last thing you want to do in times of suffering and pain is to be still. Sometimes it feels better to keep moving, keep busy, do anything to distract your mind from thinking about the difficulty at hand. The pain does not really go away, but the thought of suffering more tempts you to keep postponing the inevitable process of dealing with hurt.

God's plan for getting through suffering is for you to "cease striving" and know that He is God. What does it mean to cease striving? It means to stop trying to find all the answers on your own. Coming to a quiet place of humility and awe before your Savior is essential to allowing Him to do His sovereign work in your circumstances.

Meditate silently on these verses: "God is our refuge and strength, A very present help in trouble. Therefore we will not fear, though the earth should change, And though the mountains slip into the heart of the sea" (Ps. 46:1–2 NASB).

Lord, help me to trust in You and cease striving in times of difficulty. Teach me to be still.

Time Will Tell

SCRIPTURE READING: Genesis 50:15–20

KEY VERSE: Genesis 50:20

As for you, you meant evil against me; but God meant it for good, in order to bring it about as it is this day, to save many people alive.

Joseph was forsaken and sold into Egyptian bondage by his brothers. Years before, God had given him a clear vision concerning his future without a hint of eventual imprisonment, heartache, and brokenness. Instead, the vision had spoken of prominence and great wealth for Joseph.

Years passed in an Egyptian prison. To many, it may have appeared that God had forgotten His promise, but Joseph didn't view it that way. He remained faithful and focused on the quality of his devotion to God and not the quantity of time spent in exile.

We never read where Joseph badgered God "to hurry up and do something." Instead, he invested the gifts God had given him by serving others and waiting patiently for God's blessing.

It may take years for time to tell all we have sown into life. However, the most important thing any of us will ever do is to remain faithful to Jesus Christ. That means being faithful when it is popular and when it is not, when it is easy and when it is difficult.

What will time tell about you? Will it tell of a person who followed the way of the Cross regardless of the cost?

Oh, Lord, let it be so! May You always find me to be faithful and true to Your Word!

When the Odds Are Against You

SCRIPTURE READING: Isaiah 61:1–7

KEY VERSE: Isaiah 61:3

To console those who mourn in Zion, to give them beauty for ashes, the oil of joy for mourning, the garment of praise for the spirit of heaviness; that they may be called trees of righteousness, the planting of the LORD, that He may be glorified.

For years God had given him a dream to start a school where men and women could be trained for Christian service. In 1907, he invested the culmination of his prayers and life savings into what had been a rambling old hotel overlooking a spring-fed lake in northeast Georgia.

With enrollment increasing, plans for expansion were underway. Then it happened—the test of faith. Cinders in one of the stone fireplaces found their way through the mortar and onto the aging wood. Within moments the two-story structure was ablaze, and within an hour the dream reduced to rubble.

The next day as he poked through the smoldering ashes, Dr. R. A. Forrest came upon what was left of his books. He later wrote, "I broke down and wept like a baby. Had I misunderstood God?" Suddenly God's Word broke through: "I will give you beauty for ashes" (Isa. 61:3). And He did. Today, Toccoa Falls College remains a testimony to God's promises.

When the odds are against you and everything around you shouts: "Give up! Quit! It'll never work!" remember, God is sovereign. He has a plan for your life, and He has promised to bring it to completion.

Lord, when the odds are against me, help me to remember that You have a plan for my life.

Spiritual Surgery

SCRIPTURE READING: 1 Peter 1:3–13
KEY VERSES: 1 Peter 1:6–7

In this you greatly rejoice, though now for a little while, if need be, you have been grieved by various trials, that the genuineness of your faith, being much more precious than gold that perishes, though it is tested by fire, may be found to praise, honor, and glory at the revelation of Jesus Christ.

Have you had a medical problem that required surgery? Undergoing an operation can be a painful process, from the preparations to the time in the recovery room. Sometimes you experience pain as the area is healing, and often you must go in for a visit to have stitches or other devices removed after a period of time.

What makes the procedure worthwhile, though, is the prospect of restored health and a properly functioning body. If you keep your focus on the outcome, you are better able to endure what comes along the way.

The same is true in the area of "spiritual surgery." God allows trouble or pain or suffering into your life for a season for His special reasons, and no one's situation is exactly the same. When you are experiencing negative times, it is imperative to keep the purposes described in 1 Peter 1:6–7 in mind.

Many theological phrases describe what occurs as you learn to rely on Christ through suffering, but the simplest way to put it is this: Trials build your faith.

Dear Lord, please build my faith in the midst of trials. Give me a faith that is more precious than gold, tested by fire, resulting in praise and glory to You.

Confronting Giants

SCRIPTURE READING: Hebrews 10:35–39
KEY VERSE: Numbers 13:30

Caleb quieted the people before Moses, and said, "Let us go up at once and take possession, for we are well able to overcome it."

In times of trouble the key to victory instead of defeat is perspective. In her book, *Streams in the Desert,* Mrs. Charles Cowman quotes an anonymous writer who has the right perspective on trials and difficulties:

> Yes, they saw the giants [in Numbers 13:33], but Caleb and Joshua saw God! . . . Giants stand for great difficulties; and giants are stalking everywhere. They are in our families, in our churches, in our social life, in our own hearts; and we must overcome them or they will eat us up, as these men of old said of the giants of Canaan . . .
>
> Now the fact is, unless we have the overcoming faith we shall be eaten up, consumed by the giants in our path. Let us have the spirit of faith that these men of faith had, and see God, and He will take care of the difficulties.

The nation of Israel did not face trouble when they were standing still or thinking of retreating. Only when they moved forward, trusting God, did they face the grimmest trials. Many times a sure sign that you are doing what God has called you to do is opposition. Satan and his workers have one goal in mind, and that is to keep you from being all that God has planned for you to become.

If you sense there is a spiritual battle brewing, go immediately to God in prayer. Tell Him all you are facing. Prayer is your strength, and His Word your greatest weapon.

Lord, I am facing battles today. Give me an overcoming, victorious faith.

Never Give Up

SCRIPTURE READING: Psalm 107:1–9

KEY VERSE: Romans 8:18

I consider that the sufferings of this present time are not worthy to be compared with the glory which shall be revealed in us.

When adversity hits suddenly or hangs in tenaciously, we can lose our spiritual bearings, leading to unwise thinking and behavior. We can act erratically, and our views of God can become warped. Whatever trouble you face for however long, recall these stabilizing biblical truths:

Never lose sight of God's goodness. Nothing can cause us to doubt God's goodness more than affliction. But God can use your problem for eventual good, although you cannot see how. Affirm God's goodness, and constantly remind yourself of His unceasing love and care.

Never give up. When the struggle wearies you to the point of giving up, give in to Christ and never to your circumstances. God promises to sustain you in your trials and either bring you through them or give you His all-sufficient grace to endure them. He will never fail or forsake you, and that is truth enough to persevere.

Never deny the power of God's promises. God's Word contains promises just for your situation. Ask the Holy Spirit to put a personalized scripture in your heart. He will do it, and you will find amazing strength and peace.

God is for you and on your side. You can handle adversity because He can.

Lord, You are so good! Thank You for Your unceasing love and care.

The Eyes of God

SCRIPTURE READING: Psalm 77
KEY VERSES: Romans 8:28–29

We know that all things work together for good to those who love God, to those who are the called according to His purpose. For whom He foreknew, He also predestined to be conformed to the image of His Son, that He might be the firstborn among many brethren.

All of us have heard sermons about how God causes the circumstances of life to work together for our good and His glory. But do you believe it? Can you say in the middle of disappointment that God is at work? Sometimes it is difficult. Sudden disaster or an unplanned event can leave you wondering why God allowed you to face such turmoil.

The only way to deal with pain is to view it through the eyes of God. Ask Him to help you view the circumstances of your life from His perspective. You may not see all things clearly. But know that the same Lord who saved you loves you with an everlasting love, and He will not abandon you or forsake His work in your life.

There is a point at which you must accept that you live in a fallen world. Sin is a part of the wretched conditions of our environment. The only thing that matters in times like these is your internal belief system.

You are a beloved child of God. If sorrow touches your life, God knows all about it. He hurts with you. Yet He is strong enough to take your pain and loneliness and produce something worthwhile out of them. He will use the abuse you have suffered to help you reach out to others who have been hurt and are struggling. He will take your pain and tragedy and use both to mold you into a loving, caring individual.

Father, please take my pain and tragedy, and use them to mold me into a loving, caring individual.

The Purpose of Adversity

SCRIPTURE READING: Psalm 57

KEY VERSE: 1 Corinthians 10:13

No temptation has overtaken you except such as is common to man; but God is faithful, who will not allow you to be tempted beyond what you are able, but with the temptation will also make the way of escape, that you may be able to bear it.

God is involved in every area of your life. And while this may be easy to understand in joyful times, it is just as true in times of sorrow and heartache. God will never abandon you to the harsh forces of this world without some form of help and support.

In 1 Corinthians 10:13 (NASB), the apostle Paul told us: "No temptation has overtaken you but such as is common to man; and God is faithful, who will not allow you to be tempted beyond what you are able; but with the temptation will provide the way of escape also, that you will be able to endure it."

Let the Holy Spirit show you a deeper meaning of this word. Temptation can come in the form of a testing of your faith. It may involve something that suddenly appears and leaves you feeling helplessly overwhelmed. It may be adversity or suffering.

Often we cannot see the outcome of the testing of our faith. God stretches us in our relationships, jobs, and other areas to see if we will remain steadfast and true to Him and the others involved. Ultimately the outcome of our testing is tremendous blessing.

Is God in everything? The answer is a hearty yes! He does not cause the pain you feel or the disappointment you experience, but He promises to use each one for your good and His glory. Therefore, you can trust Him in times of rain, wind, and sunshine.

I trust You, Lord, in times of rain, wind, and sunshine.

When Hardships Come

SCRIPTURE READING: Psalm 138
KEY VERSES: Romans 8:38–39

I am persuaded that neither death nor life, nor angels nor principalities nor powers, nor things present nor things to come, nor height nor depth, nor any other created thing, shall be able to separate us from the love of God which is in Christ Jesus our Lord.

Martin Luther composed the hymn, "A Mighty Fortress Is Our God," with the idea of providing comfort to people in deep distress. He based his hymn on Psalm 46 because of its convicting message of hope and trust in God's unfailing ability.

Persecution of certain Christians was increasing, especially as some questioned the tenets of the Catholic Church in Germany during the 1500s. The suffering believers knew that Jesus was their Savior, but sought assurance and confidence as they faced growing hardships.

"The Spirit and the gifts are ours, through Him who with us sideth," Luther wrote. "Let goods and kindred go, this mortal life also; the body they may kill. God's truth abideth still; His kingdom is forever."

The Lord is your sure defense against every assault of doubt, fear, pain, loss, and rejection. When you belong to Jesus, you are protected in every way. Though hardship comes, nothing can change His love for you. Nothing can alter the plans He has laid out for you since the beginning of time.

Lord, help me realize that neither death, nor life, nor angels, nor principalities, nor things present, nor things to come will separate me from Your love.

In Times of Trouble

SCRIPTURE READING: Daniel 10:1–12
KEY VERSE: Daniel 10:12

He said to me, "Do not fear, Daniel, for from the first day that you set your heart to understand, and to humble yourself before your God, your words were heard; and I have come because of your words."

Daniel was in a difficult spot. He had received a troubling vision from God and did not know how to handle it. Finally after his human strength was gone, God's message came to him: "Do not be afraid, Daniel, for from the first day that you set your heart on understanding this and on humbling yourself before your God, your words were heard" (Dan. 10:12 NASB).

Scripture does not tell us that God acknowledged Daniel's prayer the first time he prayed. God used the time Daniel spent waiting for an answer to humble His servant and prepare Daniel's heart for God's message.

When trouble comes, our words may take on a serious tone but fade to complacency. God waits for us to get serious about His will in our lives.

There is always a lesson involved when trouble comes. In Daniel's case, God was waiting for Daniel to set his heart on God and humble himself before the Lord. Daniel was a godly prophet; yet he, like us, needed to stoke the fire of passion for God in his heart.

Adversity is a sure way for God to get your attention. He will not abandon you to hardship, but He certainly uses it to turn you back and draw you closer to Himself.

What prayer have you asked God to answer? Have you prayed casually, or have you humbled yourself before the Lord? God will answer you when you pray with a humble heart.

Lord, I humble myself before You. Please hear my prayer.

A Chance to Die

SCRIPTURE READING: Romans 5:3–5

KEY VERSE: Romans 5:3

And not only that, but we also glory in tribulations, knowing that tribulation produces perseverance.

*I*n *Living Free in Christ,* Neil Anderson writes of where our hope lies:

God does not promise to make a bad thing good, nor has He assured us that He will keep us from bad things. He has promised us that in all things—even those that are terrible—good can come out of it for all those who love Him.

In Romans 8:26–28, Paul is completing the thought he originally began in Romans 5:3–5, "And not only this, but we also exult in our tribulations, knowing that tribulation brings about perseverance; and perseverance, proven character; and proven character, hope; and hope does not disappoint, because the love of God has been poured out within our hearts through the Holy Spirit who was given to us."

In verse 3, "exult" means heightened joy; "tribulation" means to be under pressure; "perseverance" means to remain under pressure . . . God is simply trying to show us that in the midst of trials and tribulations, He intends to produce the result of proven character, and that is where our hope lies.

After overhearing a hurtful remark said about her, Amy Carmichael asked God to show her how to handle the situation. His response: "See in this a chance to die to self." Letting go of a hurtful situation may be hard, but God will handle your hurt. Submit your needs to Him, and He will surround you with His peace.

Dear heavenly Father, help me view problems as a chance to die to myself. I submit my needs to You. Help me let go of the hurt.

More Than a Conqueror

SCRIPTURE READING: Psalm 91

KEY VERSE: Psalm 91:15

He shall call upon Me, and I will answer him;
I will be with him in trouble;
I will deliver him and honor him.

Oswald Chambers wrote of God's promises:

God does not keep His child immune from trouble; He promises, "I will be with him in trouble" (Ps. 91:15). It doesn't matter how real or intense the adversities may be; nothing can ever separate him from his relationship to God. "In all these things we are more than conquerors" (Rom. 8:37).

Paul was not referring here to imaginary things, but to things that are dangerously real. And he said we are "super-victors" in the midst of them, not because of our own ingenuity, not because of our courage, but because none of them affects our essential relationship with God in Jesus Christ. I feel sorry for the Christian who doesn't have something in the circumstances of his life that he wishes was not there . . .

Tribulation is never a grand, highly welcomed event; but whatever it may be—whether exhausting, irritating, or simply causing some weakness—it is not able to "separate us from the love of Christ." Never allow tribulations or the "cares of this world" to separate you from remembering that God loves you.

Either Jesus Christ is a deceiver, having deceived even Paul, or else some extraordinary thing happens to someone who holds on to the love of God when the odds are totally against him . . . Only one thing can account for it—the love of God in Christ Jesus.

Father, I am so glad that You are with me in trouble and that through You I am more than a conqueror.

Read the Fine Print

SCRIPTURE READING: Matthew 18:11–14

KEY VERSE: Luke 19:10

The Son of Man has come to seek and to save that which was lost.

Sometimes the reason God allows adversity in your life is to deal with sin. He wants to get your attention focused only on Him and away from the transgression that besets your walk with Him. God can see the future consequences of present sin, and in His love He will send the winds of adversity to keep you from the harm that sustained sin brings.

God hates evil. Satan hates you. That is why the enemy will not share with you the ramifications of sin. He wants to keep your mind focused on enjoying the moment: Forget about tomorrow; everybody else is doing this today.

You've seen the fine print on advertisements that tout some marvelous product. The colorful adjectives atop the page describe how wonderful the product is, but the fine print below is a cold, hard recitation of the personal or financial realities of buying the hype and the product. That which is superficial and temporary most often is shouted loudest, but the truth is always the bottom line.

Satan never wants you to read the fine print. His objective is to destroy you. Jesus said He came not to destroy but to save that which is lost. He may allow adversity in your life, but ultimately it will be to your benefit if you respond properly and adhere to His Word, the finest print there is.

Let me realize that adversity will benefit me if I respond properly to it. Help me to do that, Lord.

Abandoned to Christ

SCRIPTURE READING: Galatians 2:17–21
KEY VERSE: Lamentations 3:33

For He does not afflict willingly, nor grieve the children of men.

Author Patrick Morley reminds us that God does not bring affliction upon us willingly:

He finds no pleasure in our pain. God is not the root cause of our problems; He is the solution. The reason for many of our afflictions is our disobedience to the will of God—doing our own thing, living by the desires of the sinful nature. The sinful nature leads us into good ideas that are not God ideas. One good idea leads to another, and before long we have wandered away from the Lord . . .

Because our personal relationship with Him is God's highest priority, He invariably afflicts the life of the one who strays. But He never does this willingly or with enjoyment . . . His Spirit grieves when we wander, and when He afflicts us sorrow pierces the heart of God . . .

The normal believer's expectation is that he can live twenty years pursuing the God he wanted, turn to the God who is, and twenty minutes later all the issues will be resolved. That is not how God works.

God's business is to sanctify our lives of every alien thought. When we begin to bring thoughts captive to make them obedient to Christ, we discover that deprogramming from the secular life view takes as long as the programming did. It takes as long to abandon to Christ as it did to abandon from Christ.

Father, You are the solution to my problems. I abandon myself to You.

God's Choice Tool

SCRIPTURE READING: Psalm 18:29–30
KEY VERSES: Philippians 2:7–8

But made Himself of no reputation, taking the form of a servant, and coming in the likeness of men. And being found in appearance as a man, He humbled Himself and became obedient to the point of death, even the death of the cross.

In his book *Making Sense Out of Suffering*, Peter Kreeft comments on adversity:

The most oft-repeated teaching of Jesus is the paradox that the poor are rich, the weak are strong, the lowly are exalted. It is the point of the Beatitudes, of the Sermon on the Mount, of most of His parables; it is illustrated by His whole life, by the incarnation, the kenosis, the emptying. He "emptied himself," taking the form of a servant, being born in the likeness of men. "And being found in human form He humbled himself and became obedient unto death, even death on a cross" (Phil. 2:7–8).

This is the radical counter to the wisdom of our age, of any age. The fundamental dictum of nearly all modern psychologists is to love ourselves, to accept ourselves as we are, to feel good about ourselves. When we obey this wisdom of the world, God has two choices. He can either let us stay in that state and run the risk of becoming contented, respectable, self-righteous Pharisees; or else He can mercifully slap us out of it with a dose of suffering, frustration, and discontentment with ourselves, and thus move us on to a new state . . .

Only when we are dissatisfied, only when we are weak, only when we are failures in ourselves, can God come in.

Adversity is God's choice tool in molding you into a person of tremendous potential. Even in difficult times, He is at work.

Lord, help me realize that even in difficult times, You have not abandoned me. You are at work.

Shattered Dreams

SCRIPTURE READING: Psalm 121

KEY VERSE: Job 13:15

Though He slay me, yet will I trust Him.
Even so, I will defend my own ways before Him.

Anne Bradstreet, the greatest female poet of colonial America, was a busy wife and mother. Yet in the middle of unrelenting duty and hardships, she poured out the passions of her heart in poetry that is still admired today.

On the night of July 10, 1666, she was awakened by terrible cries: "Fire! Fire!" After she and her family made their way to safety, she stood outside and watched the fast-moving flames consume everything they owned. The next morning she picked over the smoking ruins, finding the remains of keepsakes. Suddenly she was overcome with emotion and wept over the thought of the joys that were lost.

In her poem "Upon the Burning of Our House" notice what she comes to as she works through the pain of traumatic loss: "And did thy wealth on earth abide? Didst fix thy hope on smold'ring dust? . . . Thou hast an house on high erect, framed by the mighty Architect . . . There's wealth enough; I need no more; farewell my pelf, farewell my store. The world no longer let me love; my hope and treasure lies above."

Even though tragedy had struck, God was taking care of Anne and her family. She also knew He would provide for the future. Do you have this same assurance? God waits for you to bring your shattered dreams to Him. And as you do, He touches your life with restoration and hope.

Here are my shattered dreams, Lord. Touch me with restoration and hope.

The Goodness of God

SCRIPTURE READING: Psalm 30
KEY VERSE: Psalm 30:1

I will extol You, O LORD, for You have lifted me up, And have not let my foes rejoice over me.

Sometimes God hides His goodness from us. He is not cynical or a hard taskmaster, but He wants to teach us to trust Him even when there is little evidence of His presence.

Perhaps you had hoped to purchase a new home, move to another location, buy a new car, or receive a promotion. Just when you thought God was opening a door of opportunity, He led you instead into a time of waiting.

You may not see His goodness as an immediate provision that you can touch, but it is there just the same. One of the most rewarding moments comes when God pours out His blessing on your life as a result of your faithfulness.

When you cling to the love and trust you have in Him, times of darkness lose their strength. Your faith holds because it is based on truth and not what you see or feel. You don't have to live on your emotions, which can lie and deceive. Instead you live by the timeless, unchanging Word of God.

There's one way to true victory, and that is through faith and trust in Jesus Christ, not just for your salvation but for every moment of every day. Therefore, when you go through dark times, trust Him to make the way clear to you. You can expect His light to fall across your path (Ps. 119:105). His goodness is available and awaits all who walk the road of faith.

Lord, make the way clear to me in dark times. Let Your light fall across my pathway as I continue to walk the road of faith.

Stressful Times

SCRIPTURE READING: Matthew 7:25–34
KEY VERSE: John 14:27

*Peace I leave with you, My peace I give to you; not as the world gives do
I give to you. Let not your heart be troubled, neither let it be afraid.*

Each of us knows the pressure that comes from stressful times. Headaches, tight neck muscles, and even bouts of depression can come from too much external pressure and not enough peace within. There are those who right now are weathering a severe emotional storm. They feel forgotten, overlooked, and rejected. Others are struggling with going on after the death of a loved one. How do we find peace when all that surrounds us seems so dark and lonely?

Some who read these words are fighting feelings of guilt for struggling emotionally. After all, aren't Christians supposed to be strong and confident? What will people think if they see you are weak and frail? For the Christian, this is the best place to be—helpless before the Lord.

Stress can drain away your strength and joy, but God has a solution. He is your peace and strength. And when you call out to Him, He answers you. He will never refuse you. The dark trials of life are not the end but a rich opportunity for Him to prove Himself to you. If you have lost a loved one, He will comfort you. If you are struggling with a long-term illness, God will be your strength. He has healing in His hands.

Let Him take your trouble and use it to draw you closer to Him, where you can find hope and eternal peace.

Father, take my trouble, and use it to draw me closer to You, where I can find hope and eternal peace.

Keep Moving

SCRIPTURE READING: Psalm 139:11–17
KEY VERSE: Psalm 139:12

The darkness shall not hide from You,
But the night shines as the day;
The darkness and the light are both alike to You.

A deep sense of darkness and emotional fear surrounded the disciples after Jesus was crucified. That was evidenced in the lives of two disciples from Emmaus. On their way home after the Crucifixion, both talked of the sorrow and loss they felt (Luke 24:13–31). Suddenly Jesus joined their journey, but neither recognized Him. They had spent hours listening to Him teach God's Word, and yet they did not know who He was! Instead, their minds were filled with thoughts of tragedy and unrest. They had hoped that Jesus was the Messiah, but their dreams appeared shattered.

How does hopelessness get such a stronghold in our lives? For one, we become accustomed to looking for God in the sunlight. We practice seeing Him only in times of victory and peace.

But no amount of darkness can hide you from God. When you face times of darkness, pray, "Lord, remove any blinders from my eyes so that I may see Your goodness even in this season of darkness." You may think there is no way for Him to encourage you, but He always finds a way. You may have just suffered a tremendous loss. As it was with the Emmaus disciples, tragedy can cloud your eyes as well as your thinking.

But God knows the hurt you feel. Therefore, keep moving toward Him. You may be able to take only small steps, but know that He waits for you with open arms.

Lord, I am moving toward Your open arms of love. Heal my hurt.

Trusting God's Outcome

SCRIPTURE READING: Psalm 92:1–5

KEY VERSE: 1 Thessalonians 5:18

In everything give thanks; for this is the will of God in Christ Jesus for you.

One of the most difficult challenges of the Christian walk is to maintain a genuinely grateful heart in the midst of travail. It can seem almost impossible to see any positive aspect, much less find reason to give thanks, when sickness, divorce, drug abuse, or any other trial has touched your life.

But we learn from 1 Thessalonians 5:18 that it is the will of God that we give thanks in everything. How are we supposed to be thankful when we ache? First we must remember that God is in control. He knows all and has power over all. He has allowed adversity in your life for a reason, and ultimately His promise says that the reason will be for your benefit (Rom. 8:28).

Today's reading begins with Psalm 92:1. Notice the next verse: It is good "to declare Thy lovingkindness in the morning, and Thy faithfulness by night" (v. 2 NASB). It is a biblical model to pray in the morning, gratefully seeking God's guidance and protection for your day, and to pray at night, gratefully thanking Him for what He has done.

When He allows hardship in your life and you thank Him for His purposes, though you lack complete understanding, you're telling God that you trust His outcome. Then gratitude and attitude are inextricably intertwined.

Dear heavenly Father, give me an attitude of gratitude. I trust You for the outcome in the midst of trouble.

No Fear

SCRIPTURE READING: Matthew 14:22–32
KEY VERSE: Mark 11:22

Jesus answered and said to them, "Have faith in God."

There is a catchy song that speaks of one being brave and courageous, but then collapsing in fear. Peter faced that scenario when he stepped out of the boat and began walking on water to Jesus.

For a moment, he had "spirit" legs. His eyes were set on Christ, and nothing had the power to stop him. Suddenly he caught sight of the brooding, angry sea around him, and down he went in fear. We might be tempted to think it was a shame that on one of his first attempts at being like Christ, he sank in terrible defeat, but God had a lesson in mind for His eager disciple.

Principle one: Keep your focus on Jesus. Had Peter refused to consider the natural elements surrounding him, he would have made spiritual history.

Principle two: Obey God. Jesus told Peter, "Come to Me." Whenever God gives you a directive, don't be swayed. Stay focused, and refuse to allow fear to entice you to stop or withdraw from what God has given as a mighty blessing.

Fear is a ruthless enemy. It is also one of Satan's favorite tools. Stand firm by putting it into subjection to Christ, who has all authority over this very thing. In the Old Testament God told Joshua, "Be strong and very courageous." God was with him, and he had no reason to fear.

The Lord is with you. Therefore, be courageous!

God, help me keep my focus on You. Help me to reject fear, and give me courage to obey You.

The Call of a Broken Heart

SCRIPTURE READING: 2 Chronicles 20:1–30
KEY VERSE: 2 Chronicles 20:12

O our God, will You not judge them? For we have no power against this great multitude that is coming against us; nor do we know what to do, but our eyes are upon You.

Perhaps you are facing a difficult time in your life. You have received news that seems overwhelming, and you don't know how to handle the situation. Many of God's greatest saints have faced times when they did not know if they could continue. More than once, they have cried out to God for help and deliverance.

Shattered by the sudden death of her husband, Catherine Marshall turned to God in a way she never had before:

Shivering, I rose to leave the room. I knew that this would be the last time on this earth that I would look upon my husband's face. So there in the hospital room, I said my last au revoir.

Now there was nothing to do but walk out. I sensed that out beyond the door, out beyond the chilly hospital corridor, a new life awaited me. That was the last thing in the world I wanted.

Two paces from the door, I was stopped as by an invisible hand. As I paused, a message was spoken with emphasis and clarity, not audibly, but with that peculiar authority I had come to recognize as the Lord's own voice: Surely, goodness and mercy shall follow you all the days of your life. It was God's personal pledge to me.

There are some things—no, many things—that are too difficult for us to handle on our own. God promises to hear the call of our broken hearts and come to us.

Father, please hear the call of my broken heart and come to me.

Strength That Is Strong

SCRIPTURE READING: 2 Corinthians 12:7–10
KEY VERSE: 2 Corinthians 12:9

He said to me, "My grace is sufficient for you, for My strength is made perfect in weakness." Therefore most gladly I will rather boast in my infirmities, that the power of Christ may rest upon me.

Often when we face something much greater than our capability to understand or deal with, we become anxious as we wonder how God will intervene. In such a time the apostle Paul discovered a wonderful sense of security in trusting God. Paul prayed three times for the Lord to remove what he called a "thorn in the flesh."

Paul then wrote, "Concerning this I entreated the Lord three times that it might depart from me. And He has said to me, 'My grace is sufficient for you, for power is perfected in weakness.' Most gladly, therefore, I will rather boast about my weaknesses, so that the power of Christ may dwell in me. Therefore I am well content with weaknesses, with insults, with distresses, with persecutions, with difficulties, for Christ's sake; for when I am weak, then I am strong" (2 Cor. 12:8–10 NASB).

Our human nature cries out in begging sobs for God to remove the suffering. Yet it is in times of trial that God endears Himself to us in ways that we would not typically experience. Pain, once it is brought into the throne room of God, commands His personal attention.

Paul's unwavering faith brought a new sense of strength to his life, one that he had never experienced before that moment. Strength that knows it is strong is really weakness. But weakness that cries out to God for help is strength far beyond human understanding.

Lord, give me strength that is strong in You, unwavering faith that surpasses human understanding.

Greater Things

I want you to know, brethren, that the things which happened to me have actually turned out for the furtherance of the gospel.

How many of us, when faced with a painful situation, could say: "I want you to know, brethren, that my circumstances have turned out for the greater progress of the gospel" (Phil. 1:12 NASB). Most of us hope we could say these words. However, if we are honest, we would admit that finding good in bad times is difficult.

The apostle Paul might not have been so quick to say this either. He was careful to say, "I want you to know . . . that my circumstances have turned out . . ." There is an underlying progression of thought indicating that Paul, just like you, had to work through hardships with the aid of the Holy Spirit.

We have no way of knowing how God will use the trials we face. We do, however, have His promise that He will take each trial and bring good out of it (Rom. 8:28). This good is not just for our benefit. God works so that our lives become living testimonies to His love, forgiveness, and truth.

When adversity strikes, do you say, "I can't believe she did this to me"? Or "God, why did You let this happen? Haven't I served You faithfully?" Words and thoughts like these are focused on self and not on the greater good that God brings to the forefront whenever your life is totally dedicated to Him. Today, when trials come, ask Him to show you the greater good He has in mind for you.

Heavenly Father, I confess that I need You—not just in times of trial but in everything.

Circumventing God's Will

SCRIPTURE READING: Philippians 4:10–13
KEY VERSE: Philippians 4:13

I can do all things through Christ who strengthens me.

You've probably heard the saying, "There's nothing that God and I together can't handle." It places a modern twist on one of the most famous verses in the Bible: "I can do all things through Christ who strengthens me." If your ambitions or efforts are within His will, you can be sure He will help you achieve them for His great glory. But there are famous examples of man's attempts to circumvent God's will only to meet disaster.

An account of one of man's most renowned failures became a popular movie: *Titanic*. During a period of peace and prosperity, man built the largest luxury ship in history. Symbolically beating their chests, some proclaimed that *Titanic* was so large and well built that not even God could sink it. In many people's self-aggrandizing minds, they saw no way such a massive trophy of human innovation could ever fail.

But on its very first voyage the *Titanic* made it only halfway to its destination. Its hull struck an iceberg so uneventfully that some passengers didn't even notice it. A gash in the hull allowed in water.

The ship sank in the North Atlantic, famous for some of the most treacherous waters on the globe. *Titanic's* survivors said that on the night man's great prize sank, the water was peaceful. Like a still, small pond.

Lord, without You I can do nothing. Keep my efforts within Your will, and help me achieve things for Your glory.

Safe Harbor

SCRIPTURE READING: Mark 6:45–52
KEY VERSE: Mark 6:50

They all saw Him and were troubled. And immediately He talked with them and said to them, "Be of good cheer! It is I; do not be afraid."

The disciples frantically wrestled with oars and sails as their little fishing boat was tossed about in angry waves. How did they get into this mess? The answer: Jesus had sent them there. What a sobering thought: At times, God leads us along ways that seem very dark and uncertain.

Suffering of any kind can push us beyond our ability to cope. The sudden death of a loved one brings shock. The news of a mate's unfaithfulness leaves us feeling numb. Our hearts seek comfort, our minds search for answers, and we cry out in anguish: "Why does God allow us to be tested in ways that bring heartache and suffering?" One of the reasons is to uncover the level of our faith in Him.

If you remember, Jesus came to the disciples amid the storm. He didn't come when the waves were calm or before the gentle night wind changed into a seething rage. No, He came during the fourth watch of the night when the sea was at its stormiest and all hope for survival appeared lost.

"Take courage; it is I, do not be afraid," were His words (Mark 6:50 NASB). Jesus had an object lesson in mind: He is Lord over all things, and nothing you are facing is too great for God. Regardless of your circumstances, God is with you. Never be afraid to call out to your Lord. He has His eye on you, and He will bring you into a safe harbor.

Lord, I am so thankful that You have Your eye on me and You will bring me into a safe harbor.

Take a Stand

SCRIPTURE READING: Ephesians 6:10–13

KEY VERSE: Ephesians 6:13

Take up the whole armor of God, that you may be able to withstand in the evil day, and having done all, to stand.

In *The Bible Exposition Commentary,* Warren Wiersbe writes,

Satan is a dangerous enemy. He is a serpent who can bite us when we least expect it. He is a destroyer (Rev. 12:11) . . . He has great power and intelligence, and a host of demons who assist him in his attacks against God's people (Eph. 6:11).

He is a formidable enemy; we must never joke about him, ignore him, or underestimate his ability. We must "be sober" and have our minds under control when it comes to our conflict with Satan . . . Because he is a subtle foe, we must "be vigilant" and always on guard. His strategy is to counterfeit whatever God does . . . The better we know God's Word, the keener our spiritual senses will be to detect Satan at work . . . This means that we take our stand on the Word of God and refuse to be moved. Ephesians 6:10–13 instructs us to "stand." Unless we stand, we cannot withstand. Our weapons are the Word of God and prayer (Eph. 6:17–18) and our protection is the complete armor . . . Just as David took his stand against Goliath and trusted in the name of Jehovah, so we take our stand against Satan in the victorious name of Jesus Christ.

Dear heavenly Father, help me to stand in victory and withstand Satan in times of adversity.

Faith's Fixed Focus

SCRIPTURE READING: Philippians 4:6–7
KEY VERSE: Mark 11:22

So Jesus answered and said to them, "Have faith in God.

The athletes who compete in the Olympics are extremely focused individuals. As much as they may enjoy the surrounding festivities and things to do, they have to retain their sharp mental edge. During practice sessions, they run through performances in their minds, continually rehearsing the principles and concepts of movement they have spent so much time absorbing.

They even have to block out the screaming of the enthusiastic spectators as their moments in the spotlight begin. Why? Losing focus can mean the death of their dream; any distraction can make them miss a step.

God calls you, as a believer, to the same intensity of focus in spiritual matters. In addition to renewing your mind in God's Word and training it to bring every thought captive to the obedience of Christ (2 Cor. 10:5), you are instructed to remain vigilant: "Be of sober spirit, be on the alert. Your adversary, the devil, prowls around like a roaring lion, seeking someone to devour" (1 Peter 5:8 NASB).

In other words, there is not a "safe" moment when you can drop your guard. That does not mean you must be overly watchful; you're also told not to be anxious about anything (Phil. 4:6–7). The Lord wants your full attention all the time. When your focus is fixed on Him, He will build your faith during the difficult times.

Dear Lord, fix my focus on You. Strengthen my faith during the difficult times.

What It Means to Trust

SCRIPTURE READING: John 1:1–4
KEY VERSE: John 12:46

I have come as a light into the world, that whoever believes in Me should not abide in darkness.

*H*ave you ever noticed how the men and women of the Bible were drawn to Jesus? Read the Gospels and you will find that Jesus changed lives in dramatic ways. Those who experienced loneliness discovered a sense of belonging. People whose lives were shattered by sin were given fresh hope and a reason to look forward to the future.

Jesus brings new life. He revolutionizes the darkened soul with His light and eternal truth. This light goes far beyond the point of salvation. When we live within the light of God, truth and hope illuminate every area of our lives.

Mary Magdalene experienced this very thing. The enemy had tormented her with a deep, spiritual darkness. Jesus set her free from a titanic bondage (Luke 8:2). Nothing is more powerful than the strength of God. We can imagine that Mary, like so many, was brought to Jesus for healing. The Savior had compassion on this poor soul and, in touching her, provided freedom and light to her life.

What does it mean to trust in Christ? For Mary, it was an opportunity to live again. For you, it may be the same. Perhaps the darkness of sin, depression, rebellion, or adversity has blinded you to the goodness of God's love and forgiveness. No problem or sin can separate you from Him. Ask Him to touch you, and He will. Accept His love, and receive the light of His eternal forgiveness.

Lord, touch me. Let the light of Your eternal forgiveness and hope shine in my darkest hour.

Victory Over Impossibilities

SCRIPTURE READING: Judges 7

KEY VERSE: Hebrews 12:2

Looking unto Jesus, the author and finisher of our faith, who for the joy that was set before Him endured the cross, despising the shame, and has sat down at the right hand of the throne of God.

The story of Gideon reveals six biblical truths that can lead to victory in impossible situations.

1. God uses difficulties to build our faith. He wants to strip us of our dependence on anything other than Him. We are to fix our focus on Christ, the Author and Perfecter of our faith (Heb. 12:2).

2. At times God may require the unreasonable. Gideon was allowed to take only three hundred men into battle with him, a fraction of the size of the enemy's army.

3. The Lord always leads us to do what will bring Him glory. Had Israel won the battle in their own strength, the credit would have gone to them and not to God.

4. God sends encouragement when we need it the most. He is sensitive to our weaknesses and knows the proper time to send help and an encouraging word.

5. The Lord always works behind the scenes on our behalf. The night before Gideon marched into battle, God instilled confusion in the hearts of the enemy. The enemy fled in fear.

6. God provides specific instructions for victory. If we will rely on Him, He will lead us through every trial we face, step-by-step, according to His plan for our lives.

Bring your foe before God. No enemy is too great for Him.

Oh, Lord, lead me step-by-step. Work behind the scenes in my behalf.

DECEMBER

A Divine Encounter with God's Plan for the Future

Looking Back

SCRIPTURE READING: Psalm 138
KEY VERSE: Psalm 138:3

In the day when I cried out, You answered me,
And made me bold with strength in my soul.

God is always your Comforter, and there is never a time when you are alone or abandoned. One of the names of Jesus is Comforter. When Jesus left this earth and returned to heaven, He sent the Holy Spirit to comfort us.

Have you ever stopped to consider, though, when you most appreciate God's role as Comforter? You are keenly aware of His gentle encouragement and refreshment after times of great personal pain or affliction. In fact, sometimes God allows you to go through such trials so that you will learn to seek His comfort.

In John Bunyan's book, *The Pilgrim's Progress*, the main character, Christian, realizes this truth after he has passed through the Valley of the Shadow of Death:

> But now the day was dawning. Viewing the eastern hills, Christian said to himself, "God has turned the shadows of death into the morning." Looking back over the way he had come, he wondered how the Lord had gotten him through.
>
> He remembered the verse: "He reveals the deep things of darkness and brings deep shadows into the light." He was deeply moved when he saw all the dangers from which he had been delivered . . . Now he could see his way, and he went on past them all, saying, "His candle shines on my head, and by His light I go through darkness."

God knows the way through the trickiest and most discouraging circumstances. Then you have the joy of looking back on the path you have traveled during the past year and thanking Him for restoring you to safety and peace.

Lord, as I look back on the path I have traveled during this past year,
I thank You for my safety and peace. I am glad You know the way
through every circumstance.

After Death, What Then?

SCRIPTURE READING: Revelation 21:1–5
KEY VERSE: Hebrews 9:27

As it is appointed for men to die once, but after this the judgment.

He was born in a rural Southern community in 1890. He worked as a farmer and carpenter, living in a house that was without electricity or plumbing for many years. He suffered a stroke while plowing behind a mule. Partially paralyzed for several years, he died quietly in 1963. He is buried in a small cemetery in the far corner of a pasture.

Driving down a crowded interstate late at night, he nodded off. He would not awaken again. His car hit an embankment. At age seventeen, his dreams came to an abrupt end.

Death happens in many ways and at many ages, but it always happens. Is that the end for the farmer who never traveled more than a few miles from his home, for the teenager who never got his high-school diploma? Is it the somber conclusion of man?

Thankfully and wondrously no. Physical death is not final. Consciousness does not cease in the casket. But we won't have a second or third chance. We won't come back as a cantaloupe, a cow, or a comedian.

The Bible says we die once (Heb. 9:27). We will then live forever in heaven with God, or in hell away from God (Luke 16:19–26). Do you know where you will spend eternity?

Lord, thank You for assurance of my eternal destiny.

Your Heavenly Home

SCRIPTURE READING: 2 Corinthians 5:1–9
KEY VERSE: 2 Corinthians 5:6

We are always confident, knowing that while we are at home in the body we are absent from the Lord.

The feelings you have during a change in residence are many. You are excited about moving to your new home, but it's often hard to leave the old one with its memories and special places. And the physical process of moving can be burdensome as well. Boxes and tape are everywhere, and you don't know where things are. Also, it may be difficult to picture what life will be like in your new location.

Multiply those emotions many times over, and that's how many may feel about going to heaven. We know it's the marvelous place of eternal fellowship and worship the Lord has prepared for us, but we don't know exactly what it will be like.

We know that heaven will be perfect in every way, yet the familiar and everyday here on earth is all we can relate to, it seems. We have to embrace the future by faith and trust that what God has for us is best.

The apostle Paul had no hesitations about departing this world because, by faith, he understood the significance of our real heavenly home: "Therefore, being always of good courage, and knowing that while we are at home in the body we are absent from the Lord—for we walk by faith, not by sight—we are of good courage, I say, and prefer rather to be absent from the body and to be at home with the Lord" (2 Cor. 5:6–8 NASB).

Because Jesus left His home to come to earth in human form, we will someday leave this earth and go to our heavenly home.

Dear heavenly Father, thank You for the promise of my heavenly home. I can hardly wait to get there!

Receive Life

SCRIPTURE READING: 1 Corinthians 3:10–15
KEY VERSE: Revelation 22:12

Behold, I am coming quickly, and My reward is with Me, to give to every one according to his work.

The believer will live in heaven, the perfect glory and expression of a perfect God. He will live forever in the brightness, goodness, and purity of God his Father, his sins judged by God on the Cross (Isa. 53).

Those who reject Christ as Savior, who fail to receive His offer of forgiveness of sin, will live forever in hell—darkness, torment, pain—completely absent from the presence of God.

You did not get to earth on your own steam. Man was God's idea. Everyone has life because the Creator gives it. We have a spirit that is made alive by Christ or that is dead in sin and dead to God.

After physical death, the believer eventually will be judged for the purpose of rewards. God will reward him for his deeds and motives on earth. His salvation is not in question.

The unbeliever will also be judged by Christ after physical death. He will be judged for his sins. With no Advocate and no forgiveness, he will be sent away from God's presence forever.

Your eternal future can be decided today if you have not yet accepted Christ. Admit your sins, realize your alienation from God, believe in Christ's work on the Cross, and receive His everlasting life.

Thank You for life, Lord. I praise You that my future is assured.

Face-to-Face

SCRIPTURE READING: John 6:35–40

KEY VERSES: Philippians 3:20–21

Our citizenship is in heaven, from which we also eagerly wait for the Savior, the Lord Jesus Christ, who will transform our lowly body that it may be conformed to His glorious body, according to the working by which He is able even to subdue all things to Himself.

When Rajiv Gandhi was killed several years ago, his Hindu burial was described in this manner in an Associated Press article: "Gandhi's son, Rahul, was to perform the rites at the cremation ground along the Jamuma River, lighting the pyre and smashing the skull with a cudgel to release the soul of the departed."

All religions of the world, except Christianity, teach confusing, uncertain, and complex concepts of life and death. The Christian faith alone teaches, professes, and focuses on the surety of the believer's resurrection.

Because Jesus came to earth, died, and rose from the dead, proving His deity, you can be assured of your personal resurrection. The grave is not a dead end. Jesus Christ, the Son of God, was crucified for our sins and rose again from the tomb just as He promised.

When you die, your spirit is immediately with the Lord. When the Lord returns, our bodies will be joined with our spirits. It is clear we will have bodies like Christ's after His resurrection (Phil. 3:20–21).

The burial of a Christian is but a formality. He is already with the Savior, tasting the delights of heaven, seeing God face-to-face.

Dear Lord, I can hardly wait to see You face-to-face. Thank You for the hope of the resurrection.

The Good Things to Come

SCRIPTURE READING: 1 Thessalonians 4:13–18
KEY VERSE: 1 Thessalonians 4:16

The Lord Himself will descend from heaven with a shout, with the voice of an archangel, and with the trumpet of God. And the dead in Christ will rise first.

Did you know that when Jesus comes back, you'll get a new body? It's true; in a flash, in the "twinkling of an eye," you will receive a new body, a special and fresh creation of God (1 Cor. 15:52). If you're frustrated with physical problems right now, imagine the liberating feeling of a restored body.

Christian author and speaker Joni Eareckson Tada, paralyzed as a teen in a diving accident, talks about some of her physical and spiritual struggles in her book, *Heaven*. She explains how her suffering today prepares her heart all the more for that glorious day, the moment when she can look her Savior in the face.

Surprisingly, though, she doesn't want to forget her infirmities here:

I wish I could take my big old, tattered wheelchair to heaven. I would stand up in my new, strong, bright, beautiful, glorified body—brilliant and powerful and full of splendor—and I would point to the empty seat and say, "Lord, for decades I was paralyzed in that thing, but it showed me in a very small way what it must have felt like to be nailed to a cross. My limitations taught me about the limitations You endured." Then I might say, "The weaker I felt in this chair, the harder I leaned on You."

That's the right way to anticipate the good things that God has ahead for you, in this life and the life to come.

Dear Lord, I am really looking forward to all the things You have prepared for me in the future.

Your Eternal Security

SCRIPTURE READING: 1 John 5:10–15
KEY VERSE: Hebrews 7:25

He is also able to save to the uttermost those who come to God through Him, since He ever lives to make intercession for them.

Perhaps the most miserable people on earth are those who have trusted in Christ as Savior but battle harassing doubts concerning the assurance of their eternal security.

If you find yourself swinging in and out of a sense of eternal security, you can walk on the level, unchanging ground of God's truth. The ride of swaying doubt can end today. Here's why: You were saved by Christ's performance on the cross, where all your sins—past, present, and future—were forgiven. Your eternal security is grounded in the person and work of Christ, not your performance.

Feelings fluctuate, especially when we sin. But nothing can cancel the reservation that Christ has made in heaven for believers, since it was purchased once and for all by His sacrificial death.

Once you are saved, Christ takes up permanent residence in your life. He will never leave you, even if your track record as a saint is spotty. He may discipline you, and the consequences for your sin may not be pleasant. But your eternal security is not altered.

God's love for you is unconditional, unfailing, and unchanging. He has made you His child forever, and absolutely nothing can change your identity as God's son or daughter.

How I praise You, Lord, that nothing can change my identity as Your child. I am so grateful that Your love for me is unconditional, unfailing, and unchanging.

Behind the Scenes

SCRIPTURE READING: Philippians 1:12–20
KEY VERSE: 1 Corinthians 4:12

And we labor, working with our own hands. Being reviled, we bless; being persecuted, we endure it.

Endurance is not just the ability to bear a hard thing; it is the ability to turn it into glory.

You have probably discovered during the past year that periods of pain or difficulty are the hardest times to remember the basic truths of God's Word. Ironically those moments demand the light of His truth the most. While you can never anticipate all of the specific needs that will arise, you can make it a habit to view every situation through the filter of God's perspective.

Ask the Lord to help you focus on Him instead of the circumstance. Hurting does not mean that God does not care about you. You must make the commitment to cling to the truth of Romans 8:28 and similar promises. If you believe that He will bring good out of the situation somehow, then pessimistic thinking finds no permanent home in your heart. Over time, your emotions gradually align with the truth.

Part of Paul's joy resulted from his discovery of what God was doing "behind the scenes." What Paul thought was a slow time of limited contact turned out to be God's way of evangelizing one of the most impenetrable sectors of Roman society, the praetorian guards. God put Paul in a position that he never could have achieved on his own.

Always remember that the Lord will give you His perspective if you ask Him to. You never have to give in to the false friends of discouragement, worry, or self-sufficiency.

Dear heavenly Father, give me Your divine perspective. Keep me from discouragement, worry, and self-sufficiency.

DECEMBER 9

A Fantastic Adventure

SCRIPTURE READING: Matthew 14:22–34
KEY VERSE: Matthew 14:27

But immediately Jesus spoke to them, saying "Be of good cheer! It is I; do not be afraid."

Paul Tournier, the eminent Swiss doctor, wrote in his book, *The Adventure of Work,* a profound assessment of the Christian life: "Life is an adventure directed by God."

The seed of life-changing faith is contained in such a view. It can be the difference between a confident, rewarding life or a timid, fretful one. When confronted with perplexity, it can be the hinge upon which swings the response of either fear or faith.

Fear comes when we are overwhelmed by the magnitude or implications of a situation. It swells to paralyzing proportions when we think of the possibility of disastrous consequences.

But once we understand and embrace the truth that God is indeed in charge of our circumstances and has equipped us for every challenge, it is amazing how faith in Christ can change our outlook. Life isn't risk free. But God has set a divine course for every believer that He oversees and directs with perfect wisdom and love.

Our faith is in His faithfulness to us, in His power that works on our behalf, in His grace that provides all our needs. God is in charge. Life is an exciting journey in trusting Him as our Guide and Companion. Begin the adventure today, and drop your fears at His feet. He won't let you down.

Father, there may be hard times ahead, but I know that You are directing my path, and I will not fear the future.

The Nature of Sheep

SCRIPTURE READING: Psalm 23
KEY VERSE: Psalm 4:8

I will both lie down in peace, and sleep;
For You alone, O LORD, make me dwell in safety.

Have you ever fought the impulse to trust God? Have you ever gone your own way, just to prove to yourself that you could do it? It's a common impulse, but God knows the truth about your nature as His "sheep."

In her book *Single Moments,* Lynda Hunter finds this analogy in her everyday experience:

One February night when my children were young, I put them to bed at their regular time. Then I cleaned my house from top to bottom; baked a birthday cake; decorated the basement, wrapped presents, and prepared lunch for the following day.

I got no sleep that night, and I was just finishing the preparations when the children awoke the next morning. My daughter rubbed her eyes and asked, "What's for breakfast?" She had slept peacefully while I provided everything she needed for her party that day.

The shepherd may have to make many arrangements or slay innumerable enemies, but the sheep's sleep is sweet. The sheep accepts its own helplessness and knows it will always need the help of the shepherd. Likewise we can say, even in difficult circumstances, "I will lie down and sleep in peace, for you alone, O Lord, make me dwell in safety" (Psalm 4:8).

It's OK to be a sheep; that's the way God made you. But remember, as long as you resist His care, you will be vulnerable to harm you do not yet understand.

Lord, I trust You with my future. Thank You for Your loving care.

A Sheep or a Goat?

SCRIPTURE READING: Matthew 25:31–34
KEY VERSE: Matthew 25:21

His lord said to him, "Well done, good and faithful servant; you were faithful over a few things, I will make you ruler over many things. Enter into the joy of your lord."

Some people have such an obsession with the events of the end times that they forget the importance of the spiritual tasks that God has called them to today. Of course, it is important to gain an understanding of what God's Word says about the future and the coming of His kingdom, but He has not revealed some things—and for a good reason. God wants us to live by faith. He doesn't fill in all the details, endless debates about points of disagreement do not bear spiritual fruit and cause dissension in the church.

What you can know for sure is that God has all future events in His loving control. Someday everyone will be called to account before His almighty throne: "When the Son of Man comes in His glory, and all the angels with Him, then He will sit on His glorious throne. And all the nations will be gathered before Him; and He will separate them from one another, as the shepherd separates the sheep from the goats; and He will put the sheep on His right, and the goats on the left. Then the King will say to those on His right, 'Come, you who are blessed of My Father, inherit the kingdom prepared for you from the foundation of the world'" (Matt. 25:31–34 NASB).

The key question you must answer is, "Am I a sheep or a goat?" Your answer makes the difference in your eternal destiny.

God, I am Your sheep. Lead me, guide me, and protect me.

The Process of Beautification

SCRIPTURE READING: Ephesians 5:1–14
KEY VERSE: Ephesians 5:2

Walk in love, as Christ also has loved us and given Himself for us, an offering and a sacrifice to God for a sweet-smelling aroma.

Have you ever seen "before and after" photos in magazines? Cosmetics companies and weight-loss plans often use this advertisement technique. Of course, sometimes the changes seem just a little too remarkable. Yet that's what people love to see and experience, something that makes a change for the better.

The fifth chapter of Ephesians is a kind of spiritual "before and after" snapshot. It helps you understand what Jesus' grace actually does in your heart and mind as you grow in your relationship with the Savior: "Do not be partakers with them [the evildoers]; for you were formerly darkness, but now you are light in the Lord; walk as children of light (for the fruit of the light consists in all goodness and righteousness and truth), trying to learn what is pleasing to the Lord" (Eph. 5:7–10 NASB).

Can you remember what you were like before you accepted Christ as your Savior? For some people the transformation was radical and easily visible to others. But no matter what your story, you can certainly recall areas of darkness that were opened up to the light of Christ and made new.

The good news is that "beautification" is still taking place. You don't have a final "after" picture because you are always in the process of becoming more like Him.

Thank You that You are changing me, Lord. I humbly submit to the beautification process that is making me more like You.

Managing Your Time

SCRIPTURE READING: Ephesians 5:15–17
KEY VERSE: Ephesians 5:15

See then that you walk circumspectly, not as fools but as wise.

Few of us think of time with eternity in mind. Mostly we talk of time as passing too quickly or of not having enough of it to do the things we want to do. There have been volumes written on the subject of time management. But even learning how to organize our time takes time to implement.

The apostle Paul admonished the Ephesian church to make the most of their time: "Be careful how you walk, not as unwise men, but as wise, making the most of your time, because the days are evil" (Eph. 5:15–16 NASB).

What did Paul mean when he said, "The days are evil"? He was underscoring the fact that most people have their minds set on things that are fading and contain little eternal value. Ephesus was a major seaport and the largest commercial center west of the Taurus Mountains. It also was a hub of pagan activity with the temple of Diana located there.

Learning how to correctly manage your time comes down to a matter of discipline. Are you focused on the things God has given you to do, or are you being drawn away by other activities?

The church in Ephesus was dear to Paul's heart, and the believers there were sincere in their devotion to Christ. They refused to yield to the pressures around them, and as a result God gave them strength to overcome the enemy. Jesus will do the same for you.

Lord, teach me how to invest my time wisely. Give me the strength to overcome the pressures around me and set proper priorities.

The Giver of Life

SCRIPTURE READING: John 11:1–45
KEY VERSE: John 11:22

Even now I know that whatever You ask of God, God will give You.

After Lazarus's death, his sisters, Mary and Martha, were grief stricken. When Martha heard that Jesus had arrived, she went out to meet Him. Mary dealt with her feelings differently and stayed at home in seclusion. The death of a loved one can be intensely difficult to bear.

Both sisters struggled with their grief. They believed that if Jesus had been with the family, Lazarus's death would never have taken place. "Lord," cried Martha, "if You had been here, my brother would not have died. But even now I know that whatever You ask of God, God will give You" (John 11:21–22).

The scene was touching. It was obvious that Martha had learned who was responsible for the restoration of life and that it was a gift God had given through His Son. She went one step further in her faith and believed that even though her brother was dead, Jesus could restore him.

Jesus went to Lazarus's tomb and instructed those who were there to remove the stone covering, the opening to the burial chamber. Did Martha's faith hesitate at Jesus' command? "Lord . . . there will be a stench" (John 11:39 NASB).

If there was, Jesus was not bothered by it. The greater lesson had been achieved. She believed in His ability and trusted Him as her Lord. "Lazarus, come forth," was His command over the enemy of death. A few moments later, Lazarus emerged from the grave.

Lord, You are the Giver of eternal life. You are my Savior.

Facing the Future

SCRIPTURE READING: Psalm 119:169–75
KEY VERSE: Psalm 23:4

Yea, though I walk through the valley of the shadow of death, I will fear no evil; For You are with me; Your rod and Your staff, they comfort me.

Without trials, you would not know to trust the Savior. Without pain, the help He offers would go unnoticed. So many long to take the easy way. Yet this is not always God's design.

At times our pathways become treacherous, taking dark and shadowy turns. We learn to identify with the psalmist: "Even though I walk through the valley of the shadow of death, I fear no evil, for Thou art with me" (Ps. 23:4 NASB).

God goes before you into each and every trial. He leaves a trodden path for you to follow. You may walk where danger is crouched on every side, but you do not walk alone. You may face being misunderstood, overlooked, and forgotten, but God knows you and loves you greatly. Keep your eyes on Him. Fix your emotions on His promises. They are unshakable.

Once you learn to go to Him in times of sorrow as well as happiness, a new joy will spring up within you. It comes from an overflow of being in the presence of God. It has the power to change the way you feel about yourself and others. It can heal any relationship.

Don't be surprised if you find yourself praising God in desperate times. Trials bring you to your knees. From this angle all you need to do is to look up into the loving face of the Lord Jesus Christ. It is here you discover the greatness of God's love and forgiveness. Praise Him!

Father, thank You that I can face the future without fear.

Healing for Your Hurts

SCRIPTURE READING: Luke 17:12–19

KEY VERSE: Luke 17:19

He said to him, "Arise, go your way. Your faith has made you well."

The men with leprosy mentioned in today's reading were social outcasts. Few sicknesses were feared more than leprosy. In New Testament times, it was incurable and a sentence of sure death. Therefore, when the men saw Jesus, they knew He was their only chance of survival.

Perhaps you are facing something that feels as though it will be the end of you. Thoughts of hopelessness fill your mind and leave you wondering if there is a cure for what you are facing. Jesus has the power to heal you. He will touch your life and relieve the stress and sorrow of your disease. These men called out to him: "Jesus, Master, have mercy on us!" (v. 13).

Warren Wiersbe commented on this scene:

> They knew that Jesus was totally in command of even disease and death, and they trusted Him to help them . . . He commanded the men to go show themselves to the priest, which in itself was an act of faith, for they had not yet been cured. When they turned to obey, they were completely healed, for their obedience was evidence of their faith.

We would expect all ten to return to the Savior shouting words of praise and thanksgiving to God, but only one returned; he was not a Jew but a Samaritan. God may choose to heal you now or later as you stand one day in His presence. If it is now, remember to thank Him for the goodness and mercy He has shown you.

Lord, You are my Healer. You have broken the power of sin and shame in my life.

No Better Time

SCRIPTURE READING: Luke 16:19–31
KEY VERSE: 2 Corinthians 5:10

We must all appear before the judgment seat of Christ, that each one may receive the things done in the body, according to what he has done, whether good or bad.

"I've got plenty of time to make that decision," he reasoned. "Maybe in a few years I'll be ready to think about spiritual things. Right now I've got to get going and try to get my life in order." You've heard reasoning like this before. Maybe you were one of those who postponed thinking about the Lord until "some better time."

What many do not stop to consider is that they are not guaranteed a tomorrow. That's the mistake the rich man made in Jesus' parable. Only when it was too late and he was suffering the torments of Hades did he realize the importance of knowing Jesus as his Savior.

Notice what the rich man asked Abraham. He wanted Abraham to send some sort of special warning or messengers to his brothers who were still living, so that they would not meet his same dismal fate. Abraham replied, "They have Moses and the Prophets; let them hear them . . . If they do not listen to Moses and the Prophets, neither will they be persuaded if someone rises from the dead" (Luke 16:29–31 NASB).

God has already given His Word to mankind, and He says it is sufficient. The heart that is already hardened to that truth will not be receptive to more. Now is the time to listen to what God says, not tomorrow or the day after that. To put off the decision to hear Him and respond is to continue the process of hardening your heart.

Dear God, give me a tender heart and a listening ear.

An Eternal Perspective

SCRIPTURE READING: Proverbs 3:1–7
KEY VERSES: Proverbs 3:5–6

Trust in the LORD with all your heart,
And lean not on your own understanding;
In all your ways acknowledge Him,
And He shall direct your paths.

Some of the most noble and valiant events of history in many nations were born out of hearts that had an eternal perspective. The heart of George Washington, renowned Revolutionary War general and first president of the United States, was such a heart. From his earliest days, he was taught by his mother to put God first in his life. And when he went out to accept a position of leadership in the war, he had no idea how much his faith would be put to the test.

One of the most precious documents Washington ever produced as a young man was a small prayer diary that he titled *Daily Sacrifice*. He wrote:

> Oh most glorious God . . . I acknowledge and confess my faults; in the weak
> and imperfect performance of the duties of this day . . . Oh God, who art
> rich in mercy and plenteous in redemption, mark not, I beseech Thee, what
> I have done amiss . . . Cover [my sins] with the absolute obedience of Thy
> dear Son . . . the sacrifice of Jesus Christ offered upon the Cross for me.
> (Taken from *The Light and the Glory*, by Peter Marshall and David Manuel)

He made a habit of private prayer, and his faith inspired his men in the most brutal conditions. He is remembered for his great deeds certainly, but it is his faith that made his impact lasting. Only when your focus is on the eternal will your work have eternal merit.

Turn my heart to Your purposes, O Lord. Keep my focus on eternity.

I Have Fought a Good Fight

SCRIPTURE READING: 2 Timothy 4:1–8

KEY VERSE: 2 Timothy 4:7

I have fought the good fight, I have finished the race, I have kept the faith.

At the end of 2 Timothy, Paul was looking back over his life: "I have fought the good fight, I have finished the course, I have kept the faith; in the future there is laid up for me the crown of righteousness" (4:7–8 NASB).

Yet even in victory there can be a touch of sadness. In verses 9 through 18 of chapter 4, we learn that Paul was virtually alone. His life and ministry were drawing to a close. While Luke remained at his side, Paul longed for Timothy's fellowship.

Most of us think a man of Paul's stature would not suffer the painfulness of being left alone and forsaken by friends. Yet this appears to be what happened. Some, Demas for one, deserted Paul while others had followed Paul's instructions and gone on to other places of ministry.

Even though he remained physically alone, he was not alone spiritually or emotionally. Jesus was his closest companion. Dark and lonely times come to everyone, but not without purpose and design. God has special blessings stored up for those who travel the road of suffering and abandonment.

Not once did Paul speak with a tone of self-pity or resentment. He understood that he was kept by the power of God's love, especially in times of trial. He had fought a good fight and remained true to the calling of God. Now a crown of righteousness waited for him.

Lord, in the midst of suffering and abandonment, help me remain true to my calling. I want to fight a good fight!

Drifting from God

SCRIPTURE READING: 1 John 1:5–10
KEY VERSE: Proverbs 6:27

Can a man take fire to his bosom,
And his clothes not be burned?

The Holy Spirit's presence dwells within us and has regenerated our lives with purity and truth. But what hope can we find for our hearts when we yield to sin?

God has given us a tremendous promise in 1 John that provides an answer to this question. It is a verse that has been quoted many times: "If we confess our sins, He is faithful and righteous to forgive us our sins and to cleanse us from all unrighteousness" (1:9 NASB).

Here is the basis for this truth: When you were saved, God forgave all of your sins, past, present, and future. No matter what your lifestyle was, you stand forgiven before Him. However, after the point of salvation, when you sin, one of the gravest consequences is broken fellowship with Jesus Christ.

Acknowledging your sin immediately restores your fellowship with the Savior. When we yield to temptation, we open ourselves up to all kinds of evil—physical, emotional, and spiritual. Some dismiss this notion. Yet confusion, doubt, fear, and conflict are just several problems that plague those who drift from God.

Proverbs 6:27 (NIV) reminds us: "Can a man scoop fire into his lap without his clothes being burned?" Make it a habit to deal with sin immediately before the throne of God.

Lord, let me always deal with my sin immediately before Your throne where Your forgiveness covers me and embraces me with love and hope.

A Source of Refreshment

SCRIPTURE READING: Psalm 32
KEY VERSE: Psalm 62:2

He only is my rock and my salvation;
He is my defense;
I shall not be greatly moved.

It's hard to contemplate the dog days of summer in the middle of winter, but try to picture this scene. It is the hottest day in July, the humidity is high, and not a breeze is stirring. Then imagine that you are outside running on baking asphalt. Sweat is pouring off your body, and you can't wait to get to a glass of water. You feel as though you can't make another step.

That is the feeling that David described as a result of an exhausted conscience: "For day and night your hand was heavy upon me; my strength was sapped as in the heat of summer" (Ps. 32:4 NIV).

The most deeply troubling times often have little to do with external circumstances. When the Holy Spirit is nudging your conscience about a sin in your life, and you choose not to respond, the misery you experience inside can be indescribable. Do you recall such a time? Every activity in your day seemed a tiresome chore. You had to expend great emotional energy just to deny that something was wrong in your spirit.

The only cure for this kind of heart sickness is confession and repentance: "Then I acknowledged my sin to you and did not cover up my iniquity . . . and you forgave the guilt of my sin" (Ps. 32:5 NIV). If your spirit is exhausted by running from God, turn to Him for refreshment right now.

Lord, I am exhausted by running from You. I turn to You right now for refreshment.

Beginning a New Adventure

SCRIPTURE READING: Isaiah 60:1–3

KEY VERSE: Psalm 31:3

*For You are my rock and my fortress; Therefore, for Your name's sake,
Lead me and guide me.*

Remember the last time you began a new adventure? Maybe it was to visit a faraway city or to fulfill a desire you longed to achieve, such as riding horses, learning how to play tennis, writing poetry, studying watercolor painting, or climbing mountains. How did it feel to approach a new beginning? Was there a twinge of hopeful anticipation present?

The feelings can be quite different when sorrow is involved. The disappointment that comes from the loss of a job, the grief of betrayal, or the shock of a friend's rejection can leave you feeling hopeless. God wants you to know whatever your situation, He is aware of it. He knows painful circumstances can leave you wondering if you will ever enjoy a sense of hope again.

Before he became president of the United States, Abraham Lincoln was defeated for public office four times in twelve years. The last public office he held before being elected to the nation's highest office was a seat in the U.S. Congress in 1846. It was not until 1860 that he was elected president.

Lincoln dared to believe in the impossible. He refused to give up. God is your constant Source of encouragement. His strength is released in your life when you make a conscious decision not to give up but to continue in faith. If there is darkness, pray for His light to rest over your life, guiding you into a new season of hope and revival.

Dear heavenly Father, let Your light rest over my life, guiding me into a new season of hope and revival. I am ready to begin a new adventure with You!

Making Course Corrections

SCRIPTURE READING: 1 Samuel 10:17–11:14
KEY VERSE: Psalm 19:12

Who can understand his errors?
Cleanse me from secret faults.

There is a tendency to think of King Saul's life as being sinister and fore-boding. But Saul didn't begin his reign as a baneful terrorist. The Bible tells us, "He was taller than any of the people from his shoulders upward. And Samuel said . . . 'Do you see him whom the LORD has chosen? Surely there is no one like him among all the people.' So all the people shouted and said, 'Long live the king!'" (1 Sam. 10:23–24 NASB).

Saul bore God's anointing along with the love and respect of the people. The first obvious sign of erosion came in 1 Samuel 15 when Saul willfully dis-obeyed God and offered a sacrifice only Samuel was commanded to make. Pride and jealousy, combined with insecurity, led to even deeper erosion of his spiritual values. In the end, Saul's life was void of all that was godly.

Most of us think there's no way we would yield to such spiritual decline. Before you adopt this view, recall the life of Saul. He was a humble man when he first became king. But by the end of his life, disobedience and pride were his captors.

Ask God to surface any area of erosion in your life. Then pray He will give you wisdom and the ability to make the necessary course corrections in the days ahead.

Dear God, please surface any area of erosion in my life, and then give me the wisdom and ability to make the necessary course corrections.

Filling the Void

SCRIPTURE READING: Psalm 71:1–6

KEY VERSE: Psalm 71:3

Be my strong habitation, To which I may resort continually; You have given the commandment to save me, For You are my rock and my fortress.

She broke down and cried as she finished folding her husband's shirts. They had been married for twenty-five years and raised two children. Somewhere in between the Little League baseball games, drama rehearsals, and hours spent late at the office, they had lost each other.

Her children always filled the void in her life. Now that they were gone, she realized she barely knew her husband. Her pastor lovingly listened as she told of her heartache. "God created each of us with certain needs," he began, "needs for significance, security, acceptance, love, and discipline. However," he said, "no person can meet all your needs. And it's unfair to request that of anyone. The good news is that with help and time God can restore your marriage."

Many try to take control of a bad situation by filling their lives with material possessions and other people. However, when needs are not met in the proper way, emotional unrest and discontentment ensue.

Only Jesus Christ is capable of meeting your every need. If the holiday season leaves you feeling lonely and insignificant, be assured He wants to and can fill the void in your life.

Heavenly Father, thank You for the greatest gift of all, Your Son, the Lord Jesus Christ. Let His spirit fill every void of my life during this holiday season.

The Shadow of the Cross

SCRIPTURE READING: Luke 1:68–79
KEY VERSE: Ephesians 1:11

In whom also we have obtained an inheritance, being predestined according to the purpose of Him who works all things according to the counsel of His will,

As we celebrate Christmas, we are reminded of God's plan for His Son. Even before Jesus was born, God the Father had predestined Him to become an atonement for our sins. Because sin demands a sacrifice, Jesus was born with the purpose of becoming the sacrificial Lamb of God.

His death shook the gates of hell, eternally destroying the spiritual facade Satan had erected in hopes of leading God's beloved astray. When Christ came to the end of His earthly life, He lifted a cup and instructed the disciples to drink. It was to become a symbol of His blood being poured out for each one of us.

Each day He lived, Jesus understood that the goal of His life was death and sacrifice. Especially at this time of year, we love to look at artists' renderings of the birth of Christ and whisper how wondrous the event was and is. But let us never forget that even as a tiny baby, the shadow of the Cross was draped over this one child's life. He willingly drank the sacrificial cup for each of us.

His personal covenant is sure: "Whoever believes in Me shall have everlasting life." As you celebrate Christmas, know that Jesus loves you completely. He has forgiven you so you could spend eternity in the light of His marvelous love and grace.

Lord Jesus, even at Your birth the Cross cast a shadow across Your cradle. I am so thankful You came to earth to die for me.

Finishing the Course

SCRIPTURE READING: Psalm 150
KEY VERSE: Psalm 148:1

Praise the LORD!
Praise the LORD from the heavens;
Praise Him in the heights!

When you feel weak, take time to pray. When you feel lonely, take time to praise God for the things He has given. When You are angry, ask the Lord to strengthen your heart with love.

Wherever God leads you, be grateful, and you will know the encouragement that comes as a result of your faith and hope and trust in Christ.

Francis of Assisi exercised his gratitude and praised God even in difficult circumstances:

> Sing a new song to Him,
> Sing to the Lord, all the earth!
> For the Lord is great, He is worthy of all praise.
> He inspires us with awe,
> For all that He is and does is far beyond all lesser gods.
> Give to the Lord, every family, and all nations,
> Give to the Lord glory and praise!
> Give Him all the glory that is due His marvelous name!
> To do this is to offer your bodies,
> And to take up His cross for you,
> And to follow His most holy commands, from now until the end. (*Psalm for the Nativity*)

Turn your weaknesses over to Jesus, and He will provide the strength you need to finish the course.

Lord, I am weak, but I know You will provide the strength I need to finish the course!

God's Best for You

SCRIPTURE READING: Psalm 39:4–5
KEY VERSE: Psalm 31:15

*My times are in Your hand; Deliver me from the hand of my enemies,
And from those who persecute me.*

Our days are in God's hands. No matter how in control we try to be of our lives, God is over all that concerns us. We often dismiss this and face great frustration in trying to orchestrate our own destinies.

God is the only One who knows the future. Jeremiah 29:11 tells us that He has good planned for our lives. He has His best in mind for you. No matter what you have done earlier in life, God is not ashamed of you. He is faithful to protect and provide for all your needs, even in heartache and difficulty. Therefore, when the temptation comes to give up, don't give in to it.

Young Christians often become discouraged because they dislike facing faith-stretching moments. They want to grow up immediately in their spiritual walk, and they don't want to wait. But time is not an urgency to the Lord. He is aware of its value but not consumed with how long it takes you to grow into the man or woman He has planned for you to become.

Isn't it wonderful to live for Someone who knows you completely and has chosen you as His own beloved? You worship a living Savior whose love is endless and who has all the time in the world to listen to you and counsel you.

Lord Jesus, I am so thankful that You have the best in mind for me. As I look back over the past year, I see that You always knew best. Give me faith to believe for the future.

Faith for the Future

SCRIPTURE READING: 2 Timothy 1:1–14
KEY VERSE: Psalm 22:4

Our fathers trusted in You; They trusted, and You delivered them.

Timothy was a young pastor whom Paul had left in charge of the believers in Ephesus and in Asia Minor. He had a tough job guiding the new converts in a culture often openly hostile to their faith, and there was not an abundance of "fathers" in the church to encourage him. That's why Paul spent much of his two letters to Timothy doing just that.

First, Paul reminded him of his faith in the past: "I am mindful of the sincere faith within you, which first dwelt in your grandmother Lois, and your mother Eunice, and I am sure that is in you as well" (2 Tim. 1:5 NASB). Paul wanted Timothy to remember how the Lord brought him to salvation and nurtured him along the way.

Second, Paul gave him a hope-filled vision for the future: "For this reason I remind you to kindle afresh the gift of God which is in you through the laying on of my hands. For God has not given us a spirit of timidity, but of power and love and discipline" (2 Tim. 1:6–7 NASB). Timothy faced discouragement from those who felt he was too young for such a daunting task of spiritual leadership, so Paul wanted to make sure his focus was in the right direction. Timothy was strengthened by seeing this larger perspective.

Is this the kind of encouragement you need right now? Review your spiritual story, and ask God to give you a fresh sense of His involvement.

Lord, give me faith for the future. Renew my spirit.

All Is Vanity

SCRIPTURE READING: Ecclesiastes 12:1–8
KEY VERSE: Ecclesiastes 12:1

Remember now your Creator in the days of your youth,
Before the difficult days come,
And the years draw near when you say,
"I have no pleasure in them."

In Ecclesiastes, Solomon's words hauntingly draw us into a time vacuum where reality spills over to the imagined, and we find ourselves wanting to push away at the discovery he made. Surely he was wrong. There must be a way for us to indulge in the pleasures of this world and serve God at the same time, but alas, there is not. Solomon is right—all is vanity.

Therefore, his warning is true that we should remember our Creator in the days of our youth, before the years come when you will say, "'I have no delight in them'; before the sun, the light, the moon, and the stars are darkened, and clouds return after the rain; in the day that the watchmen of the house tremble, and mighty men stoop, the grinding ones stand idle because they are few, and those who look through windows grow dim. . . then the dust will return to the earth as it was, and the spirit will return to God who gave it. 'Vanity of vanities,' says the Preacher, 'all is vanity!'" (Eccl. 12:1–3, 7–8 NASB).

God wants us to enjoy His provisions. However, the key to the good things in life is not in doing or having but in living for Jesus Christ. You will find that when your affections are set on material gain, your spirit suffers. Life takes on a hopeless effect. But you avoid all of this when knowing Jesus is your aim and goal.

Dear Lord, I want to set my affections on spiritual things instead of material things. Help me to do that during the coming year.

A Clean Page

SCRIPTURE READING: John 4
KEY VERSE: John 4:4

He needed to go through Samaria.

There is nothing more refreshing than a new beginning, especially when you can start out on a clean page. This is how it is with God when you seek His forgiveness. He holds nothing against you.

Even later in life when you fall to temptation, God's mercy reaches out to help you get back on track spiritually, emotionally, and mentally. He never abandons the works of His hands. This is what you are—His workmanship—crafted in the image of His Son. You are a trophy in the eyes of God, a person who has been saved from spiritual death and given a new chance at life.

Jesus took time out of His schedule to meet the woman at the well. She had been married several times, and the man she was currently with was not her husband. Imagine the shame she felt as she talked with Someone she knew to be a teacher from God. She found it hard to accept that He would risk so much in talking to her.

The Savior will risk everything for you. Many have been saved for years, but you struggle with a judgmental attitude, jealousy, envy, and pride. You look at others and think, *My, how glad I am that is not me.*

God's forgiveness and grace change lives. After meeting Jesus, this woman ran to tell others about the saving grace and forgiveness of God. How long has it been since you have felt the freshness of His care? He is near to you right now.

Lord, thank You for a new beginning, a clean page, so I can start again.

Forever Is in Front

SCRIPTURE READING: Acts 9:1–31
KEY VERSE: 2 Corinthians 2:17

We are not, as so many, peddling the word of God; but as of sincerity, but as from God, we speak in the sight of God in Christ.

The apostle Paul encountered Jesus Christ on the Damascus road. Blinded and prostrate before God, Paul realized nothing he had learned could rival what Christ had revealed. Nor did he have a grasp of the immediate changes that would take place in his life.

Some people have shared how God removed certain sinful desires at the point of salvation. Others tell how old habits disappeared gradually. However, neither of these statements explains the depth to which God's salvation reaches. Paul wrote in 2 Corinthians 5:17–18 (NASB): "Therefore if any man is in Christ, he is a new creature; the old things passed away; behold, new things have come. Now all these things are from God."

When you accept Christ as your Savior, God immediately transfers your name from the book of sin and death to the Book of Eternal Life. He purifies your life and no longer views you according to your sin, but deals with you according to the testimony of His Son.

Don't harbor the memories of past failures and sins. Once you come to know Jesus, the past is eternally behind you and the new you—holy and pure—is forever in front of you.

Dear heavenly Father, I praise You that forever is in front! There are unlimited divine encounters with You that await me in the future.

About the Author

DR. CHARLES F. STANLEY is pastor of the 15,000-member First Baptist Church in Atlanta, Georgia, and is president and CEO of In Touch® Ministries. He has twice been elected president of the Southern Baptist Convention and is well-known internationally through his IN TOUCH radio and television ministry. His many best-selling books include *Walking Wisely, When Tragedy Strikes, Charles Stanley's Handbook for Christian Living, A Touch of His Power, Our Unmet Needs, Enter His Gates,* and *The Source of My Strength.* Dr. Stanley received his bachelor of arts degree from the University of Richmond, his bachelor of divinity degree from Southwestern Theological Seminary, and his master's and doctor's degrees from Luther Rice Seminary.

Other Books by Charles Stanley Published by Thomas Nelson Publishers

Don't Miss These Bestselling Devotionals by Charles Stanley

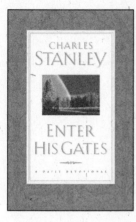

Enter His Gates

Spiritual gates are much like the gates of a city. They are vital to your well-being as a Christian and, if not maintained, leave you open to attack by the enemy. *Enter His Gates* is a daily devotional that encourages you to build or strengthen a different spiritual gate each month.

ISBN: 0-7852-7546-0

On Holy Ground

This daily devotional contains a year's worth of spiritual adventures. Dr. Stanley uses the journeys of Paul, Ezra, Elijah, Abraham, and other heroes of the Bible and his own valuable insights to encourage you to step out in faith and allow God to lead you to new places.

ISBN: 0-7852-7662-9

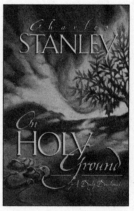

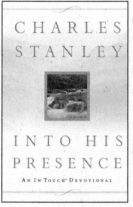

Into His Presence

Readers challenged to enter *Into His Presence* will be encouraged, uplifted, and spiritually renewed with this new devotional. In Scripture we find the Lord's people having dramatic encounters with God in mountaintop situations. There they are given revelation and transformation. To receive what He had for them they had to come away from the spiritual status quo of life and go to a higher level. That is the purpose of this devotional guide—to lift the reader to a new level of intimate, mountaintop encounters with God. Each section will have an introduction explaining the focus for that month's devotional reading and a listing of relevant Scripture along with daily devotional commentary.

ISBN: 0-7852-6854-5

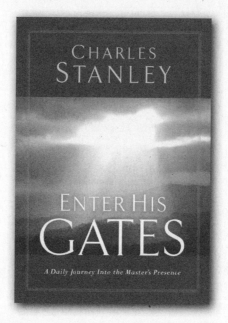

In this compact edition of Dr. Charles Stanley's best-selling daily
devotional, readers will be encouraged to strengthen their Christian
walk. Each month readers will focus on themes such as setting goals,
preparing for challenges, communicating with God,
and overcoming adversity.

Perfect for the on-the-go individual, this compact devotional fits
easily into a purse or briefcase

ISBN: 0785265805